THE TEMPEST

SHAKESPEARE AT STRATFORD

Published by The Arden Shakespeare in association with
The Shakespeare Birthplace Trust

General Editor: Robert Smallwood, (formerly of) The
                    Shakespeare Centre

Associate Editors: Susan Brock, The Shakespeare Centre Library
                    Russell Jackson, The Shakespeare Institute

SHAKESPEARE AT STRATFORD

THE TEMPEST

DAVID LINDLEY

The Arden website is at
http://www.ardenshakespeare.com

Shakespeare at Stratford: *The Tempest*
first published 2003 by The Arden Shakespeare
in association with The Shakespeare Birthplace Trust

© 2003 David Lindley

The Arden Shakespeare is an imprint of Thomson Learning

Thomson Learning
High Holborn House
50/51 Bedford Row
London WC1R 4LR

Typeset by LaserScript, Mitcham, Surrey

Printed by Zrinski in Croatia

British Library Cataloguing in Publication Data
A catalogue record for this book is available from the British Library

Library of Congress Cataloguing in Publication Data
A catalogue record has been applied for

ISBN 1-903436-73-7 (pbk)
NPN 9 8 7 6 5 4 3 2 1

THE AUTHOR

David Lindley is Professor of Renaissance Literature in the School of English, University of Leeds. He has published books on literature and music (*Thomas Campion*, 1986); on Jacobean court culture (*The Trials of Frances Howard*, 1993); and on the court masque (1984). He has edited a selection of court masques (1995), and *The Tempest* for the New Cambridge Shakespeare (2002). Currently he is contributing to the Cambridge edition of the works of Ben Jonson, and writing a book on Shakespeare and music for the Arden Companions to Shakespeare series.

CONTENTS

LIST OF ILLUSTRATIONS

Cover photograph
Penny Layden as Miranda, 1998
Photograph: Clive Barda

SOURCES

J.W.F. Cocks: by permission of the *Stratford-upon-Avon Herald*

Joe Cocks Studio: The Joe Cocks Studio Collection, The Shakespeare Centre Library, Stratford-upon-Avon
Copyright: The Shakespeare Birthplace Trust

Malcolm Davies: The Shakespeare Centre Library, Stratford-upon-Avon
Copyright: The Shakespeare Birthplace Trust

Thomas Holte (photographs 2, 12 and 27): The Tom Holte Theatre Photographic Collection, The Shakespeare Centre Library, Stratford-upon-Avon
Copyright: The Shakespeare Birthplace Trust

Thomas Holte (photograph 4): The Thos. F. Holte and Mig Holte Photographic Collection, The Shakespeare Centre Library, Stratford-upon-Avon
Copyright: The Shakespeare Birthplace Trust

Angus McBean: The Shakespeare Centre Library, Stratford-upon-Avon
Copyright: The Royal Shakespeare Company

Clive Barda

Donald Cooper

Zoë Dominic

Manuel Harlan

GENERAL EDITOR'S PREFACE

The theatre archive housed in the Shakespeare Centre Library here in Stratford-upon-Avon is among the most important in the world; for the study of the performance history of Shakespeare's plays in the twentieth century it is unsurpassed. It covers the entire period from the opening of Stratford's first Shakespeare Memorial Theatre in 1879, through its replacement, following the fire of 1926, by the present 1932 building (renamed the Royal Shakespeare Theatre in 1961) and the addition of the studio theatre (The Other Place) in 1974 (closed, lamentably, in 2001), and of the Swan Theatre in 1986, and it becomes fuller as the years go by. The archive's collection of promptbooks, press reviews, photographs in their hundreds of thousands, and, over the last couple of decades, archival video recordings, as well as theatre programmes, costume designs, stage-managers' performance reports and a whole range of related material, provides the Shakespeare theatre historian with a remarkably rich and concentrated body of material. The wealth and accessibility of this collection have sometimes tended to give general performance histories of Shakespeare's plays an unintentional Stratford bias; the aim of this series is to exploit, and indeed revel in, the archive's riches.

Each volume in the series covers the Stratford performance history of a Shakespeare play since World War II. The record of performances at Stratford's various theatres through this period unquestionably offers a wider, fuller, and more various range of productions than is provided by any other single theatre company. It may fairly be said, therefore, that a study of the Stratford productions since 1945 of any Shakespeare play provides a representative cross-section of the main trends in its theatrical interpretation in the second half of the twentieth century. Each volume in the series will, however, begin with an introduction that sets this Stratford half-century in the wider context of the main trends of its play's performance history before this period and of significant productions elsewhere during it.

The organization of individual volumes is, of course, the responsibility of their authors, though within the general aim of the series to avoid mere chronicling. No volume in the series will therefore offer a chronological account of the Stratford productions of its play: some will group together for consideration and analysis productions of similar or comparable style or approach; others will examine individual aspects or sections of their plays across the whole range of the half-century of Stratford productions' treatment of them. Illustrations are chosen for what they demonstrate about a particular production choice, a decision that, on some occasions, may be more important than photographic quality. Given the frequency with which individual plays return, in entirely new productions, to the Stratford repertoire, most volumes in the series will have some ten or even a dozen productions' approaches and choices to consider and contrast, a range that will provide a vivid sense of the extraordinary theatrical diversity and adaptability of Shakespeare's plays.

The conception and planning of this series would not have been possible without the support and enthusiasm of Sylvia Morris and Marian Pringle of the Shakespeare Centre Library, Kathy Elgin, Head of Publications at the Royal Shakespeare Company, Jessica Hodge and her colleagues at the Arden Shakespeare, and above all, my two Associate Editors, Susan Brock of the Shakespeare Centre Library and Russell Jackson of the Shakespeare Institute. To all of them I am deeply grateful.

ROBERT SMALLWOOD
The Shakespeare Centre, Stratford-upon-Avon

ACKNOWLEDGEMENTS

This book depends upon the archive at the Shakespeare Centre in Stratford, and the principal debt which I wish to acknowledge is to Susan Brock, Karin Brown, Helen Hargest, Sylvia Morris and Marian Pringle. Their unfailingly cheerful helpfulness, their encyclopedic knowledge of the materials in their possession, and their patience with my sudden impulses to go over again the very materials they had just returned to the stack, made the research not merely possible but positively enjoyable. There is no more pleasant library in which to work.

I am also grateful to the British Academy for their award from the Small Grants Fund which made it possible to spend the essential time in Stratford to undertake the research for this book. In an age where 'research excellence' tends to be measured by the volume of research funding attracted, and 'projects' take precedence, it is important to record the fact that comparatively small amounts of money enable scholars in the humanities to undertake what they most wish to do – individual research in the archives.

Conversations with Roger Howells, long-time production manager with the Royal Shakespeare Company, with Michael Tubbs, currently Associate Director (Music), with Bob Burnell, and with James Staddon, James Telfer and Roger Frost from the 2002 production of *The Tempest*, helped to fill in a number of gaps; I thank them for their assistance.

Anyone who now approaches the study of the performance history of *The Tempest* is indebted to Christine Dymkowski's *Shakespeare in Production* (Cambridge, 2000). Her authoritative survey covers a far wider historical and geographical range than this present work, but, as is evident throughout, her work has very significantly affected and assisted me at every turn.

I owe a good deal to the Arden editorial team: to Jessica Hodge and Andrew McAleer, and their successors Margaret Bartley and Giulia Vincenzi; to Hannah Hyam; and especially to Judith Ravenscroft for her scrupulous editing of the copy.

Robert Smallwood commissioned this book, patiently endured its longer than intended gestation, and exercised his customary firm and judicious editorial eye upon it. He was also, coincidentally, the general editor of my very first publication, in 1984 – and I am glad of this opportunity to thank him for conversations, advice, and help generously offered for nearly twenty years.

DAVID LINDLEY
Leeds, October 2002

INTRODUCTION

*T*he *Tempest* is in many ways a very odd play. Its action is exceptionally confined – unlike any other Shakespeare work except *The Comedy of Errors* it observes the classical unities of both place and action. But though it opens with perhaps the most dramatic first scene in the canon – a storm and shipwreck – it then seems wilfully to throw away its audience-grabbing beginning as it modulates into the longest and most static of exposition scenes. In 1.2 Prospero recapitulates the pre-history of the play in a narrative which offers a stern challenge to its principal actor in developing and maintaining momentum. The theatrical spectacle of the opening returns with the disappearing banquet and dramatic entrance of Ariel as harpy in 3.3, and is continued in the extended masque in Act 4. But where the first of these scenes is integrated into the plot and action of the play, the second, the most substantial of Shakespeare's 'plays within a play', contributes nothing directly to either. In the final act Prospero reveals Ferdinand and Miranda to Alonso, promising that he will 'bring forth a wonder to content ye' (5.1.170[1]), and it can sometimes seem as if the play as a whole is more interested in presenting its audience with a sequence of strange theatrical marvels, surrounded with music, than with sustaining narrative drive. Though the play is brief, it is made up of four distinct plot lines – Prospero's recovery of his dukedom; his daughter's acquisition of a husband; the conspiracy of Antonio and Sebastian

1

against Alonso; and the plot of Caliban, Stephano and Trinculo against Prospero himself. There is, however, little space for the development of these narratives, or of the characters within them. The figures of Ferdinand and Miranda, and of the lords, seem like brief, sketchy gestures towards character types that Shakespeare in his earlier career had explored with much greater richness, and actors do not easily find ways of animating their brief appearances on the stage.

The peculiarity of the play's dramatic construction is underlined by the fact that in Prospero Shakespeare created a character who dominates the play more completely, perhaps, than any other parallel figure. It is a long part, proportionally – according to Spevack, Prospero speaks 17 per cent of speeches, and 29 per cent of lines and words. But he also watches over much of the action when he himself is largely silent, and through his magic has virtually total control of all his island's inhabitants, with the consequence that there is little real suspense in the unfolding of the plot. Yet the motivation of this dominant character is peculiarly elusive, and, as chapter 1 demonstrates, actors have struggled to find a line through the contradictory signals the character sends out, and ways of coping with the huge technical demands of the role.

If the problematic nature of the central figure were not enough, the next two biggest parts are afforded to characters not fully human – to Ariel and to Caliban. In both cases the text is anything but clear even about the simplest details of how they might look, leaving a wide range of options for the director. In general the tendency with both figures has been steadily to make them more and more 'human', and, especially in the case of Caliban, to de-emphasize the monstrosity and deformity which the text seems to call for. Yet the result is to set up a tension between the 'otherness' they represent, and their human embodiment on stage, and therefore to articulate their relationships, especially with Prospero, in crucially varying fashion.

Anne Barton summed up the complexity of this play in the programme note she provided for John Barton's 1970 RSC production:

> *The Tempest* is the most compressed and riddling play Shakespeare ever wrote. Almost as spare as myth, it is a work of art ruthlessly pared to the bone. To perform it in the theatre, even to try and talk about it, is inevitably to add to its substance by filling in gaps and silences left deliberately by the dramatist. What did Prospero originally intend to do with Alonso and his party when he arranged the shipwreck? Do Stephano and Trinculo land on the island as part of a plan to test Caliban or by accident? Why does Prospero destroy the Masque in such anger and dismay when the conspiracy he has remembered could never in fact have been a threat to him? Exactly what does he mean when he states that back in Milan, 'every third thought shall be my grave'? Why does he seem to bully Ariel throughout the play and nag at Miranda?
>
> Like an ice-berg, *The Tempest* seems to hide most of its bulk beneath the surface. The play constantly invites conjecture and amplification, but it is impossible to be sure of the correct answers to most of the questions posed.

Barton sees the mystery and reticence of the play as essentially productive. But for many literary critics and theatrical reviewers alike these characteristics have seemed more like a fundamental weakness, preventing the play from succeeding fully in the theatre.

A way into the consideration of the play's theatrically problematic nature might, paradoxically, be found in a brief consideration of the fortunes of *The Tempest* since its first performance. 'Paradoxically', because after two recorded performances of the play in 1611 and 1613 we know nothing of its performance before the closing of the theatres during the Interregnum, and after the Restoration Shakespeare's play virtually disappeared from the stage for the best part of two centuries. It was rewritten in 1667 by Dryden and Davenant under the title *The Enchanted Island*. In 1674 Shadwell rearranged some scenes and introduced more songs, and in further recensions it dominated the stage for almost a century and a half. Garrick, between 1757 and 1776, played a much reduced version of Shakespeare's play, but only with Macready's 1838 Covent Garden production was most of the original text restored (though he still retained some of the extra songs introduced in the previous centuries).

Yet, wildly divergent from the original though it is, *The Enchanted Island*, as Stephen Orgel observed, is 'enlightening in many of the ways that a good parody can be' (Orgel, 1987, 65) since its adaptations and supplementations respond precisely to the points of theatrical strain in Shakespeare's play. The lack of narrative suspense was compensated for by adding Dorinda, a sister for Miranda, and the character of Hippolito, whom Prospero has been sequestering away from his daughters, so that his ignorance of women parallels their unawareness of men. The central 'story' of the play then becomes the discovery by the two girls of their prospective mates, and of the rivalry and misunderstanding between Ferdinand and Hippolito which leads to the latter's apparent death, and miraculous healing (by Ariel rather than Prospero). This duplication of innocent young lovers contributed narrative suspense, but it served also a distinctly salacious end – the speeches of Miranda and Dorinda are laced with unwitting double entendres, presenting their sexual ignorance as a joke to the knowing audience. This emphasizes the fragility of the representation of Ferdinand and Miranda in Shakespeare's play, and suggests the knife edge upon which modern actors walk as they attempt to project innocence and restraint to a contemporary audience at least as sceptical as those in the Restoration period about the credibility of such sexual simplicity.

By contrast, the adapters registered the problematic nature of Shakespeare's lords, not by expanding their roles, but by ruthless pruning. Penitent early, they take little significant part in the action. More interesting is the adaptation of Caliban. In *The Enchanted Island* all the ambivalences of Shakespeare's character are removed. He is simply comic; his 'conspiracy' is totally disconnected from Prospero, becoming, instead, a struggle between Stephano and Trinculo (who have become the Master and Boatswain) for control of the island, which makes straightforward negative comment upon popular government. The adaptors were, as modern producers often are, attempting to make the play speak directly to their contemporary political situation in the charged atmosphere of the Restoration. (The interested reader might follow the studies by Dobson and Maus listed in the bibliography.) But we also see from their transformation that such direct address is only achieved by writing out of the original play its teasing, disturbing ambivalence. In this respect it offers only a more extreme version of the way in which some contemporary productions achieve clarity and apparent 'relevance' by an analogous process of simplification.

But perhaps the most obvious, and most significant, transformation of all is what Sandra Clark calls the 'secularity' of the adaptation (lv). Prospero's role is leached of moral turbulence by the ready repentance of his usurpers, and of its political implications by the diversion of the plot of Caliban's conspiracy. But his magic is also shorn of much of its significance. In the prologue the authors wrote:

> But *Shakespear*'s Magick could not copy'd bee
> Within that Circle none durst walk but he.
> I must confess 'twas bold, nor would you now,
> That liberty to vulgar Wits allow,
> Which works by Magick supernatural things:
> But Shakespear's pow'r is sacred as a Kings
> Those Legends from old Priest-hood were receiv'd
> And he then writ, as people then believ'd.

> (Clark, 87)

The patronizing tone of this comment indicates that merely half a century after Shakespeare wrote, the possibility of believing in magic as a real and powerful phenomenon had evaporated and become embarrassingly old-fashioned. It remains a central problem for the modern performer. Michael Hordern, who played Prospero three times in his career (at the Old Vic, London, in 1954, Stratford in 1978 and in the BBC TV Shakespeare series in 1979), asked:

> How are we to handle the magic in *The Tempest*? This is one of the great difficulties in presenting the play and in playing Prospero. A Jacobean audience would have been steeped in superstition, magic and the supernatural and so would have been in complete accord with Prospero's conjuring. Yet no amount of abracadabra, clever lighting effects and crystal balls is going to carry a modern audience to the suspension of disbelief.   (Sales, 174–5)

Productions have approached this problem in a number of different ways, some – in 1951 and 1982 in particular – attempting to strengthen its depiction, others playing it down and focusing instead on Prospero's humanity (see chapter 1).

One final transformation which gestures towards a still-problematic aspect of the text is the way in which *The Enchanted Island* deals with the ending of the play. The narrative the authors had constructed meant that the ending had to be modified; but even when they are using Shakespeare's original they write out of it all its provisionality and uncertainty. So, for example, they cut Prospero's wry puncturing of his daughter's enthusiasm for a 'brave new world' with the dismissive ''Tis new to thee' (5.1.184); Antonio makes unforced restitution of the seized dukedom; Ariel's song, 'Where the bee sucks' (5.1.88ff.), is moved virtually to the end of the play as a celebratory hymn; and Prospero has no epilogue, but concludes the play by leaving the island as 'a place of refuge' to the 'afflicted'. The optimistic quality of the ending was further intensified in Shadwell's adaptation, which added a long celebratory masque of Neptune and Amphitrite as an afterpiece.

Even after the restoration of Shakespeare's text some of these changes were retained. Kean's 1857 script, for example, also omits Prospero's ironic intervention, and reintroduces 'Where the bee sucks' as a coda. (He also cuts Miranda's 'Sweet lord, you play me false'.) The masque of Neptune and Amphitrite was revived in Regent's Park productions as late as the 1930s. Though many recent productions have emphasized the provisionality of *The Tempest*'s final act, Peter Brook in 1957 echoed (consciously or not) a trick from the Victorian performance tradition to achieve an uplifting ending. In Kean's spectacular finale, 'Morning breaks and shows a ship in a calm, prepared to convey the King and his companions back to Naples' (Kean, 67), and it is from this ship that Prospero delivers the Epilogue. Exactly one hundred years later, as Gielgud recounted:

> Peter Brook conceived the last scene in the play as the great triumph for Prospero returning home to accept the dukedom: I had a beautiful blue robe with a coronet which I placed on my head as Ariel dressed me. At the end, as I moved to the back of the stage, some ropes fell from above, the other characters turned their backs to the audience and the scene changed and became a ship sailing away, then I turned and came down to the front to speak the Epilogue [see Figure 1]. (Gielgud, 1997, 202)

This is, however, to jump ahead. For *The Enchanted Island* was the most popular Shakespearean play of the eighteenth century. Its mixture of spectacle and song made it, as Michael Dobson has suggested, the lineal ancestor of the Christmas pantomime (1991, 102). The sense that the play was appropriate for family entertainment persisted. Beerbohm Tree in 1904 expected that children would provide a good proportion of his audience; it was a particularly popular play in the Regent's Park Open Air seasons throughout the 1930s, and in 1939 it was issued in a schools' edition since it is 'especially suited for presentation in girls' schools. The fairy element and the necessity for good dancing require the delicate feminine touch' (Gaspar, 1). More importantly, perhaps, *The Enchanted Island* continued to influence performances even after its additions had been abandoned. As Orgel observes: 'the return to Shakespeare's text was accompanied by no

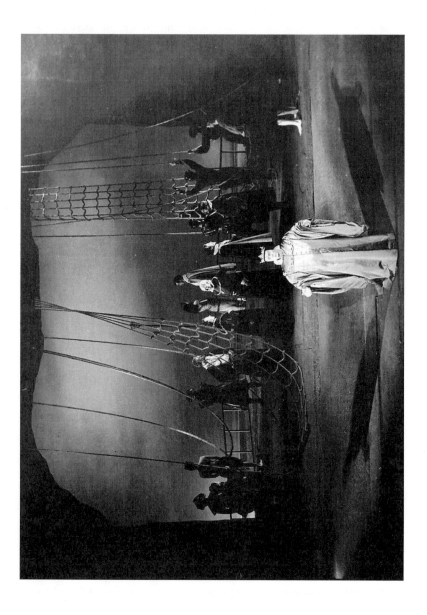

diminution of spectacular effects. *The Tempest* was still a machine-play par excellence' (1987, 72). Kean boasted that 'above one hundred and forty operatives nightly, ... (unseen by the audience) are engaged in working the machinery, and in carrying out the various effects' (ix). At the beginning of the twentieth century, Beerbohm Tree was still arguing that 'of all Shakespeare's works "The Tempest" was probably the one which most demanded the aids of modern stage-craft'. Space had to be made for the elaboration of spectacle by severe pruning of the text, at which some contemporary reviewers complained. Mary Nilan quotes Hans Christian Andersen's verdict on Kean's production:

> Everything was afforded that machinery and stage direction can provide, and yet after seeing it, one felt overwhelmed, tired, and empty. Shakespeare was lost in visual pleasure: the exciting poetry was petrified by illustrations; the living word had evaporated ... A work of Shakespeare performed between three simple screens is for me a greater enjoyment than here where it disappeared beneath the gorgeous trappings.   (Nilan, 1975, 203)

It was only at the end of the century that the reaction against spectacular staging began. William Poel's semi-professional English Stage Society production of 1897 elicited from George Bernard Shaw the comment that 'the poetry of *The Tempest* is so magical that it would make the scenery of modern theatre ridiculous' (Nilan, 1972, 117). Yet this was to be a contest continuously fought throughout the next century. One example might serve for the moment.

FIGURE 1 (*opposite*) At the end of Act 5 in 1957 the stage represents the ship which will bear Prospero triumphantly back to his dukedom. John Gielgud stands before the rest of the company in his blue gown to deliver the Epilogue. Miranda (Doreen Aris) and Ferdinand (Richard Johnson) stand at the back, and in front of them the lords: Adrian (Toby Robertson in a white shirt), Alonso (Robert Harris), Sebastian (Robin Lloyd) and Antonio (Mark Dignam). Francisco's part was cut in this production.

In 1951 Bernard Miles, in a theatre designed by Walter Stringer and C. Walter Hodges as a representation of an Elizabethan hall theatre, staged the storm scene with a minimum of rope and rigging and a swinging lantern. Critics responded with enormous enthusiasm to the revelation of what could be achieved on a bare stage. One reviewer compared it to Benthall's Stratford production in the same year, commenting that 'here the spectacle did not compete with the poetry' (Dymkowski, 78). Six years later Muriel St Clare Byrne commented rather disapprovingly on Brook's tempest:

> It was a good storm, as these storms go, if a trifle long; but nobody with an ordinary stage, and the whole box of tricks for scenery and lighting, stands much of a chance with this scene, now that Bernard Miles has shown ... what the Elizabethans probably did with it.
>
> (SQ, 490)

Perhaps the most significant new opportunity offered by the restoration of the original text came in the role of Caliban. For though adaptations had dominated the stage, Shakespeare's text had always been available to readers, and Coleridge, among others, had begun to articulate a more complicated response to the 'brute' Caliban early in the nineteenth century (see chapter 3). Malone, in 1808, had been the first to suggest that Bermuda narratives were important sources for Shakespeare's play, and thus to introduce the possibility of regarding Caliban as a figure of the colonized native. The notion was picked up by Hazlitt in 1818, and was alluded to in Kean's introduction to his performance script of 1857, and again by Beerbohm Tree in the souvenir programme for his 1904 performance. The 'colonial' Caliban was not entirely a discovery of the 1960s. It is symptomatic of the new attention afforded to this restored role that two of the principal actor–managers at the turn of the nineteenth century, Frank Benson and Beerbohm Tree, chose the role of Caliban for themselves. Benson first performed his 'pet part' at Stratford in 1891, and repeated it on many subsequent occasions. His was still, primarily, a comic version of Caliban, though informed by the notion that the character represented a Darwinian 'missing link'. (Benson researched the part by studying apes in the zoo, and swung head-down from trees in an athletic rendition of the role.) Beerbohm Tree rearranged Shakespeare's text in order to give Caliban greater prominence, and was, if not the first, then one of the most influential performers to encourage a sympathetic audience reaction to the 'freckled whelp' (1.2.283).

By the beginning of the twentieth century, then, Shakespeare's text was firmly restored. Dryden and Davenant, however, had adapted the play not in order to conduct a dialogue with a well-known master text, but simply because they thought it wouldn't work on their stage. Many readers of Shakespeare's text have thought that the play's theatrical problems were, paradoxically, a sign of its virtues. In 1823 'P.P.' wrote:

> We confess ... the very idea of *acting* such beautiful abstractions, such impalpable, shadowy conceptions as "The Tempest" and "The Midsummer Night's Dream" seem to us to be perfectly absurd. How satisfactorily are our ideas of Prospero, Caliban and Ariel embodied by a solemn stalking gentleman in a long gown and grey beard, a hairy man-o'-the-woods, and a robust young lady with a pair of painted gauze wings stuck to her shoulders?   (Oxberry, xvii)

This view is still to be found among many modern reviewers, who argue that *The Tempest* is more dramatic poem than play, and repeatedly insist upon the problems of bringing it to the stage. Derek Granger might stand for all, writing in 1957: 'One always thinks of [*The Tempest*] in the mind's eye as a favourite and then on each fresh acquaintance in the theatre one is apt to be disappointed by the result: it proves nearly always to be duller on the stage than in the memory' (*FT*). But if reviewers habitually compare the production they are seeing with the play that exists in their mind's eye, it is also the case that they frequently define the character of particular performances by setting them against some notional 'customary' rendition of the past. The inevitable tendency of reviewers (and of audiences) to employ a rhetoric of comparison in describing a particular performance usefully leads to consideration of some fundamental questions and problems concerning the nature of the evidence upon which this present study is founded.

The materials are provided by the documents, photographs and videos preserved in the RSC archive in the Shakespeare Centre, and each of these have strengths and limitations. The primary documents are the theatrical promptbooks, marked-up copies of the script which note cuts and alterations to the text, lighting and music cues, stage grouping, movement and 'business'. Other production records may include set designs, musical scores, lists of props, rehearsal records, stage manager's notes on individual performances, and so on. Not all survive for all productions – there is, for example, no surviving promptbook for the 1963 Williams–Brook production, nor any of Oliver's music for 1974. Furthermore, the promptbooks themselves are annotated at very different levels. Sometimes full and detailed (as for 1951, 1978 and 1982), they can often be frustratingly elliptical and cursory. These witnesses need to be treated with caution, too, since the same book might be used not only for the Stratford run, but for subsequent performances in Newcastle, London and elsewhere. As changes are introduced, old instructions are rubbed out, and it is often impossible to be sure at what stage these changes were made.

Photographic records might seem to offer reliable information. Yet in the earlier part of the period they were taken at specially lit photocalls, and may not represent at all accurately what the audience saw in the theatre. Even as photographs of the play in action become more numerous, they do not necessarily cover the whole production, and, furthermore, they record it as it was in its earliest stages. A similar problem affects the testimony of reviewers. In the earlier productions surveyed here, critics usually attended the opening night, and a number of those first performances were seriously marred by technical and other failures, whose influence on the minds of the critics, and on the actors' performances, can only be a matter of speculation. This is apart from the more general problem that any production takes time to 'bed down', and even though in more recent years press night has usually followed several previews, one has always to remember that printed opinion may be commenting on aspects of a production that later changed significantly. So, for example, almost all the reviews of the 1995 touring production referred to the London opening at the Young Vic, where all actors were on stage throughout, with Prospero at the side poring over a huge book – and the surviving photographs confirm that staging. Yet by the time it opened in Stratford all of this had gone.

And, of course, what none of these sources can even begin to suggest is the detail of actors' intonation and of interaction among characters on stage – the detail that is the very life of the theatrical experience. For productions since 1982 there are archive video recordings taken from a single fixed camera. They are invaluable, and do repair some of the gaps that other records leave, but they have all the limitations that one might expect from recordings under such conditions – they cannot always cope with the variation of theatrical lighting, so that details are frequently lost, and the actors seem even more remote than they do to a spectator sitting in the Stratford balcony. And they record only one arbitrarily chosen performance. Finally, it is generally true that documentation of all kinds grows richer as time passes – and this means that my commentary on later productions is generally much fuller than it can be on those at the beginning of the period. Nonetheless, despite the limitations, these records are unusually dense. And the aim of this study is, after all, not to give a blow-by-blow account of each production, but selectively to compare and contrast approaches to the central challenges of this most elusive of plays.

Rather than following the play sequentially through its successive acts, I have chosen to organize the greater part of this book around characters. This decision is an attempt to reflect one of the distinguishing features of *The Tempest*: the way in which its various groups barely meet until the play's ending. Their separation one from another is, indeed, fundamental to the play's thematic as well as its dramatic structure. It is not an unproblematic organizational decision, and the reader will find that there is considerable cross-reference between the chapters. After an initial focus on the central and commanding figure of Prospero, each of the four following chapters places its titular subjects in relationship to him. The spectacular and musical elements are so important to the play, and so pervasive, that it is appropriate to consider them separately in two final chapters.

As prelude to this discussion, I give a general sense of the character of the fourteen productions at Stratford since World War II (those of 1946 and 1951 were each repeated in the following season, with different actors and in the case of the first a new director) in a chronological sketch that focuses principally on one central decision that every *Tempest* must take – how to represent on stage the nowhere-land that is Prospero's island. It is a strange place, perceived very differently by its different inhabitants. It is either 'lush' or 'tawny' (2.1.55–6), a 'fearful country' (5.1.106) or 'of subtle, tender and delicate temperance' (2.1.44–5); its natural inhabitants include jays, marmosets and scamels (2.2.166–9), and Antonio's allusion to the roar of lions (2.1.316–17) seems to be accepted as entirely plausible. In the seventeenth-century Globe or Blackfriars, none of this mattered, since the bare stage was itself everywhere and nowhere. But in the modern theatre – or at least, in the main house at Stratford – decisions have to be made, locations created, and, as Dennis Kennedy observes: 'There is a clear relationship between what a production looks like and what its spectators accept as its statement and value' (Kennedy, *Looking*, 5).

The Tempest initiated the new season of 1946, and with it a new company policy, overseen by the recently appointed director, Sir Barry Jackson. For the first time (and to considerable opposition)

FIGURE 2 In 1946 an episcopal Prospero (Robert Harris) chastises a Caliban (Julian Somers) whose webbed hands and feet and 'monster' ears place him firmly in the old tradition of the part (1.2). They stand before Prospero's cell in which can just be seen books and an astrolabe, symbolizing his magic powers.

plays were introduced gradually during the season, and each entrusted to a different director. Eric Crozier was the director, and Paul Shelving (who had worked with Barry Jackson on his controversial modern-dress productions of Shakespeare in the 1920s at the Birmingham Repertory Theatre) was the designer. These were the days when the Shakespeare Memorial Theatre, despite its modest front apron, was still treated essentially as a proscenium-arch stage, complete with curtain. Shelving's design might be characterized as 'standard fairy-tale illustration', its vocabulary of rocks and tree roots owing something to Arthur Rackham. It offered a solid and distinct cell for Prospero, in which were books and an astrolabe, symbols of Prospero's magical powers that reappear frequently over the years (Figure 2). Locations in subsequent scenes were clearly differentiated. The set was, in fact, one of the few aspects of this production to attract positive notices. The *Birmingham Post* enthused:

> Magic casements were set ajar and we were allowed to glimpse the enchanted isle where a fantastic landscape reared in a series of coloured crags, and the many-hued features of the scene glowed beneath a sweeping arc of the rainbow.

Yet when the production was revived the following year, with a substantially different cast, H.S. Bennett and George Rylands commented that: 'it was re-produced by Norman Wright, using the same *décor* and costumes. Here he was unlucky, for nothing he could do could alter the gloomy setting' (*SS*, 109). Not for the first time, or the last time, two reviewers apparently contemplating the same object report upon it in totally contradictory terms.

The production imagined the play very much in the familiar terms of the earlier part of the century, with a dignified (though unbearded) Prospero, and an apelike Caliban. But in one respect the production was noteworthy for an experiment never again repeated, of using a boy actor to play the part of Ariel. Though his costume placed him in the tradition of winged Ariels stretching back into the eighteenth century (Figure 11), the fact remains that a young boy would almost certainly have played the part in 1611 – and to have such an Ariel profoundly colours the dynamic of the relationship between Prospero and his servant. This is one of the most important – and problematic – relationships in the play, and a good deal rests on the age and gender of the actor playing the spirit (see chapter 2). In this case the experiment seems to have failed – though it cannot have been helped in the reviewers' eyes by the fact that:

> when Prospero says farewell, ... [Ariel] was to walk a few paces, turn back to Prospero, tears in both their eyes, turn away again then actually fly up into the air ... But something went wrong. Instead of disappearing silently he crashed into the scenery and came swinging back to Prospero, before being yanked off his feet again to take some of the scenery with him as he was propelled into the wings.
>
> (Sinden, 1982, 75)

This was not the only disaster which befell the first night – the set for the shipwreck got stuck, took twenty-five minutes to change and, as Sinden reported, 'the audience grew restive and it was impossible for anyone, even Robert Harris as a superb Prospero, to recapture their attention' (75). If these two mishaps were not enough, the other innovation of this production, the use of recorded music by Lennox Berkeley, had threatened to lead to a musicians' strike, and, in the event, did not work; the programme boasted that 'the loud-speaking equipment in this Theatre is the first of its kind to be used', but it was 'badly timed and often inaudible' (*D. Herald*). In the production's 1947 revival Harris's Prospero was virtually the only continuity in the casting, with the 1946 Miranda (Joy Parker) replacing David O'Brien as Ariel. Though the set remained the same, the new director, Norman Wright, aimed at greater speed – in part by introducing a significant number of cuts in the opening two scenes. The overall tenor of response, however, was scarcely more positive than it had been the previous year.

The play was next revived in 1951, under the direction of Michael Benthall, who had made his name at the Old Vic, as a director 'the most likely not to fail in bringing a Shakespearean fantasy to the stage as pure spectacle' (*Scotsman*). The design was entrusted to the Australian, Loudon Sainthill, who 'provided something between a shell-encrusted landscape and a rocky seascape in which all things seemed to aspire to the shape of a cactus' (*Times*). 'Blending greens, whites, and browns, the single setting uses flats at the sides and a backdrop to give the effect of island scenery in perspective, and a gauze scrim at front and back added the mist of enchantment' (*SQ*, 336). The front of the apron was decorated with shells, and found space for the trusty astrolabe as a sign of Prospero's astrological power, as well as for a sun floating in the sky, a motif adopted by several later designers. The shapes of which this set were made reminded different critics of stalagmites, or of the anthills of the antipodes, and its overall effect was felt by many to be subaqueous – Robert Speaight in

1963 recalled that it 'suggested that Mr Loudon Sainthill had spent rather too long on the Great Barrier Reef staring through the glass bottom of his dinghy' (SQ, 424). It was certainly, by later standards, a crowded production. The stage was peopled with Prospero's spirits in various monstrous forms; the promptbook somewhat disconcertingly tells us that Prospero's magic robe was removed, at 1.2.24, not by Miranda but by a 'barnacle and a hedgehog'. Spirits carrying candelabra traced out the magic circle at the end, suggesting to one reviewer 'several centenarians awaiting the final touch to their birthday cakes' (SA Herald). Both 3.3 and the masque were staged with full effect, employing allusion to the scenic and costume designs of Inigo Jones, Ben Jonson's partner in the elaborate spectacles of the Jacobean and Caroline court (Figure 3). This influence was to be felt in later productions elsewhere. Peter Hall, in 1974, based his production at the National Theatre, London, on the idea that this play's generic allusion in Act 4 can be developed as a principal underpinning for the play as a whole. Sainthill attempted to find a balance between the strange, the threatening and the exquisite which delighted many of its audience, though Dennis Kennedy later characterized it as 'febrile', 'overripe' and 'busy in the extreme' (Looking, 175). Prospero was played by Michael Redgrave (who had nominated Benthall as his director). Richard Findlater suggested that 'the co-operation of Redgrave and Benthall – who stood, as it were, for the conflicting elements in this poetic masque – resulted in a successful union of spectacle and meditation, naturalism and formalism' (108). When the production was revived the following year, however, Ivor

---

FIGURE 3 (*opposite*) In Loudon Sainthill's 1951/2 set of pointed rocks, Ariel (Alan Badel) emerges as a harpy in 3.3 to chastise the 'three men of sin', Antonio (William Fox), Alonso (Jack Gwillim) and Sebastian (William Squire), who cower, left to right, at the front of the stage, watched by Adrian (Brendon Barry) and Francisco (Alan Townsend), with Gonzalo (Geoffrey Bayldon) on the right. The monstrous 'shapes', and Ariel's extravagant wings, owe something to the designs of Inigo Jones for the Stuart masque.

Brown, though recognizing that the setting had been much praised, yet objected: 'What we chiefly see at Stratford is a stony space with stalactites growing the wrong way up: it is as monotonous as shiversome ... To me [it] seems both gloomy in its grey monochrome and nonsensical in relation to the coral-tints and gold-glitter of the poet's rocks and beaches' (*Observer*). With hindsight, it is precisely the eeriness of the set which looks forward to the dominant tone of many later productions.

This is the last time we shall encounter a single production remounted with different actors, and there is some interest in observing how its internal dynamics were modified by the change of personnel in 1952. Peter Fleming wrote:

> The difference ... is due to the difference between Mr. Redgrave's Prospero and Sir Ralph Richardson's. The former was a magician, the latter is an illusionist ... his performance is throughout flat and naturalistic; ... and his Prospero, though human and likeable, is dangerously deficient both in power and in the quality of wonder.
> (*Spectator*)

In part it may have been this less powerful reading which enabled Michael Hordern's Caliban to emerge more strongly than that of his predecessor, Hugh Griffith, but even more interesting is the fact that the Ariel of Alan Badel in 1951 was replaced by Margaret Leighton. She was to be the last woman to play the part at Stratford until Bonnie Engstrom in 1995, and, in the opinion of Harold Conway and others, Richardson's understated Prospero allowed Ariel to 'take possession of the island and the play' (*E. Standard*).

If Benthall and Redgrave had begun to explore some of the darker possibilities of the play, the next production, in 1957, broke the traditional mould. For John Gielgud it was his third Prospero (he was to play the part once more on stage, and in Peter Greenaway's film, *Prospero's Books*, 1991). Its director was Peter Brook, for whom it also became a play to which he repeatedly returned. It is one of the most frequently cited of all the performances we are considering, though it seems, in part at least, to have acquired its reputation in retrospect. At the time of its first performance many were not happy with the set, with the music, with the extended slapstick comedy, or with the masque. This production transferred to Drury Lane for a season after its Stratford run – and it is revealing to see how the tone of the reviewers changes as they return to a production which was modified in certain respects (particularly in the masque), but in others had merely, as most productions do, grown in the intervening months.

The young Brook was an innovative and iconoclastic director, not least in his taking control of all elements of the production, including its design and music. As Dennis Kennedy remarks, Brook 'ensured that the look of his Shakespeare radiated the interpretive stance ... the "resuscitation" of the play progressed from making a new set of images for it' (*Looking*, 168). The *Nottingham Guardian* noted that 'the great Stratford stage and its equipment are used to their uttermost capacity; caves change their shape and size before our very eyes; the trap door sucks down Prospero's victims, and spirits are high fantastical'. But where the *Times* grumbled that 'Mr Brook's scenery is bare to the point of dullness', Milton Shulman commented that 'manipulating twanging noises and coloured lights with consummate dexterity, he has made of Prospero's island a producer's paradise' (*E. Standard*). This, indeed, is how Brook himself recalled the production a quarter of a century later:

> My first production in Stratford had followed the accepted view that *The Tempest* is a spectacle and therefore had to be brought alive by elaborate stage effects. So I enjoyed myself, designing striking visual moments, composing atmospheric electronic music, introducing goddesses and dancing shepherds. (Brook, 104–5)

What struck everyone, however, was Gielgud's reimagined Prospero. His reading of the role, and especially his emphasis on bitter anger and resentment, was to initiate the sequence of angry (and younger) Prosperos which reached its peak in the 1980s. For at least one critic, set and conception went together. Roy Walker wrote: 'the interpretation of Prospero superbly delivered by John Gielgud, a man whose wrongs haunted him through the winding caverns and overgrown jungles of the mind, largely justified the strangely subterranean settings and tangled hothouse vegetation' (*SS*, 135). The same might be said for the music, produced by Brook himself, a *mélange* of distorted recorded sounds which emphasized the island's alien character (see chapter 7). In other respects, however, Brook's reading of the play was a 'conservative' one. Caliban was still weighed down with a heavy animal suit, and the comic was emphasized, rather than the colonial. The play was concluded, as we have seen, on a note of reconciliation and harmony.

Brook was involved in the next *Tempest* at Stratford, in 1963, as associate director with Clifford Williams, though he seems to have had very little to do with the play once it got into production. Williams told David Addenbrooke:

> When it was decided that I would do the play, he said 'Look, I've done the thing several times before, and if I'm around can I help you do some work on it?' And so we hit on this formula whereby I was completely responsible for the end product, but he worked 'in association' with me.   (Addenbrooke, 247)

Williams's programme note suggests that there had been a fairly major rethink since 1957: 'at one time we thought of lifting all the scenery away at the end ... or of putting all the characters of the finale in clown's costumes, to underline the derisory nature of the play's resolution'. The design, by Abd'Elkader Farrah, created an abstract, alien, even alienating world. A vast, vaulted cyclorama was the single permanent setting, and, as the designer explained in his programme note:

> the bottom half of the circular wall ... is made of perspex, the top half of cinema-screen plastic lit by four projectors on trolleys. I wanted to give the idea of a magic wall, a mirror which splinters whenever and wherever you look at it.

He also commented: 'that eclipse at the start of the play, I wanted it to grow and spread over the entire cyclorama; but it costs four hundred pounds to put a zoom lens on a projector'. This programme was issued in June, a month after the play's opening – and it is not difficult to hear the note of self-justifying complaint here, for the expense of Farrah's set led to some very uncomfortable correspondence between the Technical Manager and the Board of the Royal Shakespeare Theatre, explaining cost overruns. Nonetheless, the abstraction of this translucent setting, 'on which strange suns and moons wax and wane with alarming frequency and enthusiasm' (*D. Mail*), pointed the way to the future. In front of this setting there were self-consciously 'stagy' tricks – including a conveyor belt which delivered mysterious objects, and some of the characters, on to the stage. Williams later felt that 'it was too far in advance of what people could take at the time ... many of the things that were turned down in that *Tempest*, bits of stage practice, have been subsequently accepted by audiences and critics' (Addenbrooke, 247).

Whether or not this was the principal reason for the lack of success may be doubted – few reviewers found Tom Fleming's Prospero powerful, and a number commented on the ponderousness of the production as a whole. But, even more than Brook's, this staging explored the possibility of a darker and more uncomfortable *Tempest* than most critics at the time expected. Some were able to detect in Roy Dotrice's blacked-up Caliban a hint of the colonial reading which elsewhere, if not in Stratford, was to become a dominant interpretation of the role in the last decades of the twentieth century (see Figure 19).

The play's next outing, in 1970, had a complicated genesis. Ian Richardson told Judith Cook:

> I was to have played Ariel in a production by Peter Hall ... with Michael Hordern as Prospero, then Peter couldn't do it and it had to be put off. Michael Hordern then dropped out and the project was taken on by Trevor Nunn and he asked me to play Prospero ... I accepted the challenge only to find that Trevor, too, had to give

up, but I was fortunate in having John Barton take it over, assisted
by Robin Phillips.   (Cook, 164–5)

Shortness of time may have necessitated a minimalist set, not
dissimilar to that for the previous season's *Twelfth Night* by the
same designer, Christopher Morley, which contained the action in
a tunnel of 'plain blue walls sloping inwards to meet a vast wedge-
shaped shutter suspended overhead. The effect is like looking
down a dark corridor, with at the end a square black door'
(*D. Telegraph*). The 'latticed white roof heaves and bellies
ingeniously into sail, ceiling or clothes-line for Prospero's magic
cast-offs' (*Observer*), and 'naked-looking spirits vaguely undulate
behind the transparent blue walls of the long, bleak passageway in
which the production is strangely set' (*New States.*). This led to
particular problems in the staging of the masque, and more
generally reviewers felt that the design contributed little to the
effectiveness of the performance as a whole.

Ian Richardson (at thirty-eight still the youngest actor to
undertake the part at Stratford) was aggressively dressed down (see
Figure 14). This did not please many reviewers, and his tendency
to put his hands in his pockets came in for especially severe
criticism from the well-mannered. But in this fairly 'glum'
production, in which Prospero's bitterness was again emphasized,
the relationship between Prospero and Ariel figured particularly
strongly – an anticipation of what was to become increasingly the
norm in later productions. In the same year Jonathan Miller had
offered a challenging attempt in his Old Vic production to render
the play in the light of Mannoni's influential analysis of the work
as a myth to characterize the psychology of colonization. His
employment of black actors to play both Caliban and Ariel
radically challenged perceptions of Prospero's servants, both in
their relationship to their master, and to one another. By contrast
Barry Stanton's Stratford Caliban was marked by a withered arm,
and an inability to stand up, so that he oared himself, horizontal,
about the stage (see Figure 26). He suffered from physical

deformity rather than monstrosity, and so was placed many leagues away from the racial reading that Miller and others were making central to the play. (See Hirst for an account of Miller's production.)

There is a further problem, however, in evaluating the not very positive reviews of this production, for the first-night gremlins struck again. The actor playing the Boatswain had forgotten that performances on press nights began early, and was not in the theatre when the play should have started. This would not perhaps have mattered too much, were it not that the sound of a ticking clock preceded the beginning of the storm (this emphasis on time had, incidentally, been present also in Redgrave's urgent and frequent consultation of an hour-glass, and Brook's introduction of the figure of Father Time into the masque of Act 4 – see Figure 39 – as well as in the changing moons of Farrah's design). Nobody, however, seems to have countermanded the starting of the clock, or to have explained the problems to the audience, whose growing impatience with the delay can only have been increased by the relentless *tick-tock*.

Even more minimalist – but necessarily so, since it was staged at The Other Place – was Keith Hack's 1974 production, which has left little trace in the archive. There are no photographs, and it was scantly reviewed; Stephen Oliver's music (though praised) is lost. Sheila Bannock described the set as 'an irregularly shaped raked wooden platform from which rises a single scaffolding tree, and sea and sky are represented by a silvery-grey-blue curtain running across the back, upon which are projected from time to time Prospero's magic visions' (*SA Herald*); Eric Shorter noticed the 'spiral of wooden steps' which connected its levels (*D. Telegraph*). It seems, like its predecessor, to have been a production beset with internal problems – a late change of casting for the part of Prospero the most obvious of them. Nonetheless, in casting Jeffrey Kissoon as Caliban this was the first Stratford production to afford the part to a black actor. The reaction of the reviewers was, paradoxically enough, to object that he was far too handsome and noble a figure to be taken as 'monstrous'. This, of course, might well indicate a political naiveté on the part of the critics – that Caliban's monstrosity is, precisely, the construct of the colonizer could be strongly implied here. In the same year, in Peter Hall's National Theatre production, this double focus was made explicit. Denis Quilley as Caliban was given a bisected make-up, 'on one half the ugly scrofulous monster whom Prospero sees, on the other an image of the noble savage' (Irving Wardle, in Dymkowski, 59). But the discomfort which these reviews evinced in interpreting the significance of the colour of the actor's skin, rather than of Caliban's, persists, and has become more problematic as colour-blind casting has become the norm. (Interestingly, Kissoon in 1994 played Prospero in a production by Bill Alexander at Birmingham, where Caliban was played by a white actor; see Dymkowski, 69.)

In the 1978 production, once more by Clifford Williams, David Suchet played Caliban explicitly as the 'noble savage', justly angered at the theft of his island. But in his account of his development of the role he notes that the director 'didn't really have any concrete ideas, except that I might be half-fish, half-man (presumably I would wear fins) or possibly something deformed, like a thalidomide child' (Suchet, 169), and he records the gradual evolution of his own interpretation, which Williams seemed happy enough to go along with. But in developing this view of the character he was not assisted by his Prospero. Hordern recorded later that 'there are those who read anti-colonialist sentiments into *The Tempest*. I can't go along with that, although Shakespeare does present Caliban's side of things with some sympathy' (Sales, 175). This was not the only problem, for as he himself made plain in an interview during his time in Stratford, and even clearer when drawing on that interview for his autobiography, he felt out of temper with Clifford Williams, unhappy with the company as a whole – or at least with the fact of being in a company – and seems simply to have taken himself off fishing whenever possible. This cannot have helped the production to arrive at a coherent reading of the play. Indeed, John Velz reported that Clifford Williams told his cast at the first rehearsal that it would be a *Tempest* 'without a conception' (*Cahiers Elis.*, 104).

There were, however, some continuities with his earlier production, particularly in its setting. Ralph Koltai, like Farrah, provided an abstract set in which 'the island itself ... is featureless and barren, a flat plain with a dark curve of black plastic at the back' (*FT*) and either a blood-red sun or a silver disc floated ominously in the sky (Figure 4). Characterized by reviewers as 'vaguely lunar' (*Cahiers Elis.*, 104), or having 'the disembodied eeriness of modern surrealism' (*Oxf. Mail*), its darkness was contrasted with the bright colours of the costumes of the lords, and of the spirits in the Act 4 masque. There were practical problems with this set. It may have been visually impressive in an austere way, but the trap doors set into it were, during blackouts, barely visible to the cast, who wandered round in some trepidation. They were also noisy. The promptbook notes that 'music or sound should <u>start before</u> traps move to eliminate noisy traps noises'. The hollowed 'rock' in which Hordern sat for much of 1.2 squeaked audibly when he moved. Ruby Wax later remembered that 'I went into the RSC at the lowest level. I played a piece of seaweed in *The Tempest*. The play was done on a garbage bag representing timelessness. The production didn't have a chance' (Wax, 57). Germaine Greer described it as

> an extra-galactic landscape with curved red cruds upon it, around mechanical craters whence Prospero's baseless visions, only too clearly fashioned of plastic, would noisily emerge. Upon this desolate planet the sun never shone and no filbert or scamel ever grew. (*Spectator*)

Only John Barber saw any real connection between setting and concept, when he wrote:

> Prospero's island is no pretty vision of magic banquets, of fairy lakes and groves. It is a place of torment and trouble – 'this fearful

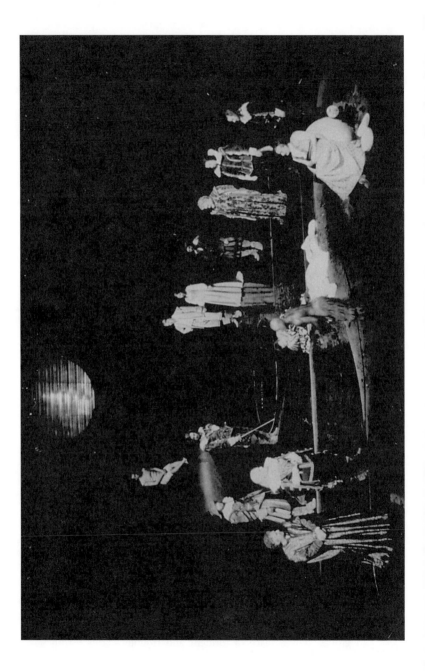

country' [5.1.106], Gonzalo calls it. Ralph Koltai has designed a
plain black cubic room. The sparse decorations are of steel, and Ariel
looks like a man from outer space. *(D. Telegraph)*

But in general this was a classic example of the way in which a set
designed and largely constructed before the rehearsal process
began imposed itself upon a production which, in the event,
derived little sustenance from it.

The perilousness of the set was evident on the opening night,
when the main lighting board failed, and the emergency board
had to be used. In the backstage dimness Miranda collided with
the black 'wave', and appeared as if 'someone had just made a
spirited and largely successful attempt to saw her nose off, her
right profile being so extensively coated with gore that she looked
like a refugee from *Titus Andronicus* rather than Milan' (*S. Times*).
It is astonishing how few of the reviewers comment on this
disaster, or on the problems with the lighting.

After four visually spare and abstractly designed productions,
Maria Bjornson's 'beautiful and appropriate' setting for Ron
Daniels's 1982 production came as a complete contrast (see
Figure 32). As Roger Warren described it:

As the great prow of Alonso's sinking ship disappeared into the
forestage, it revealed behind it the bleached skeleton of another ship
– presumably the 'rotten carcass of a butt' in which Prospero had
arrived on his island years before, and serving both as his 'cell' and
as the permanent set. *(SQ, 85)*

FIGURE 4 (*opposite*) Caliban (David Suchet) and his co-conspirators have
just emerged from a centre-stage trap to confront Michael Hordern's
Prospero (5.1), on the left. The black floor of Ralph Koltai's 1978 set,
presided over by a disc that changed from white to blood-red, curls up at
the back into a 'wave' on which Ariel (Ian Charleson) sits. Sitting in the
seat which Prospero had occupied in 1.2, Antonio (Paul Brooke) casts a
baleful eye on the proceedings. The gorgeous costumes of the lords made a
striking visual contrast to the dark setting.

This 'hyperrealistic wreck' (*Cahiers Elis.*, 117) dominated the stage visually, and physically – the Prospero, Derek Jacobi, complained that 'there is not one piece of the stage on which you can tread with ease' (*Cahiers Elis.*, 117), and several reviewers felt that it cramped the play's action. The majority, however, were not only delighted by its spectacular appeal, but saw it as a design to which the production as a whole was successfully keyed. Michael Coveney discerned 'a pleasing emblematic flair' in the production, where 'Prospero's island is ... a broken ship of state ... This is a strong visual conception that underlines the political upheavals back home in Milan and establishes Prospero as an exiled magician rather than an eccentric conjurer' (*FT*). But, as Dymkowski points out, the very physical presence of the ship left 'the audience unsure whether to read the image on stage as literal, metaphorical or both' (90). Daniels cut Prospero's characterization of their 'butt' as 'not rigged, / Nor tackle, sail, nor mast' (1.2.146–7), implying that it was indeed the boat upon which he had arrived, but at the simplest level the transformation of the ship carrying Alonso into a ship which (might have) carried Prospero neatly brought together the past and the present, providing an apt environment for Jacobi's performance, dominated by a convincing sense of the present reality of past hurt.

The visual richness of the production – the most luxuriant since 1951 – was complemented by aural plenitude in Stephen Oliver's score, which rose to a through-composed operatic setting of the masque and thereby established the hope embodied in Ferdinand and Miranda as a real alternative to revenge and intransigent evil. Desmond Pratt commented that 'for the first time in my memory, the young lover pair makes the centrepiece of the play' (*Yorks. Post*). Whereas Guy Woolfenden's fine score in 1978 seemed, stylistically, to struggle against the severity of Koltai's setting, Oliver's pastiche musical language exactly complemented Bjornson's 'historical eclecticism ... which regularly combined lavish visuals with disjunctive temporality' (Kennedy, *Looking*, 294). Less successful was the representation of Caliban in

Rastafarian dreadlocks, where any political point was diffused in comic effect. But the production commanded far more enthusiasm than any since 1957. Michael Billington commented: 'Ron Daniels has raised *The Tempest*. Not since Peter's Brook's production 25 years ago has there been a first-rate revival of this stubbornly undramatic play in the main house at Stratford' (*Guardian*), while Jack Tinker declared: 'Never before in my memory have all the elements of masque, magic, vengeance and retribution combined with such force on one stage' (*D. Mail*).

If 1982 was splendid in costume and setting, Nicholas Hytner's 1988 production seemed deliberately to set out to establish its difference from its immediate predecessor by returning to the spareness of the 1970s. Robert Smallwood described David Fielding's set:

> A grooved, steeply raked white disc serves up the performers, as it were, on a plate to the audience. The center stage occasionally opens up for Prospero's cell, and for the first half a great boulder (which one must not allow to remind one of a baked potato) lies beside it. This is the rock in which Caliban is stied, but after his initial entry it is hardly used ... Apart from this, the stage is a starkly empty white space in front of a blue cyclorama with nowhere to hide and no mysteries to conceal. It is saved from visual monotony only by the rouched curtains that go up and down in front of the cyclorama to suggest clouds ... and by the lighting ... On this uncompromising flying saucer of a space, this disk of a desert island, Prospero appears in simple white shirt and tweedy trousers like a businessman ready for a weekend at his gardening ... and the courtiers in high-Renaissance costume including (unwisely, really, for a shipwreck) full armor. Is the director suggesting a time warp, an island set apart temporally as well as geographically? The question is not pursued. (*SQ*, 85–6)

If the curtains at the back of the stage suggested to Michael Billington 'the old Regal Cinema in Leamington Spa' (*Guardian*), Kate Kellaway was rather more positive about the design, which gave her 'a marvellous sense that the island is decorated only by characters. Each seems a discovery washed up on the shore, a curiosity to be inspected or a miracle to be wondered at' (*Observer*). The bare space and white and blue light, the 'lunar landscape', as Michael J. Collins described it (*SB*, 9), was not softened by Jeremy Sams's modernist musical language, which underlined the fearful quality of the island. The effect was to throw the attention firmly on John Wood's mercurial Prospero as the centre of the production. Despite the coldness of the setting, this was a reading which emphasized the tormented humanity of Prospero, suggesting to Billington that he 'is a Freudian wreck whose battles are all internal' (*Guardian*). His performance provoked very different critical reactions, but reading the reviews is complicated, since there were no less than three important productions of *The Tempest* in the UK at the same time, and many critics organized their reports to compare the various versions. Of the three this was by far the least political – Jonathan Miller at the Old Vic was having a second go at a post-colonial reading, and the harshness of Michael Bryant's Prospero in Peter Hall's National Theatre production reflected a bleak view of the play as unambiguously about power. As Virginia M. Vaughan commented, the RSC production 'follows an old tradition in its emphasis on mercy and forgiveness'. But she concludes that though 'it may seem to be a throw-back to earlier, pre-colonial interpretations, in the private sphere it bears un-mistakeable signs of our own time' (*SB*, 11).

If the two productions of the 1980s turned upon strong performances by their respective Prosperos, the two main-house productions in the 1990s were much less centred on the Duke of Milan. In 1993 Sam Mendes's production derived its central visual and thematic impetus from the consideration of *The Tempest* as a play about theatre, and Prospero's magic as a specifically theatrical magic. This was evident right from the beginning of the play, as Russell Jackson described it:

> The play began with a bare boarded stage, in the center of which was
> a large property basket. An orange disk of sun lowered from a

> backdrop. As the house lights dimmed, a [blue]-suited figure, Ariel,
> emerged deliberately from the basket, closed the lid, then stood on
> it and raised his hand to start the swing of a lantern lowered to him
> from the flies.   (*SQ*, 343)

This theatrical basket was later to function as the route of Caliban's entry on to the stage, and into it the 'low-life' characters were shoved at the play's end. Prospero observed the storm perched upon what was later revealed as a stage electrician's ladder and the emphasis on metatheatricality was evident both in the single folding screen set centre stage, just in front of a trap, from behind which characters emerged, and in the 'pop-up-book' theatre which was let down to contain the masque. As Prospero's cell was revealed at the beginning of the second scene it not only contained huge piles of books (seen by some as a deliberate allusion to Peter Greenaway's film, *Prospero's Books*, released a couple of years earlier), but Prospero's desk, as Robert Smallwood noted, bore

> an odd resemblance to the assistant stage-manager's properties
> table and we are not at all surprised when the bunch of marigolds
> on it turns out to be a designer's scale model for the eight-foot
> sunflowers among which King Alonso's party will later wander.
>
> (Smallwood, 195)

This concern with theatre as metaphor for power led to a preoccupation with matters of service and freedom. At crucial points Mendes altered the text, so that, for example, Prospero's speech commending Ariel's performance as a harpy (3.3.83ff.) was moved – as it had been in a number of earlier productions – to the end of the scene. Mendes, however, cut the final three lines and ended the speech with the words 'they now are in my power'. The interval followed immediately, underlining the directorial emphasis still further. So too, at Stratford, Prospero's offer of pardon (5.1.293–4), and Caliban's intention to sue for grace (296) were both cut, and Prospero sent him back, not to 'my cell' (292), but to 'thy cell'. (The lines were restored for the London transfer.) The production, however, was rather muted by Alec McCowen's intelligent but underpowered Prospero. Peter Holland noted that the very device intended to emphasize his supervisory role – his frequent overseeing of the action from the top of a ladder at the back of the stage – put him in a position 'from which I would defy any actor, even Robert Stephens, to dominate that stage' (171). The effect, indeed, was to strengthen even more the force of Simon Russell Beale's Ariel, perhaps the most striking and extreme reading of the part as 'resentful servant'. It was he who literally stage-managed everything in the play, instructing the white-clad attendants in scene-setting, and initiating action with a clap of his hands. In this, as in the whole production, there was plenty of evidence of the most completely conceptualized reading of the play since Brook's in 1957. Robert Smallwood used it as his first example of 'directors' Shakespeare', defined as offering 'an approach to the play that is likely to be of particular interest to those who already know *The Tempest*' and one which not only presents Shakespeare's play, but offers 'something of an inter-pretative essay upon it, showing its awareness of other critical essays, academic and theatrical' (176–7).

The self-conscious intellectualism of Mendes's *Tempest* did not continue in the next production. David Thacker, the director in 1995, wrote in his programme note: 'I've always believed – and I know that this isn't a particularly innovative, radical or new insight – that *The Tempest* is an autobiographical play.' This was the first *Tempest* since 1974 not to be produced in the main house. It opened in London, at the Young Vic, and came to the Swan before setting out on tour. The play was paired with Edward Bond's *Bingo*, a play about Shakespeare himself in retirement. Paul Jesson played both Prospero and Shakespeare, underlining Thacker's view of *The Tempest*. In pursuit of the autobiographical concept, the production in London opened with all the actors on stage (as had been the case in 1974), with Prospero sitting at the side poring over a huge book. The narrative of 1.2 was then illustrated by the actors playing out the conspiracy as it was recounted. The general effect was one of clutter; as Paul Taylor commented, it 'looks like some congested dossers' hostel because of the misguided idea of having all the characters in Prospero's power slumped in sleep on the stage whenever they aren't acting' (*Independent*). Roz Symon, the Education Director of the tour, noted that Paul Jesson was not happy with the continuous presence of Prospero, and the actors were relieved when much of this was cut on the transfer to the Swan (74–5). All that remained was the idea that the spirits themselves became the logs which Ferdinand carried, and the 'trumpery' which lures Stephano and Trinculo away from their conspiracy. According to Symon, 'the idea behind the spirits therefore ... was that they were exactly equivalent to the writer's creative imagination' (76). If that was the idea, then it signally failed to cross to the audience. The continued presence of Ariel and the spirits, reacting, for example, to Caliban's freedom song 'like sufferers with acute migraine' (Holland, 229), seemed distracting rather than thematically justified.

Because this was a touring production, its setting was necessarily very simple. Some trunks and boxes were the sole furnishings of the stage. The recollection of 1993, as Caliban appeared from one of the trunks, yet emphasized the difference between the two. In this 'underimagined' production (Holland, 227) the concepts were undeveloped, and the central box, upon which Ariel stood effectively enough during the storm, uttering the master's words before shafts of fire played about the stage, became in later scenes something of an obstacle. In 2.1, for example, Ariel was uncomfortably perched on this box through-out, getting in the way of Antonio and Sebastian's dialogue; in the perfunctory masque in Act 4 the same confinement to this fixed point did nothing to assist the creation of a ceremonious atmosphere for the celebration of Ferdinand and Miranda's betrothal. In the costuming a very clear distinction was made between the Jacobean dress of the lords, and the drab costuming of the inhabitants of the island. As one reviewer remarked: 'If there's any statement being made here, it's how to dress for the next Glastonbury festival. Miranda shows the way with her cut-off leggings, baggy shirt, tattoos, wrist-bands, big hair and bare feet' (*Time Out*). In emphasizing the tattiness of the island's inhabitants the production suggested that this was decidedly a place from which Prospero and his daughter might be very ready to escape.

The most interesting feature of the production was the simple fact that for the first time since 1952 Ariel was played by a woman, and, as Peter Holland suggested, 'If a female Ariel seemed like a throw-back to an old theatre tradition long out of fashion, Engstrom at least made something significant of it, using her gender to create an additional layer to the master–servant relationship' (Holland, 229). It is worth remarking that the reviews of this production improved significantly when it moved to Stratford (Peter Holland excepted), with Martin Esslin describing it as 'an extremely effective, fast-moving and plausible performance' (*Plays Int.*), and even in generally dismissive accounts the Miranda of Sarah-Jane Holm, and David Fahm's Ferdinand, attract more positive attention than is often the case. It is a pity that this, together with the 1974 attempt to perform the play on the kind of bare stage for which it was originally imagined, should not have succeeded, for the next production, Adrian Noble's in 1998, illustrated the weaknesses, as well as the strengths, of the elaboration the technology of the main house makes possible, and the appetite of its audience demands.

This was a striking production visually. As Russell Jackson describes it:

> The set was a disc of pebbles resembling a Zen garden, bounded by a semi-circular cyclorama at the back, with access from the sides and a flower path through the stalls (down the left-hand aisle). Apart from a log fire, which rose from the floor for the first appearance of Prospero and Miranda, and an outsize conch, brought on as Caliban's cell, this was a bare island. A diaphanous curtain ran

across the front of the stage on a curving track, marking the ends of scenes like a cinematic wipe. A curtain at the back, lowered in front of the cyclorama and attached to Prospero's shoulders, suggested a magic cloak directly connected with the skies: he put it off after the tempest itself and reassumed it just before summoning the powers he was about to relinquish ... All this fabric took light wonderfully, giving a sense of the island's magical variety. At the opening, the downstage cloth was lit from the front, making it a translucent but opaque greenish-blue wall.   (SQ, 196–7)

Dazzling though the effect was, reviewers were less than confident that it reflected a coherent conception of the play as a whole. Michael Billington, noting the echo of Giorgio Strehler's famous Milan production of the play in 1978, wondered whether the dominant idea of Noble's staging was 'that this is a play about reality and illusion and the wonderment of theatre itself' (*Guardian*). He lamented (as usual) the absence of 'an exploration of the play's colonial politics or psychological darkness', yet Charles Spencer, describing it as a 'solid, beta-double-plus production', managed to find 'a dutiful nod to the fashionable theory that *The Tempest* is a study of colonialism. The black Ferdinand is placed in shackles like a slave, and both Ariel and Caliban cry for freedom, though with different degrees of resentment' (*D. Telegraph*). Russell Jackson, calling it an 'effective' production, yet felt a 'lack of engagement' with the play's ideas (*SQ*, 197).

The contrast with Mendes's production is instructive. There the concern with metatheatricality was pursued throughout; here it was gestured towards as Prospero's magic was symbolized by the huge silk curtains he attached himself to, but, apart from that, the swishing gauze was simply a theatrical sleight of hand that drew attention to itself, but did not connect with the actors and action. Interestingly, this is one of the rare cases when watching the production again on the video changed my impression of it. In the theatre I had found it rather vacuous, would have agreed with Peter J. Smith that the 'design extravagances were offered in an attempt to disguise the shortcomings of the performances' (*Cahiers Elis.*, 125), and would have concurred with Robert Smallwood's wish that David Calder's Prospero had been 'just a little bit bigger' (*SS*, 238). On the video, which minimized the design effects in all kinds of ways, the intelligence of Calder's performance was strikingly more evident, for all the film's blurriness and bleached colour. In 1993 Peter Holland suggested that 'In the Swan, McCowen ... would have been magnificent; on the main stage the performance lacked the authority this theatre, as much as the part, demands' (171). The same might be said of Calder's Prospero, which ultimately seemed to be drowned in silk.

The next production, by James MacDonald in 2000, presents an interesting paradox. As in 1974 and 1995 this was a small-scale production, designed to fit in the 'module' which would enable it to tour to leisure centres and halls across the UK and abroad. Its basic design was therefore very simple; the space was arranged with

> seating on three sides of a white platform. Its surface consisted of three gentle undulations curving up at the back to a white screen, with a narrow platform crossing it about ten feet from floor level and allowing entrances and exits above from either side of the rear wall.   (*SQ*, 113)

The steep drop at the back 'like a funfair water chute ... as well as allowing Ariel his abrupt, tobogganing descents, provides gradients that are a formidable obstacle to the drunken characters' (*Independent*). The closeness of audience to actors enabled Philip Voss to involve them in his long narrative without effort, and without much movement; elsewhere it assisted in the communication of the problematic lords' scene of 2.1, and permitted a quiet intensity in Ferdinand and Miranda's wooing. It facilitated, just as the earlier small-scale productions had done, whatever the merits of individual performances, a close engagement with the narrative and with verbal detail.

FIGURE 5 Video images of the sea were projected on to the steep fall at the back of the white set in 2000 so that Ferdinand (Oliver Dimsdale) appears to be drowned on his first entrance in 1.2. Ariel (Gilz Terera), with a gold lamé dress over his suit, representing a sea nymph, sits on the raised walkway at the back.

But Jeremy Herbert's 'clean minimalist set' (*S. Times*), was simultaneously a screen for 'multiple video projections that are a key feature of this staging' (*Independent*). Whereas in 1974 Keith Hack had to be content with four photographic slides to project abstract images of the banquet and the goddesses of the masque, here the storm was created by film of 'real' rolling waves, which returned as Ariel sang 'Full fathom five' poised above a Ferdinand who seemed to be literally drowned at the bottom of the ramp (Figure 5). Among other effects Ceres, the goddess of harvest, played in front of hugely magnified ears of corn; Stephano and his co-conspirators were accompanied in 4.1. by a 'ground-level chase through long grass [which] captured the sense of panic arising from the directionless pursuit' (*Cahiers Elis.*, 106); and scarlet flowers waved as Ariel sang of lying in the cowslip's bell. Reviewers' reaction to these visual pyrotechnics varied wildly. Paul Taylor thought that the 'notion of the eerie provisionality of everything on the island is communicated well by the dream-like filmed images' (*Independent*), whilst Susannah Clapp felt that 'Many of these images are pleasing, but they're effects rather than ideas: they illustrate what's being said. The video film makes the human flesh in front of it look clumsy, as if cellulite were a staging-post on the way to celluloid' (*Observer*). Lynn Gardner argued that 'We see the storm, but we never experience the emotional tempests and transformations of the characters. The visuals ... take precedence over the actors, who are only allowed to be efficient puppets' (*Guardian*), but Peter J. Smith thought it 'an excellent design, evocative without being intrusive, economical and, despite the diminutiveness of its scale, fittingly amazing for such a miraculous play' (*Cahiers Elis.*, 108).

For some, then, this 'elegantly arty' production (*E. Standard*) was an appropriately dreamlike and 'hallucinogenic' creation of the nowhere land that is Prospero's island (*What's On*); for others it was an externally imposed visual concept which had no roots in a strong idea of the play itself, distracting rather than revealing. The same divided reaction attended Orlando Gough's musical score. Performed by musicians we could see, who also functioned as scene-shifters and spirits, it was largely made up of vocalizations on nonsense syllables. Robert Gore-Langton complained that 'songs are complemented with a lot of unscripted chanting and whatnot which gets on your wick' (*D. Express*), and Charles Spencer similarly objected that:

> The only major irritant is Orlando Gough's score, in which six
> vocalists cluster round the stage and perform nonsensical 'mouth

> music'. 'Ong, ang, ing, ong!' they chirrup, squeak and drone ... One
> fervently wishes that they would put a sock in it.   (*D. Telegraph*)

But Russell Jackson felt that 'the "noises" and music of the island
... complemented these simple but richly atmospheric projections
and light effects' (*SQ*, 113), and Kate Bassett found it 'inspired,
blending eerie bird-like cries with tribal drums and rhythmic
breaths' (*Indep. Sun.*). That I consider it one of the three finest of
the scores discussed in more detail in chapter 7, whereas in the
end I found the video distractingly overemphatic, says as much
about my own predilections as anything else, and is a useful
reminder that, even in a book which attempts to give as objective
an account of performances as is possible, the writer's prejudices
are as significant a distorting factor as any of the other problems
with interpreting the evidence that have been set out here. More
central to what follows is the way in which this production's use
of 'real' images rendered insubstantial by their video projection,
but of musical sound constructed of nonsense syllables yet uttered
by real musicians, encapsulated a central problem for directors
and actors alike in finding a way of articulating the play's
otherworldliness in the corporeal reality of the stage.

Michael Boyd's 2002 production was designed originally for
the Roundhouse in London, and, on its transfer to Stratford,
brought the Victorian engine shed to the RST. An apsidal wall of
brick, rising to a hint of a domed ceiling, made a severe and
abstract backdrop. The storm was played out on a circular silver
disc, with ladders and ropes rising to the flies; as it ended the disc
moved backwards and came to rest tilted against the back wall.
(This was a redesign of the original, where the floor was of wood,
and, according to the actors, worked much more securely.) The
severity of the set corresponded to Boyd's harsh view of the play in
general, and of Prospero in particular. Malcolm Storry's Duke
emphasized throughout the bitterness of his anger, both at
Caliban and at his political enemies. In 1993 Carole Woods, in
What's On, had complained, of Mendes's production, at what she

perceived as a lack of 'any resonances with the play's latent themes of imperialism and power. It's as if the past decades – and the reassessments they have brought – had never existed.' In the same year, however, Ralph Berry commented: 'I suspect that directors have become bored with Caliban as a victim of colonial oppression ... the colonial framework is a constriction of the play, which may have outlived its usefulness' (129). But it was only in 2002 that, finally, Stratford saw a *Tempest* in which its potential to sustain a colonial reading was explored with any real determination. Caliban was played by a black actor, and additional lines and business emphasized his position as dispossessed king of his island (see chapter 3). But the colonial reading was crossed, and perhaps somewhat diffused, by the production's equal emphasis on Prospero's fear of sexuality, which provoked his treatment both of Ferdinand and of Caliban, and was embodied in the way that the eroticism of the aerial 'dance' of nymphs and reapers spurred him to end the masque. It was further complicated by the fact that, for the first time on the main stage since 1952, Ariel's role was entrusted to a female actor, playing the part very much as a boy. Though her colour and her accent might have prompted suggestions of a parallel between her servitude and that of Caliban, she actually presented a reading of the role less resentful than any for the past fifty years – with the significant exception of Engstrom in 1995. Billington called it 'a truly terrific *Tempest* ... a truly great production' (*Guardian*), though, as usual, some others were much less impressed.

The Tempest is a repetitive play, insistently replaying conspiracies, and underlining parallels of one kind and another between its characters. Boyd responded with a production which itself emphasized continuities and similarities: the Mariners became shapes; the Boatswain's whistle turned into Ariel's pipe; Ferdinand and Caliban were identically harnessed; the 'trumpery' which distracts Stephano and Trinculo consisted of the robes and coats of Alonso, Antonio and Sebastian. In the end, however, the production did not, to me, quite cohere. The very clarity with which different strands were underlined seemed to inhibit their blending into a larger vision – but then, that is precisely the difficulty which confronts any and every production of this most elusive of plays.

NOTE

1 All references to Shakespeare's plays are to the Arden editions.

PROSPERO

The fortunes of *The Tempest* on stage depend, if not entirely, then disproportionately, on the actor playing Prospero. Ian Richardson called it 'the most difficult role I have ever undertaken' (Cook, 164–5), and indeed in no other play did Shakespeare confront his principal actor – presumably, in 1611, Richard Burbage – with a greater challenge. The problems derive, in the first place, from the curiously unfocused nature of Prospero's ambition in the play's narrative. In his conversation with Miranda he rejoices that his enemies are now in his power (1.2.178–84) – thus making him sound like the standard revenger of Elizabethan and Jacobean drama, and suggesting that the arc of the play might be taken as Prospero's achievement of the restoration of his dukedom. But at the same time he also assures his daughter that he has 'done nothing but in care of thee' (1.2.16), suggesting a rather different spring for his action. To combine, or to reconcile, these two stated motivations for the action – the 'tough' and the 'tender', one might say – is problem enough. It is complicated further, however, by the ambivalence that attends Prospero's crucial change of heart in 5.1. Whereas he responds to Ariel's challenge to him to forgive in a brief half-line (5.1.20), without much apparent sense of struggle, the decision to renounce magic generates, shortly afterwards, one of the most powerful and emotionally fraught speeches in the play. The decision to 'drown my book' (5.1.57) seems to cost him more than the forgiveness of his enemies. To focus on Prospero the magus, or to place the human duke at the centre – or to manage a reconciliation between the two – is one of the major decisions the actor must take. But whatever approach is adopted, the fact that Prospero controls virtually all the play's action means that it is only through and in him that real dramatic tension can be generated.

The question of how to approach the part is one which a number of Stratford Prosperos have addressed in print. The modern actor is trained to found interpretation upon an imagined psychological consistency. Yet Michael Redgrave argued, after playing the part in Benthall's 1951 production, that 'Stanislavski was mistaken to follow so psychological an approach to Shakespeare's characters ... the full truth of this was only lately made fully clear to me when playing Prospero' (Redgrave, 73–4). Even as he disowned this method, however, he acknowledged that it was still important for the actor to find some starting point which would animate and shape his own performance. Redgrave found it in the lines:

> And thence retire me to my Milan, where
> Every third thought shall be my grave.
>
> (5.1.311–12)

He saw them as a 'clue to some kind of theatrically effective Prospero in which I pictured him as a very old man who was uncertain that he could accomplish his task in time' (75). Redgrave commented that this was very much his own, individual approach, and he rightly observed that the actor's stimulus might or might not communicate itself directly to the audience.

In this same chapter Redgrave acerbically dismissed the 'silly, literal assumption that if [Prospero] had a daughter of 14 he *need* not be so very old', yet in 1970 the same sense of a Prospero on the edge was important to the young Ian Richardson. He struggled with 'those unaccountable rages – the sheer impatience of the man', and reported that:

> I was still puzzling over it when I saw Trevor Nunn and I explained
> my difficulty to him and he thought for a while and then said, do
> you know I think Prospero probably knows there is something very
> wrong with him medically, something like a cancer. Now he didn't
> suggest for a moment that we put out a programme note saying that
> this was the view which was to be taken, but he felt it might help
> illuminate all sorts of areas for myself. So I decided to imagine that
> Prospero has severe pains inside and that he knows – as he is so wise
> and mysterious a man – that it is something very serious. So he
> knows that he has to move very quickly because he hasn't got long
> to live. It worked very well for me.   (Cook, 165–6)

What both actors share is an effort to render Prospero's anger
comprehensible, even justifiable, at least to themselves, by
concentrating on the sense of time running out that is so marked
in the repeated references to the hour of the day that are sprinkled
through the text.

In the last forty years or so the dominant portrait of Prospero
at Stratford and elsewhere has generally taken his irascibility as its
starting point, but it is not the only choice. The older convention
of seeing Prospero more benignly is to be found in a number of
performances. Michael Hordern in 1978, for example, offered: 'by
far the kindest performance of this role I have seen. Ascetic
aloofness, unapproachable authority, arbitrary severities, and its
other forbidding aspects are all subdued in the portrait of a wise
and caring father' (*Times*). This concurs with Hordern's own
account of the key to the role as he saw it: 'one often finds a line
early on, a text you might almost say, on which to hang one's
characterisation and performance. "I have done nothing but in
care of thee" [2.1.16] is, for me, just such a line' (Sales, 173). Philip
Voss in 2000 similarly felt that 'Miranda and Ferdinand are at the
centre of my performance of Prospero. Through them and their
offspring I will accomplish my revenge over my brother.' In thus
reconciling the motivation of revenge and of paternal care,
consciously or not, Voss echoed the Stanislavskian analysis offered
by David L. Hirst, who wrote:

> Prospero's super-objective is the handing over of Naples and Milan
> to the joint heirs, Ferdinand and Miranda. His particular objectives,
> therefore, are essentially the bringing together of the lovers and the
> attempt to make the guilty restore to him his rightful inheritance.
>
> (Hirst, 56)

The effect, however, was to generate a performance which, like Hordern's, struck many reviewers as 'serene and sweet, paternal and kind' (*Times*).

In both cases many reviewers were less than happy with a kindlier rendition. This is both a mark of the way in which the dominant interpretation has shifted over the years, and at the same time a register of a real, central problem with the figure of Prospero. For modern habits of mind depart from those of the seventeenth century in ways that profoundly affect our responses to the play's central character. In the first place, we do not accept, as Shakespeare's society generally did, that the authority of duke over subject, master over servant, father over child, is fundamentally unquestionable. How that power should be exercised was certainly a subject of seventeenth-century debate, and is explored in many of Shakespeare's plays, including *The Tempest*, but its essential legitimacy was incontrovertible. And, whether or not one also thinks the question of the domination of colonizer over colonized is important in *The Tempest*, the modern transformation of attitudes to authority complicates our response to Prospero's demands for unquestioning obedience, and to his unhesitating imposition of the threat of physical punishment when it is not forthcoming. The more forcefully the actor gives full rein to anger, the more he risks alienating the audience; yet to tone it down risks appearing merely disagreeably tetchy, or 'schoolmasterly', or else, as in the case of Hordern and Voss, invites critical disapprobation for what is seen as a softening of the text.

Secondly, our response to Prospero is complicated by the simple fact that magic is no longer a reality, but is almost inevitably seen only as symptom of, or metaphor for, something else. As we have seen, this has been a difficulty at least since the

Restoration, but in the last half-century the general tendency to humanize Prospero and to explore his inner emotional turbulence has also tended to diminish the significance of Prospero-as-magician, or else to convert magic into a metaphor for theatrical transformation (as in the productions of Mendes in 1993 and Noble in 1998). Yet without some sense of Prospero's intellectual and emotional investment in the acquisition of knowledge, and recognition of the control of Ariel, inevitably precarious, that follows, one risks a serious diminution in the power and energy of the role.

As if all this were not enough for the actor playing Prospero to deal with, it is also an extremely demanding part technically, especially in the narrative of 1.2. It is not just its length, or the syntactical contortion of its language, which issues a challenge to the actor, but its curiously unfocused address. For throughout his first scene Prospero, though ostensibly speaking successively to Miranda, Ariel and Caliban, is also providing the past history of the island's inhabitants which is essential to the audience's understanding of the action to come. Prospero, however, seems not quite to be speaking either to us or to them, but delivering an extensive monologue, one which establishes his own nature and motivation in the audience's mind, and which the actor must therefore animate from within.

Prospero, then, is neither an easy nor an obviously grateful role. But a number of actors have returned to the part more than once in their careers. Redgrave and Hordern were playing it for the second time in their Stratford appearances, Gielgud for the third. For all the difficulties Hordern felt at Stratford in 1978, he yet claimed that '*The Tempest* is a splendid challenge, a sublime play, and I am sure I will never get to the bottom of it. The character of Prospero has so much appeal' (Cook, 167), and he went on to take the part again in the BBC TV version in 1979. Derek Jacobi played the part again at Sheffield in 2002. Ian Richardson claimed that 'it is the one part, above all, I would really love to do again' (Cook, 164–5). Something of the appeal of the part was suggested by Alec

McCowen in 1993. He declared in an interview with Peter Lewis that 'the fascination of Prospero is that he's such an emotional jigsaw puzzle, lovable one minute, hateful the next, then vengeful, then sentimental. His moods change like quicksilver, which is very attractive to an actor.'

It is that variety which any Prospero must attempt to reflect, and in different renditions the qualities will be very differently balanced. There is, therefore, no simple way of categorizing Stratford performances since 1945, and it has seemed best to begin with an outline account of the successive Prosperos, rather than imposing a schematic frame upon them. Of course, as with any dramatic character, much depends on the relationship between the actor's individual conception of the role and the ways in which it is worked out in dealings with other characters – especially with Miranda, Ariel and Caliban and, in the final scene, with Alonso and Antonio. These relationships will be considered primarily in the chapters which follow; in this discussion my major concern is with the routes individual actors have found through the role, and with the ways in which that interpretation has been embodied physically and visually.

In 1946 Robert Harris presented Prospero 'not as a he-ancient, but as a man of middle girth and serene nobility' (*Observer*). Though this seemed at the time something of a challenge to the older representation of Prospero, 'whereby the father of the young girl Miranda is so often represented as a doddering, bearded creature of 80' (*News of the World*), the performance clearly belonged at the benign end of the scale, 'too deeply touched by sweetness and light for the sterner hints of majesty' (*Man. Guardian*). Harris's Prospero was characterized by the *Times* as 'a fine, faded ecclesiastic gracing with weary dignity some familiar ritual', and his costume assisted in creating this impression (Figure 2). He wore a long cassock-like garment buttoned down the front, and the magic cloak, embroidered with astrological symbols, accompanied by a substantial staff ornamented at the top, further suggested the episcopal. The *Birmingham Post* reported that 'Mr Harris speaks beautifully, moves with calm dignity, and admirably suggests the human intellect equipped with the attributes of a Providence', though suggesting that 'these praiseworthy qualities would gain by contrast if patient calm were more frequently ruffled'. More curtly W.A. Darlington thought him 'sonorous and soporific' (*D. Telegraph*). Clearly this rendition was consistent with pre-war tradition, and a reviewer who required that Prospero be 'the soul of paternal urbanity' (*Birm. Mail*) could find it attractive. When the production was revived the following year, indeed, Harris was commended precisely because 'Prospero ... goes on a royal progress through the island, unchallenged lord of it, instead of the bitter victim of human wickedness that Prospero can so easily become' (*Stage*). There is little sign of any exploration of Prospero's darker potential, nor any sense of internal conflict.

Michael Redgrave in 1951 also projected a humane reading of the part. T.C. Worsley commented that 'from the first Mr Redgrave distils an extraordinary warmth and a dominating largeness of heart' (*New States.*). Peter Fleming, claiming that 'whatever Shakespeare may have intended Prospero to be, he made him a bully and a bore', yet found that:

> Redgrave, with extraordinary skill, glosses over this tetchiness and his tendency to pontificate, leavens his intolerance with humanity, and gives us a nobleman with whose wrongs we sympathise and a magician – a practising, an empirical magician, not a mere ringmaster with a wand instead of a whip – whose art we follow with curiosity and admiration.   (*Spectator*)

It is on the last part of this description that virtually all reviewers concur. Unlike his predecessor, Redgrave attempted to suggest that the magic really mattered. Harold Hobson (who thought Shakespeare's Prospero a 'disagreeable old man') noted that Redgrave dealt with the problem 'by pretending that Prospero performs his tricks with difficulty. His hands tremble and his shoulders heave with effort whenever Prospero goes into action,

FIGURE 6 Prospero (Michael Redgrave, wearing a false nose in 1951 for the first time in his career) enjoins chastity on Richard Burton's Ferdinand (4.1), with Hazel Penwarden's Miranda holding his hand. Prospero's Druidic costume, with the largest magic staff ever seen at Stratford, contrasts with the 'juvenile lead' period costumes of the others.

and he is an exhausted man when he comes out of it' (*Theatre*). The centrality of Prospero-the-magician to this production was aided by the way that Redgrave was dressed as a cross between Druid and Old Testament Prophet, as Figure 6 shows; 'bearded, grey and burdened by the weight of his own remorseless magic, with a sea-bleached wand that is branched like the tentacles of the monster crabs and shellfish that rise to do his bidding when the wand is raised' (*Man. Guardian*). If it was part of his success to take Prospero's enchantments seriously, this enabled at least one critic to feel that there was a certain menace in this magic power, remarking: 'Bad as was usurping brother Antonio, one suddenly felt that Milan may have been better off without the "rough magic" of this darkened art' (*Man. Guardian*).

The effect of this concentration on magic power was emphasized by contrast the following year when Ralph Richardson took over the part. For him Redgrave's imposing costume was much simplified; intimations of vegetation were confined to some sprigging on the sleeves of a much plainer tunic, and the prophetic beard shrank to a modest goatee (Figure 29). This seems to have been in tune with Richardson's effort to play 'a very human Prospero', one who 'observed with grave wonder the smooth workings of the magical powers which he has acquired in exile, and leaves the impression that he is as much surprised as Bottom the Weaver' (*Times*), reminding J.C. Trewin 'of an anxious cook, glancing at the cookery-book in one hand while with the other, clutching his staff, he proposes to stir the cauldron' (*Sketch*). The redeeming feature that some found was the 'tenderness shown to youth' (*Times*), a response which, indeed, is often to be remarked in the comment on less angry Prosperos, as we have seen in the case of Hordern and Voss, and which had earlier been noted in the 'deep tenderness for Miranda' exhibited by Harris (*Stage*, 1947). Most reviewers, however, shared John Gielgud's view of his friend's performance. He is alleged to have said to Richardson: 'I think I hated you more in the first half than I did in the second', and when asked why, to have replied 'because there is more of you in the first half'. With great generosity, in 1957 Richardson sent a note to Gielgud, the next Prospero on the Stratford stage, saying: 'magnificent, I felt I was back with giants, the best Shakespearean acting I have ever seen, and I am sure that WS would have been delighted' (Morley, 284).

For all their significant differences, the previous three Prosperos had been benignly intentioned; Gielgud instead offered an altogether more tormented and problematic figure. His reading was 'wonderfully clear of insipidity or boredom. Here is no bearded wizard but an exile, the hurt, watchful outcast, first cousin of Timon of Athens but heading toward serenity and release' (*Man. Guardian*). Many commented on the way in which Gielgud generated a sense of conflict in his Prospero, the *Times*, for example, remarking that:

> we are almost invited to wonder if forgiveness will after all triumph over lower feelings. For through the performance the actor throws out a persistent suggestion that though Prospero intends of his own accord to surrender the omnipotence which he has only valued as the instrument of impersonal ends, he nevertheless has an inner battle of his own to fight.

The *London Evening News* felt that 'from the start Peter Brook's production ... signalled that this was going to be Shakespeare with a difference. And different – wantonly, astonishingly different – it certainly was.' Part of that difference was that Gielgud appeared unbearded, and dressed in a knee-length tunic of rough fabric which left one shoulder exposed, 'rather like the symbolic figure of a workman about to strike the anvil' (*Times*), or 'a Roman warrior' (*D. Mail*) (Figure 7). Hope-Wallace, despite his approval of Gielgud's performance, complained that 'his costume was not happy, a tattered toga; nor was his magic robe, all too like a plastic "mack". At times this wonderful-sounding Prospero failed to command the eye and thus to suggest the awe he is supposed to inspire.' Kenneth Tynan commented: 'Instead of a venerable Mosaic figure, we have an austere and bookish hermit, who wears a brief, mud-coloured toga and whose life is wholly of the mind. At first Sir John seemed embarrassed by his semi-nudity. ("The costumes," one felt him signalling, "are arriving to-morrow")' (*Observer*). But the costume, far from embarrassing the actor, had been suggested by him as fitting his concept of the part: 'a sort of El Greco hermit with very short hair' (Gielgud, 1997, 94).

Dymkowski claims that this was the performance which decisively broke the legacy of the benign, otherworldly tradition (19). It was, nonetheless, a performance ultimately in the service

FIGURE 7 Prospero (John Gielgud) chastises Ariel (Brian Bedford) in 1.2. Behind are the rocky caverns of Peter Brook's 1957 set: his stage lighting suggested water in the distance.

of a production which ended in forgiveness and redemption. In 1963, Tom Fleming attempted to continue the emphasis on Prospero's hurt and anger in a generally less optimistic reading of the play. Robert Speaight characterized him as 'a formidable Victorian headmaster, steering his course majestically between the Bible and the birch'. He thought it 'a magnificent performance, and very moving at the end in its painfully achieved humility' (*SQ*, 425). This positive view was not widely shared; reviewers complained particularly at the slowness of Fleming's delivery 'which hyphens every word as though it were from *Chick's Own*' (*S. Telegraph*). Visually, however, Prospero was something of a throwback. Fleming resumed the beard, the heavy, full-length gown and magic cloak, and his magic staff – if it didn't remind one of a television aerial – had the same weightiness as Redgrave's a decade earlier, and made him look like 'a mixture of Thomas Carlyle and Wotan' (*Man. Guardian*) (see Figure 12). The attempted synthesis of sonorous speech (Fleming was later to become the commentator on state occasions for the BBC), imposing physical presence and an emphasis upon Prospero's disciplinary tendencies does not seem to have worked convincingly in a production which generally represented the island and its magic as unrelievedly disturbing and threatening.

Over the next decades, with a general tendency to emphasize more and more Prospero's humanity at the expense of his magic powers, his dress tended to become much less symbolic, much more a 'realistic' representation of the clothes that a duke cast away for twelve years might still possess. In 1970 Ian Richardson brought youth to the part, but maintained some of the anger that had come to characterize it.

> He plays the part, a youngish man with dark, hidden eyes, his hands casually thrust into his pockets. He's not the grim island potentate most actors offer us, but a very private man: withdrawn, wry, contemptuous of show, self-mocking . . . It is clearly difficult for him to surrender a beloved daughter, and scarcely less to forgive enemies who disgust him.   (*New States.*)

Magic was not significant in this rendition; instead he was

> very much the Victorian parent, proud of having done the right thing by his daughter under trying circumstances. His self-esteem stems not from his magical powers but from his learning . . . [Richardson] is by no means grand: the cloak is nothing but a dun-coloured artist's smock.   (*Times*)

It was not only the magic cloak that was understated, but the basic costume of breeches and shirt struck the *Birmingham Evening Mail* as looking like the dress of 'a slightly diffident landowner' (see

Figure 14). The unemphatic costume seems inordinately to have upset reviewers, challenging their preconceptions about the character's 'nobility' more severely even than had Gielgud's tunic. At the same time the inwardness of the performance and the detachment reflected in comments on 'a cold, weary creature, withdrawn, shambling' (*D. Telegraph*), or 'a Lear who has mastered passion, learning to let go his power over his daughter and kingdom' (*Observer*), perhaps account for Hope-Wallace's sense of this as 'a very small scale and ordinary Prospero' (*Guardian*). Richardson was responding to the isolation of Prospero which is very much present in the writing, yet, despite the generally acknowledged excellence of his verse-speaking, he seems not to have found a way of communicating to the audience the tension he himself imagined as motivating his reading.

Though comparatively little survives of the 1974 production, some reviews suggest that Michael Aldridge continued with a Prospero of 'nervy paranoia' whose tyrannizing of Ariel and Caliban suggests that he 'was banished from Milan because he was a dictator' (*Times*). Sheila Bannock speaks of 'the expression of a flayed sensibility' and noted that the actor 'contrives to suggest at the end that even acceptance of this wisdom does not bring tranquillity; his final speech to the audience is delivered as a kind of challenge rather than a prayer' (*SA Herald*). But there is little unanimity in the scanty record – others saw a 'noble and weary Prospero' (*D. Telegraph*) and a 'sad wise man' who used magic arts 'not for a display of power and the discomfiture of his enemies, but more for the sober carriage of justice' (*Coventry E. Tel.*).

In 1978 Hordern offered a much quieter 'study of a man who has seen enough havoc caused by greed, carelessness and cold hearts, and has opted for kindliness in full knowledge of his precarious position' (*Times*). Only John Barber managed to find 'a weather-beaten, vigorous avenger, clean-shaven and gnarled as a tree' (*D. Telegraph*). Majesty and magic were very much down-played. His ordinary costume was a plain and simple jerkin and breeches (Figure 8). The designer's original intention had been to

FIGURE 8 Michael Hordern's 1978 Prospero narrates the story of the past to Sheridan Fitzgerald's attentive Miranda in 1.2. The relationship of schoolmaster and pupil is suggested by their positioning; for Hordern the relationship with his daughter was the key to the role.

make his magic robe, like the costumes of the lords, a striking visual contrast both to the black set, and to Prospero's 'normal' appearance. This is the robe worn in the production photographs, but it never appeared in performance. Hordern reported that:

> Ralph Koltai ... appeared at the dress rehearsal with a tiny little baton arrangement and a cloak so encrusted with decoration that when I put it over my shoulders I sank to the floor. I am not good at making a fuss but, after some discussion, a decent stick appeared, and the decorated nightmare disappeared to be replaced by a plain schoolmasterly cloak.
>
> (Hordern, 144)

Its rejection may just have been a practical matter of freedom of movement; it may have been a consequence of Hordern's generally uncooperative feelings; but the understated magic garment suited the way in which the actor felt more generally about the representation of the supernatural. It certainly validated B.A. Young's opinion that 'Michael Hordern's Prospero, in his grey knickerbocker suit, his magic garment a black school-master's gown, suggests some wandering Mr. Chips' (*FT*). The rejection of the elaborate cloak can only have intensified the ordinariness of this human Prospero.

The 1982 production made a striking contrast. Perhaps for the first time since Redgrave, Prospero-as-magician was central to the play. The designer gave Derek Jacobi a magic cloak of impressive proportions, covered in astrological and cabalistic signs, and clasped over the chest like an episcopal cope (Figure 9). The importance of magic to the production was signalled by the image of the cloaked Jacobi on the first page of the programme, and the inclusion of a substantial section on 'ritual magic' in the background material provided for the audience. For the actor himself, too, magic power was vital to his conception of the role. Where Ian Richardson had imagined terminal illness as a way of reconciling himself to playing a younger Prospero, Jacobi said:

> I am sure he is not old in body. I think he has grown old in his mind. His researchings into magic and his workings with the elements have made his brain old ... it has almost burned him out.
>
> (Cook, 167)

His 'normal' costume was elegantly tattered, and the contrast with his gorgeous magic cloak echoed the way his performance manifested 'an internal struggle between omnipotence and humanity', in which Prospero, 'even in renouncing magic, clearly relishes it' (*Guardian*).

At forty-three, Jacobi was the same age as Redgrave had been when he took the part, but, unlike his predecessor, he played Prospero at his own natural age, and was therefore able to suggest that it could still matter to him that he regain the dukedom he had lost. As Jack Tinker, reviewing the London transfer, wrote:

FIGURE 9 In 1982 Derek Jacobi's Prospero, in a striking cloak, boasts of his past exploits, before promising to 'drown my book' (5.1.33–57). The book was a vital prop, frequently consulted by Prospero throughout, and used almost as a weapon to ward off Caliban in 1.2.

there is no mistaking this Prospero's deep bitterness at his betrayal. This is no grizzled wizard whiling away his twilight years on an enchanted island. He is a man who has clearly been deposed in his prime and is willing every demon in nature to extract his revenge. It is a formidably commanding performance which, despite its power, never loses sight of the man's humanities and frailties.   (*D. Mail*)

Michael Billington compared Jacobi's performance to Gielgud's, and like Gielgud he was able to suggest the anger and resentment that gnawed his soul. Paul Vallely, indeed, disliked Jacobi's reading of the role precisely because 'his wrath is so turbulent that we can never believe that he is as genuine in those moments of compassion which show us the other side of Prospero' (*Mail Sun.*). But for most reviewers the sense of forgiveness narrowly achieved was, as it had been in Gielgud's reading of the part, one of its major achievements. Not all agreed; others found it a 'powerful but low-key interpretation' (*TLS*), with Jacobi 'temperamentally remote from the severity and revengefulness that dictate [the play's] rhythms ... [he] screws himself up for bursts of aggression, but only to fall into soft lyrical contrition immediately afterwards, extremely eloquent, but not the man' (*Times*). My own memory, and viewing of the archive video, makes me wonder whether these reviewers were attending the same production; it seemed to me that Jacobi was able to convey bitterness and anger, to give a real sense of the centrality of magical power and control, and yet not to lose an underlying humanity. Judith Cook asserted that 'Derek Jacobi's Prospero must be one of the finest of our times' (*Scotsman*); its impressive quality derived from the way that, more than most, he managed, with cloak, staff and book, to suggest something of the 'reality' of Prospero's magic power, his readiness to use it and the cost of surrendering it.

John Wood's performance in the next production, in 1988, received from some reviewers an equal praise. Michael Coveney called his Prospero 'the best I have seen' (*FT*), and the *Sunday Express* trumpeted that 'you will have to live another life-time if you want to see a more memorable Prospero than John Wood's'. Christine Dymkowski selected this as the performance which 'most successfully embodied the complex potential of the role' (32). Visually his white shirt and breeches recalled Ian Richardson (see Figure 10). His magic cloak was a dressing gown, his rough wooden staff slotted nonchalantly upright into the surface of the stage. Some reviewers used images that recalled Hordern's performance – Alex Renton reaching into the cliché-bag to characterize Wood as 'a kindly professorial figure, a doting father ... a stooping, dishevelled Mr Chips' (*Independent*). To Stanley Wells he projected a 'likeable image of the role. This gaunt figure with an amiable, self-amused grin, loping round in baggy trousers obviously unpressed since he left Milan, conveyed a basic naivety and innocence which easily explained his usurpation' (*SS*, 147). Others, however, saw him as 'suspended between smouldering rage at his usurpation and unbridled glee at his alternative ethereal power' (*FT*) or as 'a wounded rather than angry man' (*S. Times*). Dymkowski argues that these divergent reviews are testament to Wood's capacity to move easily 'between Prospero the thoughtless task-master, the gentle guardian, the outraged aristocrat, the socially inept man, the loving father, the blinkered judge of past actions, the lonely child still carried within the adult being' (33).

A good deal depended on the reviewers' reaction to Wood's delivery of the verse. Eric Shorter hated the way 'the actor barks and whinnies and whispers the verse until it sometimes sounds unintelligible' (*D. Telegraph*). But Irving Wardle characterized his voice as 'a super-sensitized instrument responding to the smallest pressures of the verse with a musical intensity that lights up the text like an electric storm' (*Times*, May). The virtuoso quality of Wood's verse-speaking might make one think of the actor as self-consciously standing at a distance from the words, watching himself perform them 'like a pianist with scant trust in the ability of the score before him to hold the attention of his hearers' (*S. Telegraph*). If one could surrender to it, however, then it could powerfully suggest a self-absorption in words fashioned to articulate a deep and personal hurt. It was that quality of introversion that a number of reviewers picked out as the performance's distinguishing feature. Compared with Jacobi's turbulent rage, Wood seemed 'distressed' (*SS*, 154); his narrative 'a re-run of his agony, a condensation of long-endured grief' (*FT*). Wood's reading echoed elements of Gielgud's (to whom his verse-speaking was more than once compared), and of Ian Richardson's in its isolation, though it more readily encompassed human warmth.

Complementary as they were in a number of ways, Jacobi's and Wood's Prosperos were perhaps the best received of any since the war, with the sole exception of Gielgud's in 1957. Those who followed in the last decade of the century generated less enthusiasm. In 1993 Alec McCowen was sixty-eight, the oldest actor to undertake the part at Stratford. Less informally dressed than Wood, and provided with a passably gorgeous coat as his magic cloak, he yet seemed 'a donnish, avuncular, mildly eccentric figure – a conjuror who'd go down well at a children's party but not a man who would have to struggle desperately to conquer vengeful desires' (*Independent*). In a production which, as a whole, made more of theatrical magic than most, its central magician seemed less directly involved than many of his predecessors. One reviewer commented that 'the magician Prospero is presented as a godlike impresario – the Cameron Mackintosh of a coral island' (*D. Express*). The focus therefore shifted to his executant, Ariel, as 'Alec McCowen sits on a ladder as impartial as a Wimbledon umpire' (*Observer*). Michael Billington commented: 'the concept of Prospero as the ultimate theatrical illusionist makes it difficult for McCowen to suggest, as Wood and Bryant [at the National Theatre, 1988] did, a man wrestling with his own inner demons' (*Guardian*). Whilst McCowen's delivery was frequently commended, he was, as Kate Kellaway put it, 'a Prospero determined to make his magic plain' (*Observer*). This very clarity of address contributed to the sense of 'a cerebral Prospero, both scholarly and introspective but perhaps a bit too subdued to convey the enormous power he possesses' (*SB*, 13). The 'schoolmaster' image, never far from reviewers' minds, was used by a number to characterize this Prospero.

If McCowen was not rapturously received, Paul Jesson fared even less well in 1995. Peter Holland described him as 'a genial father, a benign aristocratic castaway but with no glimmering of energy or imagination. There was nothing to hint at the magus, the duke, the plotter, the embittered victim. Jesson's Prospero was a thoroughly nice chap' (Holland, 227). Russell Jackson was one of very few who were able to view this rendition more positively, characterizing Jesson as 'a humane, feeling, well-spoken Prospero'

(*SQ*, 321). There was, however, one element of the conception of the role that was original, at least in intention. Roz Symon noted that 'Paul Jesson was adamant that Prospero's magic was of the island, inherited from Sycorax' (67). This concept was embodied in a staff which was 'simply a piece of drift wood ... something Prospero had found on the island', and a cloak 'decorated with island memorabilia' (Symon, 71). The idea that Prospero's magic in some way doubles or reflects the magic of Sycorax is one that has attracted literary critics in recent years (see Orgel, 1986). Jesson claimed that 'he was attempting to try and get some darkness and evil, something blacker, into the play'. He had 'at one point, and only for a few performances ... produced a black tarred skull from one of the trunks on stage ... It was a real human skull which, he liked to think, belonged to Sycorax' (Symon, 67). But this feeling of menace did not cross to the audience, and, once the idea of having Prospero at the side of the stage throughout, poring over a huge book, was discarded, the force of his enchantments seemed lost.

David Calder in 1998 returned to the fiercer, angrier Prospero that characterized most of the performances of the 1970s and 1980s both at Stratford and beyond. He also eschewed the white shirt and trousers which had served as the basic costume for Prospero in 1988 and 1995 (and was to do so again in 2000). His dark-green, full-length gown and long staff managed to persuade one reviewer to dust off comparisons not encountered since Redgrave and Fleming, commenting that Prospero seemed 'like an Old Testament prophet or patriarch' (*S. Telegraph*). He was a Prospero who 'feelingly and movingly suggests a man painfully caught between a festering sense of grievance and a recognition of the need for forgiveness' (*D. Telegraph*); though he didn't have

> the ascetic, guru-like figure of a John Wood, Derek Jacobi or John Gielgud ... he makes you realise what he means when he says he has a 'beating mind' ... and leaves you feeling that his decision to forgive his evil brother and the treacherous King of Naples is a close-run thing. (*Times*)

But to Nicholas de Jongh Calder's anger marked him as 'indelibly stamped with dyspeptic frostiness. [His Prospero] has caught such indigestion of the soul that his protestations of forgiveness and reconciliation come listlessly across' (*E. Standard*). In this rendition 'the progress from vengeance to virtue [was] clearly marked, particularly in the precariousness of that progress, the fear that the vengefulness of the man might triumph after all' (*SS*, 238). As in 1993, much of the 'magic' in the production was developed in and through visual, theatrical means. But much more than McCowen, Calder managed to imply that power mattered to him, for example in the way his staff became a physical weapon not only warding off Caliban, but flailing at the 'three men of sin' in 3.3. He was 'no confident magus but an infirm and unsure ruler frantically laying down the law in a bid to protect his own standing' (*Cahiers Elis.*, 124). The effect was, however, rather confused than helped by the conceit of Ariel being invisible to him throughout (see chapter 2).

As has already been remarked, Philip Voss reverted to a less aggressive view of Prospero in 2000, in a performance 'weighted towards kindly beneficence' (*Indep. Sun.*). The Victorian dress of the production (like the early nineteenth-century costuming in 1993) actually went some way to limiting the possibility of a real focus on magic. Voss describes 'my all important magic cloak' as

> based on an old Byzantine priest's vestment, but made of a very loose weave linen . . . embroidered by a craftsman whose normal job is to emboss the clerical robes of the church. He has decorated the entire garment in gold thread, with accepted magic symbols . . . It is extremely light, which means that I can wear it for longer and more frequently than many Prosperos.   (Voss)

Yet, in competition with the exuberant video projection which dominated the visual effect of the production, Prospero's own magic was somewhat eclipsed. Voss's eloquent speaking was praised – Peter J. Smith remarking that he 'possesses a voice of the most extraordinary range – by turns fruitfully resonant, movingly gentle and intensely angry' (*Cahiers Elis.*, 107), and Russell Jackson commenting that his 'musical voice and careful nuancing of every phrase – although sometimes a little too elaborate – seemed to come from a precision of thought and a lively apprehension of the sensuous quality of words' (*SQ*, 114). But for many reviewers, it was a performance that remained 'very generalised' (*Independent*), and 'kept emotions too tightly buttoned up' (*Mail Sun.*). As Wood in 1988 had competed with Bryant's bitter Prospero in Hall's National Theatre production, so Voss was up against McDiarmid's rendition at the Almeida. Benedict Nightingale contrasted the two, and concluded that:

> the usually excellent Philip Voss suffered by comparison. Ian McDiarmid is such a bitter, vindictive Prospero that his conversion to merciful guru has the impact the play demands. Voss's duke has moments of anger yet comes across as what he says he was before his exile: a lover of liberal arts, happiest with his books. (*Times*)

This verdict indicates how far the standard expectations of Prospero have shifted since 1946; where Gielgud's angry rendition was revolutionary, it is now the expected norm.

In 2002 Malcolm Storry fulfilled that expectation, offering a 'tremendous, craggy Prospero, whose progress to forgiveness is exceptionally hard won' (*D. Telegraph*). Though Nicholas de Jongh objected to his (as he had to Calder's) 'generalising fury' (*E. Standard*), Michael Billington argued that 'it is precisely because Storry is so initially ferocious that his access of charity is so powerful' (*Guardian*). There was little kindness in the characterization – even Miranda was clearly afraid of him – and, in his red, tattered tunic with an academic gown for a magic cloak, little majesty in the magus. This was a performance in which the transformation of 5.1 was absolute, and absolutely central.

But whatever overall view an actor takes of the part, the first hazard he confronts is the technical challenge of negotiating the long narrative in 1.2, 'which might almost be taken as a test of the actor's power to arrest his audience's attention' (Redgrave, 73). Under the weight of this virtual monologue of 200 lines many a production has collapsed almost before it has begun, and many a Prospero has bored his audience into indifference. Within the narrative of the play this retrospective account is occasioned by Prospero's desire to quieten Miranda's anxiety, and reassure her that he has 'done nothing but in care of thee' (1.2.16), even though, 160 lines later, she is still asking him 'your reason / For raising this sea-storm' (176–7). Against any criterion of realism one might object that these are things of which Prospero should long ago have informed his daughter – and there is a severe danger that, punctuated as it is by injunctions to Miranda to pay attention, it can seem like a very prolonged lecture to a wayward child. At the same time, of course, it is essential that the audience understand the narrative clearly, since we, as much as Miranda, have been bemused by an opening scene which has not even supplied us with a character's name. The actor's job, as Voss recognized, is to make it become dramatic. 'He has to re-live the betrayal. He has to tell his daughter what she is. He has to suppress his anger and finally he has to admit that fate has handed him the gift and opportunity for reprisal.' Voss also knew that 'if I don't succeed in this, I know I will have nowhere to go. It sets up the evening and the audience must be taken along and they have to understand it.' But the tangled syntax makes that an extremely difficult task. Voss comments memorably on lines 89ff.: 'It might just as well be Hungarian, but it has a meaning although it is tortured. I don't think anyone hearing that for the first time could understand it, but from the actor the audience will understand the anguish and the hurt.' This is the actor's problem – to reconcile clarity with tempestuous feeling, to persuade us of Prospero's love for Miranda even as he chides her for inattention.

Some actors have placed a premium upon intelligibility. Fleming in 1963 managed to achieve a 'dignified and measured clarity which is a pleasure to hear' (*E. Standard*), but at the cost of 'taking Prospero so slowly at times that he might have been chiselling words on a headstone' (*Birm. Post*); there seems to have been no compensatory warmth for his daughter, nor much sense of anguished recollection. Thirty years later McCowen delivered his narrative with impeccable lucidity and sense of narrative drive – one really seemed to be hearing this story for the first time. But the cost was that he seemed to talk to his daughter 'like a stiff, fussily pedantic schoolmaster' (*D. Telegraph*) or 'a slightly patronising consultant at a hospital, giving her a benign diagnosis' (*Observer*, Aug). This was emphasized by the fact that there was no physical contact between them until her weeping at lines 132–5, and he only demonstrated any real warmth at 'O, a cherubin / Thou wast' (152–3). Nor did the recollection of past injustice stir great anger. At 'Twelve year since, Miranda' (53) he took a ducal crown from a box on his prop-laden table and blew the dust off in a gesture which seemed one of melancholy nostalgia rather than bitter resentment. In 1978 Hordern, who brought to this scene his 'enviable gift of speaking the verse so that it is at the same time great poetry and every day communication' (*FT*), had much closer physical contact with Miranda, and she seems very much to have been the focus of his narrative, but he delivered much of it from his seat as she sat on the floor beside and below him, so that despite the 'easy relaxation and extensive experience [that] enabled him to sustain the enormous second scene' (*SS*, 203), he seemed to offer a 'mildly tetchy headmaster figure with a soft spot for his star pupil' (*Guardian*) (Figure 8).

Other actors have focused the narrative much more on the recreation of bitterly remembered experience. In 1970 Ian Richardson joined Miranda in sitting on the floor at 'Canst thou remember' (38), but for all the closeness of the embrace 'during the narration the eyes never light on Miranda but move away to some distant spot' (*Times*). Richardson explained:

> I thought that if I sank down on my knees with Miranda beside me with her head in my lap and I held my staff beside me with the cloak upon it, it would look reminiscent of the position we would have

> been in, in that little boat; ... with Miranda in my lap, I physically
> relived the whole event. (Cook, 165)

In fact, photographs show no staff or cloak, and the promptbook suggests that they maintained this position less long than Richardson suggests. But Philip Hope-Wallace, though he praised the 'full understanding and great deliberation' of Richardson's speaking, felt that one reason for its remaining 'a very small scale and ordinary Prospero' had to do with 'the whole style of sit on the floor Shakespeare, expressly shorn of glamour, and seeming unwilling to rise from a leaden jog-trot' (*Guardian*).

In 2000 Philip Voss again sat on the floor beside Miranda for much of this exposition (Figure 28), and perhaps the lack of movement contributed to the way in which a number of reviewers, as we have seen, again managed to praise the eloquence, but despite his clear intention, were less persuaded of his anger. In 1957 Gielgud dealt with 'what has been written off again and again as the most boring passage in Shakespeare' with 'no tricks, but simply the words as the cue for passion ... living and suffering the experience while he narrates it' (*SQ*, 488–9). He seems to have made a clearer distinction between speech directed to Miranda, and that which expressed his own inner turmoil. He knelt beside her to explain 'those being all my study, / The government I cast upon my brother' (74–5), but then rose again as he recollected the way Antonio had 'new created / The creatures that were mine' (81–2) to pace about the stage, only returning to her at 'Hear a little further' (135), where he sat, with Miranda leaning on his knees. One reviewer felt that 'the speeches of harsh intemperance are more characteristic of this Prospero than those which give rein to his parental and human tenderness' (*Times*), but Gielgud could yet modulate to a tone of 'much pride and profound emotion' (*Morn. Adv.*) as he answered Miranda's question as to why they were not killed with the words 'Dear, they durst not, / So dear the love my people bore me' (140–1). Though one reviewer thought his question to Miranda as to whether she 'attended' was 'a waspish challenge to any Father's-off-again attitude that might spoil self pity's satisfaction' (*Punch*), Muriel St Clare Byrne lauded 'the skill with which the actor fuses past and present, and makes us as aware of the anger then felt as of the control now achieved . . . The narrative becomes a condensed action, and we live the experience with him' (*SQ*, 489). In an analogous fashion, David Calder, in 1998, though pacing the stage in 'animated anger' (*Cahiers Elis.*, 124), 'looking deep into a wound that is still open, still raw' (*Times*) and insistent that Miranda understood what was at stake, punctuated his tirade with embraces of his daughter, touchingly, for example, as he reached out to reassure her at her uncertain observation that 'Good wombs have borne bad sons' (120), and thereby persuading us that he was 'constantly struggling with the hurt and resentment of past memories' (*SS*, 237).

Perhaps the most complex articulations of this enormously problematic narrative (at least since video recordings became available) were achieved by Jacobi in 1982 and Wood in 1988. The former began the scene with his back towards the audience, trembling with the effort of raising the storm (see chapter 6); and his immediate concentration on his magic book established firmly that the arc of the scene was for him to reach the moment when he could put his plans into execution. It was his 'slowness to shake off the effect of such a mighty act of magic that g[ave] impetus to his finely calculated performance' (*Times*). To him, Miranda's question was an unwanted interruption, and, though sitting down with her at line 32, his anger was directed at her, as well as at the memory of his usurpation. When he spoke of 'My brother, and thy uncle, called Antonio' (66) the gesture of compassion with which he had taken her hand as she exclaimed 'O, my heart bleeds' (63) was transformed as he kneaded her fingers throughout the ensuing speech. But even though he could be intemperate with Miranda – rising to anger as he reminded her of his success as her schoolmaster (172) as if to compel her gratitude – he managed both to be 'a very bad-tempered father' and yet to be 'gentle in his constant reminders . . . to pay attention' (*FT*).

FIGURE 10 The warmth of John Wood's 1988 Prospero towards Miranda (Melanie Thaw) is touchingly conveyed as he carries her across the stage before gently laying her down as she falls asleep (1.2.185–6). His magic staff, seen in the background, was fixed in a notch in the stage.

Wood's affection for his daughter was more obvious, and his dependence upon her was palpably evident from the moment when he wiped her eyes (with her own hair, according to the promptbook, with the cuff of his sleeve according to reviewers) until he gently picked her up at line 179, cradling her until he put her down asleep at 187 (Figure 10). 'More maternal than fatherly, this is a Prospero who practises not a "rough" but a gentle magic . . . when Prospero claims that all he has done is motivated by care for Miranda it is convincing' (*Observer*). His rendition of this scene attracted more notice than that of any other actor, and (apart from those who couldn't tolerate his delivery) meets with constant approval. Unlike Jacobi, whose anger and impatience propelled the scene forwards, Wood focused upon the articulation of past events, speaking 'as though the memory of them were still so raw that he can only succumb now to grief and now to rage as he relives them' (*S. Telegraph*) and 'repeatedly holding his hand to the side of his face as if to pillow memory' (*Observer*). As he asked Miranda 'Canst thou remember / A time before we came unto this cell' (38–9) he inserted a pause before and after 'remember' as if to underline the centrality of memory to the account he was about to give. At 'Twelve year since, Miranda, twelve year since' (53) the repetition elicited a haunted surprise and a drifting off into a virtual trance, from which Miranda had to drag him back by shouting her question: 'Sir, are you not my father?' (55). His recollections of his brother's treachery were not simply angry; rather he suggested an astonishment that Antonio could have thought of him as he did. So variously modulated was his delivery that it is hard to believe that each performance did not new-mint the lines, even if the total effect was always to suggest a mind in action, a narrative that he had not prepared but which was elicited precisely by the fortunate chance which brought his enemies into his power and therefore suddenly made it necessary.

Boyd's production in 2002 attempted to marry clarity with fierce projection of remembered hurt by bringing the characters of Prospero's narrative on stage as he named them. This is a device others have used (see chapter 5) but here, as they walked slowly from the back, passing between Prospero and Miranda and disappearing into the auditorium, Malcolm Storry seemed to be speaking directly to them; berating Antonio and Alonso, warming to Gonzalo. This 'solution' to the problem of the narrative, however, came at a cost. In the first place many in the audience must have wondered at the status of these figures – there was faint laughter at one of the performances I attended as Miranda said of Gonzalo 'Would I might / But ever see that man!' (168–9). More significantly, as they became the actual, physical objects of Prospero's speech so their very presence tended to lessen the sense of remembered hurt that other actors have managed to convey, and inhibited the possibility of any interaction between Prospero and his daughter.

The task of this narrative over, Prospero must then negotiate the encounters with Ariel and Caliban. In each of them he again provides the audience with past history, accounting for his attitude to his servants by recollection first of the obligation Ariel owes him and then of the injury Caliban has done him. The tone of self-justification is strong, and the exchanges are discussed in the chapters which immediately follow. In the scene's final movement, as Prospero feigns anger at Ferdinand, disarms him and rejects Miranda's pleas, some Prosperos have lightened the tone. Gielgud's 'manner soften[ed]' (*Yorks. Post*); Hordern 'found much humour' in Prospero's explanation to his daughter that Ferdinand is indeed a real man (*SS*, 203); Voss was notably indulgent towards the couple, inviting the audience's complicity by speaking his asides directly to them. Wood prepared for his amused presence in 3.1 (see chapter 4) as he 'extract[ed] an unusual amount of laughter from the incongruities of a Prospero who organises his daughter's love-match, must appear to resist it, gets worried by its growing intensity, yet still wishes it to progress' (*Punch*). Characteristically he softened the rebuke of 'One word more / Shall make me chide thee, if not hate thee' by touching her cheek at 'Hush' (476–8). Even the angry Jacobi, with thunder accompanying the moment of his disarming of Ferdinand, was able to persuade us that this was a simulated anger compared with the very real bitterness he had just shown towards Ariel and (especially) Caliban. Calder, by contrast, seemed angry indeed as he threw Miranda to the floor at 'if not hate thee' in 1998, and Storry in 2002 prepared for his later fixation on his daughter's chastity by allowing little warmth into his asides (and he put her to sleep with an aggressive embrace). In 1957 the severity of Ferdinand's punishment was emphasized by his being locked in fetters (see chapter 4), but no Stratford production has shown the sadism which had Ian McKellen's Prospero, despite his obviously warm feelings for his daughter, force Miranda herself to lock Ferdinand in chains as he was pushed down into Caliban's 'sty' (at Leeds, 1999).

After the Herculean effort of 1.2, Prospero is offstage during Act 2, and appears only as an observing presence in Act 3 (though there are some few opportunities both in 3.1. and 3.3 for varying interpretations, as discussed in chapters 4 and 6). At the beginning of Act 4 he has to negotiate the stern injunction of chastity on Ferdinand – much more problematic in the late twentieth century than one might think it would have been in earlier times – though Dymkowski notes that it was actually cut in most nineteenth-century productions, and at Stratford until 1934, presumably for reasons of prudishness rather than any objection to its senti-ments. It has since been retained; though in 1998 Noble attempted to give it more dramatic point by delaying Prospero's joining of Ferdinand and Miranda's hands, which the text suggests occurs at line 5, until after he had given his warning and Ferdinand had replied satisfactorily. Some comic effect has been extracted from line 32, where both Hordern and Jacobi firmly emphasized 'Sit then and *talk* with her' (my italics), and from the subsequent reminder of their promise at lines 51–6. Voss underlined his kindly concern by firmly sitting between Ferdinand and Miranda to watch the pageant. For Storry, however, as the staging of 3.1 had made explicit (see chapter 4) chastity mattered, and his anxiety was underlined by the utterly improbable reading of 'No tongue' (59) as an injunction against 'French kissing'. But it is at the masque's ending that Prospero really returns to dominate the stage in his own person, rather than through the agency of Ariel.

Prospero dissolves the masque because he recollects the conspiracy of Caliban. Voss felt that 'it is not the fact that I am in danger that makes me end the celebrations so abruptly, but the fact that for once ... I have lost control of events and *forgotten* the threat to my life'. Serious though any such lapse might be to this memory-obsessed figure, in a number of productions his anger has been more directly motivated. In 1974 the promptbook records that cries of 'Caliban, Freedom' were heard off stage; in 1993 Mendes had one of the dancing reapers lift his straw hat to reveal the face of Caliban; in 1995 Caliban was 'increasingly controlling the action ... making the dance less and less a vision of order and harmony and more a wild, subversive carnival' (Holland, 229). In 2002 it was the erotic nature of the 'dance' that precipitated Storry's intervention.

Then the actor faces the challenge of rendering the perhaps all too familiar speech: 'Our revels now are ended' (146–63). This is a rhetorical set piece, framed by Prospero's anger, but delivered as if to console the distressed Ferdinand, since he begins with the words 'Be cheerful, sir' (147). Gielgud, one feels, would have had little embarrassment at giving the speech its full, measured, poetic weight. For though in his 1974 National Theatre performance he apparently spoke 'urgently and at speed' (Dymkowski, 287), in 1957 the masque dissolved and 'we hear, as if from far off, the words "We are such stuff as dreams are made on" [156–7]. The air becomes still, there is no sound but the lovely voice' (*Stage*). It came 'with an overwhelmingly moving effect' in 'the great moment' of the production (*D. Telegraph*). David Calder also achieved 'spellbinding' effect (*Cahiers Elis.*, 124) through slow and deliberate speech – though with a delivery much less self-consciously poetic than Gielgud's – in 1998. But actors (and perhaps audiences) now are more likely to want a 'realistically' motivated rendition. Hordern, in 1978, treated 'Prospero's great speeches not as operatic arias but as products of a particular situation, so that "Our revels now are ended" is an urgent reminder there is pressing business to be done' (*Guardian*). His angry delivery, however, prompted one reviewer to object that he 'need not speak in tones of rage merely because in the course of [the speech] he says he is vexed' (*S. Times*). Hordern himself said of his rendition for the BBC TV performance a year later 'he has recently seen an apocalyptic vision of the fate awaiting humanity. My Prospero saw the mushroom cloud [of Hiroshima] as he spoke' (Sales, 176) – but either his reading had much changed, or else he failed signally to communicate any larger resonance to reviewers in 1978. The note of anger, however, was to be found again in

McCowen's performance where it was delivered as 'a statement of baffled fury' (*Guardian*). Both of these actors were responding primarily to the fact of the conspiracy; Jacobi and Wood each focused upon a reaction to the dissolution of Prospero's work of art. In 1982 Jacobi delivered what seemed to one reviewer 'a murmured reverie by a man who seemed pleased to shed the burden of his magic' (*SS*, 154), and to another contained 'relief mingled with the resignation in his voice' (*TLS*). As he concluded, near to weeping, however, it was possible to hear something less resigned, more powerfully troubled as Prospero spoke rather to the audience than to Ferdinand, in an appalled realization that the knowledge and the magic which meant so much to him were, like all things, finite. The pain of the speech perhaps registered all the more powerfully because of the way the masque which preceded it had risen to a note of high triumph (see chapter 6). In 1988 the masque, imagined as dreamed by Prospero lying on stage before it, was rather less successful, but Wood, who brought to this most familiar of speeches the 'vital quality of seeming to mint the thoughts and images anew' (*Times*, May) with a note of amazed recognition that '*We* are such stuff / As dreams are made on' (156–7; my italics), also delivered it quietly. Here, perhaps, the introversion of the delivery could be seen as a mark of Prospero's own recognition of the failure of the masque; Robert Smallwood suggested that this was actually 'his motive for dismissing it, the conspiracy of Caliban, which he can obviously handle with perfect ease, merely an excuse' (*SQ*, 87). But, again with his characteristic ability to switch tones in a moment, Wood built up a quick crescendo as he spoke of his vexation. In Wood's and Jacobi's performances the interiority of the set piece's delivery suited their overall readings of the character. It also served a simpler function in the architecture of the last movement of the play in distinguishing it from the next set piece, the invocation of magic powers in 'Ye elves . . .' (5.1.33ff.).

But between the two comes the crucial moment when Ariel challenges Prospero to forgive the enemies within his power:

> Your charm so strongly works 'em
> That, if you now beheld them, your affections
> Would become tender.

PROSPERO

> Dost thou think so, spirit?

ARIEL

> Mine would sir, were I human.

PROSPERO

> And mine shall.
> Hast thou, which art but air, a touch, a feeling
> Of their afflictions ...

(5.1.17–22)

It is a very curiously written exchange. Prospero's decision to relent is joined into a single verse line shared with Ariel, and his reasoning follows after the momentous choice is already made. We might have expected, if Shakespeare wished to dramatize the turmoil in Prospero's mind and the difficulty of his decision, that the order would be reversed. Yet in 2000 John Peter thought it the 'one weak point' of the production that 'Voss's response is immediate: no pause for thought, no sense of inner struggle' (*S. Times*). In fact, Voss was not only at one level respecting the writing, but also indicating that the decision to forgive had already been taken, and that the release had begun the moment Ferdinand and Miranda fell in love. But this is not the standard view, nor the most dramatic. In most productions, in one way or another, this is represented as a real turning point. In 1951 Redgrave responded 'with a sudden shamed repentance and strong prayer for the power to forgive, turning a speech which sometimes seems merely smug self-righteousness into a decisive, victorious struggle of the "nobler reason" towards divine aid' (*SA Herald*). Gielgud asserted that 'I tried to play [the part] with strength and passion – as a revenge play, which I think it is. The whole action of the play is Prospero's gradually being convinced that hatred and revenge are useless' (Hayman, 198). It was presumably this moment which T.C. Worsley had in mind when he said that 'we feel this change of heart more intensely than is common on this occasion' (*New States.*). In 1970 Richardson, according to the promptbook, responded to Ariel's challenge by kneeling to him, which suggests a prolongation of the moment and a real change of heart. Wood was taken aback by Ariel's implied rebuke, his response a surprised moment of real self-revelation. Robert Smallwood commented: '"And mine shall" he replies, a sharp change of mood from the sardonic tone of his previous "Dost thou think so?" indicating his relief at finding a course less angry than the one he had embarked on' (*SQ*, 86). Dymkowski, however, felt that the exchange was played 'for ambiguity ... it was not clear whether Prospero had always intended mercy or was prompted to it by Ariel' (301). In 1998 David Calder was much less ambiguous, his amazement at Ariel's remark (delivered without particular emphasis by Scott Handy) leading to his own astonishment 'to find himself renouncing vengeance' (*Times*), and suggesting a real turning point for this angry Prospero. For the equally ferocious Storry in 2002 it was the absolutely key moment; his Ariel spoke with real feeling in suggesting 'your affections / Would become tender' (5.1.18–19), but he first emphasized 'Dost thou think so, *spirit*' with ironic near-contempt, only to hold a long pause before responding positively to Ariel's parallel emphasis on 'Mine would, sir, were I *human*' (19–20; my italics). Jacobi also looked wonderingly at Ariel as he spoke, but the struggle to come to terms with the necessity for forgiveness persisted throughout his speech, and the precariousness of his decision to espouse the 'rarer action' was emphasized later by the fact that it was only the prompting of Ariel, appearing silently at his side when confronting his brother, which 'checks his ungovernable fury and leads to a hard-wrung "I do forgive thee" [78]' (*Guardian*, Aug).

Immediately after coming to the decision to forgive, however, Prospero must gird himself up to the renunciation of the very magic that has made the choice possible. The 'Ye elves' speech is closely based on Ovid, where it is spoken by the witch, Medea. Its classical original would have been familiar to any educated member of Shakespeare's audience; not only would this clearly bracket it off as a 'set piece', but its close association with black magic would have rendered it frightening, potentially blasphemous. It is disconcerting that Prospero suddenly claims for his magic an extensiveness which we have scarcely seen in operation – especially the ability to raise the dead – and it is awkward for the actor that the grammar of the speech collapses, since the elves who are invoked at its beginning are given nothing to do as Prospero diverts the syntax into the recreation of his own magical operations. Benign Prosperos have particular difficulty with the speech – Hordern, in 1978, couldn't convince Desmond Pratt that he was a master of potent arts (*Yorks. Post*), though J.W. Velz thought that through the 'realistic reading ... we felt the enactment of a second abdication in this renunciation of magic' (*Cahiers Elis.*, 104). The director did not necessarily help by leaving the lighting unchanged for the speech (almost all productions darken the stage), nor by introducing music under it (as had also been the case in 1951). In 1993 McCowen, according to one reviewer, seemed only 'to be indulging in Mittyesque fantasy' (*Guardian*). Philip Voss, in 2000, also chose not to unleash his considerable vocal powers here, but his quiet intensity suggested a regretful amazement at what he had done. John Wood, however, in 1988, beginning in a whisper, produced 'an extended operatic crescendo that leaves us, not him, breathless' (*Independent*) in an astonishing *tour de force*, which yet still did not convince Stanley Wells that we could quite believe his claims (*SS*, 147). David Calder, in 1998, once again draping round his shoulders the huge silk sheets reaching beyond the height of the stage, recalling our first sight of him, brought out 'very strongly the character's exuberant delight in his own creativity: he describes how "graves at my command have waked sleepers" [48–9] in the tones of a man exhilarated by that old black magic' (*Guardian*). At its end he collapsed, exhausted with the effort of renunciation. But perhaps the performance which brought the greatest conviction to this speech was Jacobi's in 1982. Coped, with book and staff in hand, he circled the stage, building to an enormous climax with thunder and dry ice, trembling with the same intensity he had manifested on his first appearance in 1.2 (see Figure 9). The effect had been worked for throughout the performance, and it was all the more compelling for its contrast with his delivery of 'Our revels now are ended' (4.1.146–63). Magic power to this Prospero was the bulwark against human frailty and despair – and yet it must be renounced.

Then into the circle that he has made – of stones in 1988, of magic dust in 1993, of smoke in 1982, by the sudden appearance of nymphs carrying candelabra in 1951, simply by the actors standing in a circle in 2002 – come Prospero's enemies. He contemplates them, and then asks Ariel to robe him as he was 'sometime Milan' (5.1.86). In 1957, though 'at the prospect of coming face to face with his old enemies [Gielgud's] Prospero is visibly agitated' (*Times*), this was the decisive moment, described by Muriel St Clare Byrne:

> [Gielgud] assumes his ducal robe, his Dantesque coif and coronet, and placing the magnificent 'rapier' in the crook of his left arm stands holding it as if it were indeed the Sword of Justice – the Ruler, called to his election and accepting the burden. It is difficult to say why the brisk, formal, almost sacerdotal gesture with which he took the sword from Ariel and placed it should have been so moving and impressive; there are certain things in the actor's art that cannot be explained, that can only be felt; and this was one of them.
>
> (*SQ*, 490)

Reviewers noted both the pride with which Gielgud delivered his 'Behold, sir King / The wronged Duke of Milan' (5.1.106–7) and a transformation and relaxation of mood at this moment (Dymkowski, 307), and though his Prospero forgave his enemies 'with some asperity', the course was set for the production's final image of reconciliation as the scene changed (see the Introduction) and Prospero moved slowly upstage with a 'proud carriage of his head and almost imperceptible, perhaps barely conscious, drawing up of himself to full height' (*SQ*, 490) before turning back to deliver the Epilogue (Figure 1).

In 2000, though on a much smaller scale, Prospero's resumption of his 'ducal' robes – in this Victorian-dress production a full set of bow tie, waistcoat, tail coat and overcoat with an impressive top hat – transformed him into 'a Verdi-looking figure' as Voss described himself. There is one detail that this production shared with 1957; in each case Prospero broke his magic staff early – in the former before 'Where the bee sucks' (88–94), in the latter just after it, and in both handing the pieces to Ariel. Placing this highly charged symbolic moment so early suggested that the hard work had been done, the mind made up, and that the final confrontation with his enemies was now a matter of secular political will.

Most modern Prosperos, however, have been rather less confident in facing Alonso and Antonio. Even though Jacobi's ducal robe was almost as impressive as his magic cloak, his forgiveness was by no means certain, needing Ariel's prompting, and when he contemplated his former enemies 'the old bile return[ed]' (*Guardian*). It was not just that he found it hard to forget; his icy glare at Antonio as he undercut Miranda's optimism with ''Tis new to thee' (184) underlined his contempt, and his suspicions were maintained right to the end as his declaration of his retirement to Milan (311) was again aimed at his brother 'making clear that he still regarded him as a threat; indeed, at "my Milan" Antonio had looked up sharply and he and Prospero looked each other in the eye' (Dymkowski, 325). (In 1995 the gesture was repeated, though with less preparation, and therefore less effect.) Jacobi offered perhaps the most unresolved of endings, but in their different ways many productions since 1957 have all qualified the play's final harmony. In 1970, Ian Richardson's solitariness, his representation of a Prospero who has learnt 'to let go his power over his daughter and kingdom' meant that it was almost a matter of indifference whether or not they responded to his forgiveness of them. Something of the same weariness was evident in Hordern's performance in 1978, where 'he effectively surrender[ed] his powers on the line "They shall be *themselves*"

[32], restoring to his enemies their freewill in full awareness of what they are likely to do with it' (*Observer*). A decade later Wood chose the same emphasis, though here, perhaps, the sense of resignation was of a piece with a view of the part which suggests that 'Prospero does not want his dukedom back: his earlier rage and grief were for betrayal, not for usurpation' (*SQ*, 86), his 'desire for revenge coupled with a Hamlet-like awareness of its final futility' (*Guardian*, May). But this final scene was complicated in its effect by the way 'Prospero, true to his brooding, self-absorbed nature, thinks of this forgiveness as entirely his own affair and expects it to be accepted as eagerly as he's offering it ... the embarrassed passivity of the guilt-ridden Alonso and the reptilian Antonio makes for one of the subtlest moments of the production' (*S. Times*) (see Figure 34). But then this Prospero's ducal attire consisted (at least after the very first performances) solely of a circlet for his head and a rapier on a belt that, in business introduced during the Stratford run, Wood buckled round himself only to find that it was now rather too small. Resumption of political power scarcely seemed a significant (or even a credible) goal.

There is one more major decision to make – for however Prospero deals with his long-term adversaries, he must also cope with Caliban. The crucial phrase here is 'this thing of darkness I / Acknowledge mine' (275–6). Prospero may be doing no more nor less than accepting that Caliban is his servant as Trinculo and Stephano belong to Alonso; but, depending partly on the subsequent response to Caliban's suit for grace and the tone of his dismissal, more can be suggested. In psychoanalytic critical readings of the play, this acknowledgement can be taken to indicate Prospero's acceptance of the dark side of himself. This is, in fact, an extremely difficult notion to convey on stage – though Dymkowski quotes reviews of a production in Minneapolis, 1981, which seems to have succeeded (321). Jacobi apparently intended some such interpretation. He commented on the peculiarity of the line 'we must prepare to meet with Caliban' (4.1.166):

what a strange thing to say. We know he has been meeting Caliban
all the time for fifteen years (*sic*), but this time it is as if he has to
force himself to formally confront just what Caliban is, that other
side of man. (Cook, 168)

Yet in performance, though the line was slowly delivered, there
seemed no sign of such recognition. The tone of Prospero's offered
pardon and the reception afforded to Caliban's repentance has
been significantly varied. Sam Mendes's production in 1993 was
exceptionally severe in cutting Caliban's intention to sue for
grace, and offering no pardon. By contrast, Voss's tone softened
notably as he spoke 'Go, sirrah, to my cell' (5.1.292); Wood in
1988 reached down to pat a thoroughly repentant Caliban on the
head. In 1998 Charles Spencer thought that 'when a broken-
voiced Prospero says of Caliban, "this thing of darkness
I acknowledge mine" [275–6], the production does seem to
approach the play's mysterious heart' (*D. Telegraph*). Calder
accepted the hand that the crouching Caliban offered as he sued
for grace – revising his own first refusal of Caliban's hand in 1.2,
and achieving a touching reconciliation. Storry, in 2002, paused a
long time before acknowledging Caliban, then awkwardly doffed
his hat to him. Here it was less an acceptance of Caliban than an
acknowledgement that he must cede the island back to him, in
keeping with the production's emphasis on their quasi-colonial
relationship.

The parting with Ariel, discussed in the next chapter, in almost
all productions leads immediately to the moment when Prospero
finally breaks his staff, surrendering his magic power. (Again, in
most productions the final line 'Please you, draw near' is either
cut, or else moved to before the parting with Ariel – 1988 was an
exception, with Wood addressing this final line to the audience as
preparation for the Epilogue.) The moment may be accompanied
by a clap of thunder or flash of light (as in 1982 and 1988, for
example) before brief darkness. But in 1998, in the production's
'best sequence', Ariel was freed, and ran slowly away; as he did so:

his song of 'Where the bee sucks' was heard on the air and Prospero caught and hummed it to himself, several registers lower, standing looking into the distance, his staff across his back. Then, all of a sudden, when we weren't ready and, more important, when he wasn't ready either (for he'd liked being magic, this Prospero), he snapped the staff with a crack across his shoulders and we were into the very simple, direct speaking of the Epilogue. (*SS*, 238)

There is, in fact, not a lot that an actor or director can do, or should attempt to do, with the Epilogue, though there are two notable and similar exceptions. In 1970 the promptbook indicates that during Ian Richardson's melancholy rendition, with a heavy emphasis on 'despair', Caliban entered at the words 'Now I want / Spirits' (13–14), 'picked up wand', and exited upstage behind him. The fact that there is no comment in the reviews suggests that this was business introduced after the production's opening. In 2002 Caliban entered from the auditorium during the speech, finally standing on stage facing Prospero, who was positioned on the tilted disk towards the back. Storry looked hard at him before uttering the final word 'free'. This was clearly a Caliban who had his island back, and a rendition which deliberately counter-manded the normal focus on Prospero. But these are exceptions. Gielgud, who delivered the Epilogue with the other characters still on stage (Figure 1), was, in his own word, 'grandiloquent' (1979, 202). McCowen, by contrast, delivered the lines 'close to tears, a lonely old man who has failed to pluck the mystery out of life and has only death to look forward to' (*D. Telegraph*). Voss was 'magnificently poignant' (*Indep. Sun.*), as for virtually the first time in the production the video was completely shut down and he stood on the bare white stage so that 'there was an ingenious complement between the unadorned set on which he stood … and his frank, plain-spoken sincerity' (*Cahiers Elis.*, 108). But in 1974 Michael Aldridge contrived 'to suggest at the end that even acceptance of wisdom does not bring tranquillity; his final speech to the audience is delivered as a kind of challenge rather than a prayer' (*SA Herald*).

The Epilogue, however, for all the numinousness that is often attributed to it, was almost certainly not delivered at every one of the play's original performances. In the Folio the play ends with '*Exeunt omnes*', and the 'Epilogue spoken by Prospero' is printed below a double ruled line, which suggests its detachability. It was cut throughout most of the nineteenth century, and by Ben Iden Payne at Stratford in the late 1930s, but never since. I have a sneaking wish to see a production which leaves it out; one wonders how different the ending might appear without the ineluctable focus on Prospero as solo figure of some pathos which it almost always engenders. For central though Prospero is to the play, there are many ways in which his relationships with the figures who surround him and are controlled or manipulated by him can be worked out – and it is to those relationships that we now turn.

2

ARIEL

riel, of all the play's characters, is the one most inextricably linked to Prospero. He spends virtually the whole play invisible to everyone except his master; his only public appearance is disguised as a harpy in 3.3. In Renaissance magical theory, the ability to command spirits was the sign that the adept had reached the highest level of wisdom – though such control was precarious at best. He is therefore crucial to Prospero – the executant of his designs throughout the play, and, at its end, the figure he claims he will 'miss' on his return to Milan (5.1.95). How their relationship is to be construed is one of the fundamental decisions any production must take – though first it must be decided how this otherworldly spirit is to be represented, and the text sends out conflicting signals. Ariel, it might be argued, is the island's only true indigene, unlike Prospero or Caliban, except that, as the final song indicates (5.1.88ff.) and his name suggests, Ariel is a creature of the air, not the land (contrasting with Caliban, who knows and lovingly names the natural properties of the island). Able, his final song suggests, to couch in a cowslip, he is explicitly not human, as he acknowledges (20). Ariel is weightless, invisible and inhuman, yet must be embodied visibly by a human actor on stage. In 1611 the part would have been played by a boy actor, but in the modern theatre this is rarely an option, and it is worth briefly considering the implication of that fact, since shifts in casting convention have profoundly shaped the perception of the role.

Ariel unambiguously refers to himself as male – he speaks of 'Ariel and all *his* quality' (1.2.193; my italics) (and for convenience I will retain the male pronoun throughout this chapter, even when discussing female performers), yet the disguises he adopts at Prospero's instigation – sea nymph, harpy and Ceres – are female. This androgynous quality would have been readily managed by a boy actor, who might equally have performed as Miranda, and easily accepted by an audience familiar with such cross-dressed roles. Though the Dryden/Davenant adaptation initially kept Ariel as a male figure, from early in the eighteenth century the part was given to female actors, conventionally dressed in gauze and wings, comfortably corresponding to a theatrically traditional notion of the 'fairy'. Only in 1915 was a male actor again cast as Ariel (Dymkowski, 39). Even then it was some time before Ariel was customarily seen as a male part – Leslie French's numerous performances as 'an unearthly male Mercury-figure' in the 1930s (Dymkowski, 40) did much to establish the orthodoxy of an adult male Ariel, scantly clad, which persists down to Scott Handy's Ariel of 1998.

There have only been five Stratford exceptions to the adult male casting of Ariel. It has been played four times by women: Joy Parker in 1947 (having performed as Miranda the previous year), Margaret Leighton in 1952 (taking over the part from Alan Badel), Bonnie Engstrom in 1995 and Kananu Kirimi in 2002. Christine Dymkowski has argued that the gender of the performer significantly conditions an audience's response to the central questions raised in Ariel's relationship to Prospero, and suggests that it is no coincidence that the emergence of the male Ariel occurs in parallel with the increasing humanization of Caliban.

> As Caliban became a representation of oppressed humanity, Prospero became less God-like and the parallel between Caliban and Ariel became clearer. Or, to put it another way, as Prospero became less God-like, it was possible to see the oppression of Caliban and Ariel as undeserved. Or, to put it in yet another, once Ariel became male (for whatever reason) within a modern cultural

context, it was difficult to be entirely comfortable with Prospero's
treatment of him ... to suggest that the oppression of both Caliban
and Ariel is in some way unjust, the one had to become human and
the other *male*. Just as a bestial Caliban was seen to deserve
Prospero's punishment and restraint, the service of a female Ariel
was too culturally normative to be disturbing.   (Dymkowski, 44)

Her argument is supported by the way in which Joy Parker's
'ballet-like Ariel' (*Wolverhampton E. & S.*), though embodying a
'Peter Pannish spirit of independence and pride, which shines
through the subservience' (*Birm. Mail*) seemed a welcome return
to a traditional view of the part. Even in 1995, when one might
have thought that the servitude of women had ceased to be
'culturally normative', Bonnie Engstrom's Ariel was perceived as
unproblematic in her relationship with Prospero. As Michael
Billington remarked, 'the master–servant tension ... [was]
conspicuous by its absence' (*Guardian*). This was not, perhaps,
surprising, since the director, David Thacker, thought of the
spirits as embodying 'Prospero's creative imagination' (Symon,
75), but it marked a decisive break with the immediately
preceding Stratford productions. Dymkowski discusses other
recent *Tempest*s which have had a female Ariel, and privileges
feisty, feminist performances, while by implication condemning
as 'conventional' performances such as Engstrom's, or the
'willing and dedicated servant' offered by Rakie Ayola in
Birmingham, 1994 (Dymkowski, 45–7). But to imply that Ariel
'should' resent his service is not a necessary, even if it has become
the dominant, reading of the role. Ariel might, after all, function
not as a parallel to Caliban, but as his antithesis; in which case a
ready acceptance on his part of Prospero's power and a sadness at
leaving his command, might not be an inappropriate representation of the relationship. And, indeed, if Ariel is played by a
woman, then, just as in the original performances, the potential
exists for some kind of correlation to be set up between the spirit
and Miranda. Peter Holland commented: 'Engstrom's Ariel was
clearly envious of Miranda, always ready to dart angry, jealous

looks at her ... and she turned "Where the bee sucks" (5.1.88ff.) into a sad anticipation of parting from her beloved Prospero' (Holland, 229). Nancy Meckler's Shared Experience production in 1996 also explored the parallel as her central focus upon Prospero's difficulty in dealing with the emerging sexuality of his daughter was complemented by the 'repression' of the female Ariel's body in a tightly encasing tabard until the very end of the play. Indeed the parallel may be taken further by doubling the parts of Miranda and Ariel.

The possibility of drawing comparison between Miranda and Ariel is also significantly affected by one variable that Dymkowski's discussion does not consider – Ariel's age. If in 1995 the actresses playing Miranda and Ariel were much of an age, the same must have been true of the boys playing the parts at the Blackfriars in 1611. If Ariel is young, then this makes readily comprehensible the terms of affection which Prospero uses towards his spirit – 'chick' (5.1.317) and 'bird' (4.1.184), for example, are both terms Shakespeare uses elsewhere to refer to children – and a parent–child relationship between Prospero and Ariel becomes possible. In such a light Prospero's chiding of his servant might acquire a very recognizable parental exasperation at having 'Once in a month' to repeat the same story to ensure docility (1.2.262), and might enable a credible 'childish' swift turnaround in Ariel's reaction as he asks eagerly: 'What shall I do? Say what? What shall I do?' (1.2.301). In the post-war history of the play at Stratford the truly exceptional decision was the casting of a fifteen-year-old boy, David O'Brien, in 1946. He was dressed in a costume owing something to Leslie French's characteristic habit, with a helmet and wings vaguely suggesting a Mercurian god (Figure 11). But though the *Observer* felt that 'we gain an Ariel of eager buoyancy who is never criticised', the *Manchester Guardian* commented that O'Brien was 'less of an airy spirit than a dutifully drilled boy'. The promptbook suggests that he spent a good deal of his time on his knees in subservient acquiescence. Of subsequent Ariels Ian Holm, in 1963, managed to suggest

FIGURE 11 In this very obviously posed photograph, David O'Brien, the only boy actor to have played the part at Stratford, wears in 1946 a costume which gestures towards the traditional fairy Ariel.

some kind of boyishness, at least to one critic. Robert Speaight thought his playing 'blazed with angelic innocence. It confirmed all my feelings that Ariel *must* be played by a boy, or by an actor clever enough to look and behave like a boy' (*SQ*, 425) (Figure 12). Rather more enigmatically, Philip Hope-Wallace saw him as 'an Ariel with the strange look of a starved Victorian waif', commenting that this was a 'curious conception and yet it seemed perfectly right at the moment when Prospero turns upon this androgynous sprite and calls it "Malignant thing" [1.2.257]' (*Man. Guardian*).

FIGURE 12 Ian Holm, Ariel in 1963, in a tight-fitting suit, speaks to a forbidding Prospero (Tom Fleming), whose costume seems a throwback to Redgrave in 1951. Holm, with his pageboy haircut, conveyed an impression of boyishness to some reviewers. The plastic back wall of Farrah's stark, abstract set can just be seen. (1.2)

In 2002 Michael Boyd provided an imaginative solution by casting a female actor, Kananu Kirimi, as Ariel, but dressing her as a boy in breeches and jerkin (Figure 13). This costume was also that of the Mariners, who were transformed into the spirits simply by adding green face-paint. Ariel was, then, nicely placed between spirit and human worlds. There was no parallel with Miranda here, for though the production emphasized Prospero's rigid command of Ferdinand and Caliban's sexual desires, Ariel seemed

FIGURE 13 In 2002 Kananu Kirimi, on the right, was the first female actor since 1952 to play Ariel on the main stage at Stratford, but her dress is distinctly 'boyish', enabling her to deal effectively with the androgyne nature of the part. Caliban (Geff Francis) entered at the beginning of 2.2 carrying spirits as logs (here James Hyland is over his shoulder, Dan Crute waits his turn). His gaberdine is an impressive garment, suggesting the rather worn cloak of a tribal chieftain very much in keeping with the production's emphasis on his dispossession.

fascinated by their sexuality, and, in added business, gleefully mimed sexual activity very much like the naughty adolescent schoolboy. The actor's diminutive stature also enabled her to be convincingly 'boyish', as had Holm's slightness of build in 1963. Particularly in the reviews of earlier productions, one tends to find complaint at an actor who is felt to be too bulky for the part – for example at Brian Bedford, 'a more solid Ariel than is usually seen' (*Oxf. Mail*), in 1957.

More significant, however, is the way in which the actor chooses to respond to Ariel's first speech:

> I come
> To answer thy best pleasure, be't to fly,
> To swim, to dive into the fire, to ride
> On the curled clouds. To thy strong bidding, task
> Ariel and all his quality.

> (1.2.189–93)

Followed, as it is, by his narration of his actions in the storm, this suggests a spirit willing in service, fleet of foot and light of body. Yet this display of dutiful eagerness immediately precedes his grudging reaction to Prospero's demand for more work, which in turn precipitates Prospero's anger and the recapitulation of their previous history. No matter that, compared with Prospero's repeated curses of Caliban, this is a single rebuke; no matter that Prospero repeatedly compliments his servant on work well done; it is this resentment which has tended to dominate the conception of the part in Stratford performances. As Dymkowski suggests, it is the very fact of an adult male casting which makes this focus plausible, even necessary.

Even before a production decides how to characterize the Prospero–Ariel relationship, it must choose how to dress the spirit. Or, perhaps one should say, whether or not to undress him, for one tradition is, paradoxically, to represent the immaterial spirit in very bodily form. Alan Badel, in 1951, was clad only in 'grey-green rubber trunks with palm leaf design' according to the

FIGURE 14 Ben Kingsley, Ariel in 1970, narrates his raising of the storm (1.2) to Ian Richardson's very plainly dressed Prospero. Kingsley's costume (or lack of it) and white body-paint is characteristic of one strong tradition in the representation of Ariel's otherworldliness. He stood behind Prospero for much of this narrative (as some other Ariels have done), as if to imply his invisibility.

costume plot (see Figure 3); in 1970 Ben Kingsley wore a G-string with a minimal fronded sporran for modesty (Figure 14); in 1988 Duncan Bell was naked to the waist, though wearing rather more substantial breeches, decorated with tufts of material suggesting leaves or feathers, and in 1998 Scott Handy sported only a loin-cloth (Figure 17). Unearthliness in all of these representations was suggested by body-paint, on which the lighting might play in different ways. The photographs suggest that Badel was silvery, but one reviewer thought that he 'suggests in every movement the blowing breeze, as he weaves among the other elements and blends his small green body with the tree trunks or the waves' (SQ, 335). There is some disagreement among reviewers as to whether Duncan Bell was white, grey or blue, precisely demonstrating how his make-up, together with the lighting, could provoke 'a loss of focus and make him the most transparent Ariel I can remember' (*Cahiers Elis.*, 104), as his body 'toned into the backcloth' (*SS*, 147). In similar fashion, Scott Handy, 'blanched so he resembles a resuscitated ghost' (*E. Standard*), exuded 'unearthly calm from a bare body' (*Times*), supporting the production's conceit that not even Prospero could see him.

More fully clad Ariels have been more varied. When Margaret Leighton took over from Badel, her costume was less revealing, but still created a 'truly ethereal, a gliding, almost transparent spirit' (*Man. Guardian*). In 1963 Ian Holm's tight-fitting body-stocking suggested 'an athletic Martian from out of space' (*E. News*) (Figure 12). In 1982 Mark Rylance also wore a tight-fitting costume, but here the body-stockings were 'patterned with veins, as in the anatomical images of Vesalius' (*SQ*, 85) (Figure 15). (On the production's London transfer, though, Rylance reverted to a loin-cloth, with veins suggested only by streaks of make-up.) Brian Bedford's costume in 1957, covered with tendrils, implied rather Ariel's affinity with nature, reminding one of the tree from which he had been freed (one reviewer characterized him as looking 'like a leprechaun recently emerged from cold storage', *Liv. D. Post*) (Figure 7). In 1995 Thacker seems to have thought rather of

FIGURE 15 (*opposite*) In 1982 Mark Rylance's 'moody' rejection of his servitude (1.2) was echoed by his attendant spirits, identically clad, who imitated his gesture of defiance, as Prospero (Derek Jacobi) grew angry at his disobedience. The spirits' body-stockings were coloured with blue and red 'veins' and grey piping, colouring that was continued in streaks in their hair; the costume was redesigned for the London transfer.

Prospero's appellation of Ariel as 'my bird' (4.1.184), since Engstrom's costume, and that of her attendant spirits 'link[ed] the spirits to creatures of flight, of the air' (Symon, 75). Engstrom enforced the analogy with her staring, unblinking eyes (Figure 31). By contrast, Ian Charleson's costume of white tabard and below-knee trousers in 1978 (Figure 20) seemed to bemuse reviewers as they sought to describe it – as that of an 'acrobat' (*E. News*), a 'skin diver' (*Yorks. Post*), 'an etherial compère of "Cabaret"' (*Morning Star*), a 'space-voyager' (*S. Times*) or an 'all-English cricket captain' (*New States.*). In 2000 Gilz Terera was very different – a 'grey-suited aide-de-camp' (*FT*), a 'clerk-like' Ariel (*Guardian*) – whose normal costume was not distinguished from the late-Victorian dress of the production, and who therefore failed 'to convey that sense of the unreachable otherworldliness' that Paul Taylor desired (*Independent*).

This representation of Ariel may have been affected by one of the most distinctive of all Stratford Ariels, Simon Russell Beale in 1993. Beale's interpretation 'was informed by childhood experiences of servants in the former British colonies of Malaya and Singapore' (Symon, 128). Barefoot, he wore a high-collared, buttoned jacket and trousers, which suggested to Russell Jackson the uniform of 'a steward on a rather nerve-racking cruise' (*SQ*, 343), to a number of others a Mao suit (see Figure 16). The one connection with earlier representations was the unearthliness of a pale white face and Kohl-rimmed eyes (which also echoed the whitened Caliban of David Troughton in this production). This costume was emphatically of a piece with his overall reading of the role. Paul Taylor described the performance with brio:

> Beale pads about barefoot making 90-degree turns and looking like a *Stepford Wives* equivalent of Wishee-Washee. God knows what his mind is picking up on its far-flung frequencies, but the beady remote hauteur of his stare suggests that, compared with him, Jeeves is in the grip of a gibbering inferiority complex.   (*Independent*)

FIGURE 16 The weary impassivity of Simon Russell Beale's 1993 Ariel as he endures the chiding of Alec McCowen's Prospero in 1.2 was characteristic of his whole interpretation. The suit he wears suggests the household servant.

Though different in many ways from anything that had preceded it, Beale's performance at the same time represented the culmination of the emphasis upon Ariel's servitude which had begun in 1951.

Before considering the evolution of that tradition it is worth commenting on the aspect of Shakespeare's Ariel which has been least successfully rendered in Stratford productions – his meta-morphic quality. Ariel is instructed by Prospero to make himself 'like a nymph o'th' sea' (1.2.302) in order to bring on Ferdinand. There is no clear instruction in Shakespeare's text for the removal of this 'disguise', though generally he returns to his 'normal' appearance in 2.1. There has been considerable uncertainty, even embarrassment, about the sea nymph. Ian Charleson (1978) adopted a large white ruff; Duncan Bell a decade later assumed a blue curled wig which seemed to one reviewer 'like a soiled paintbrush on his head' (*Independent*). A sheet of iridescent perspex for Mark Rylance was a not entirely convincing cape – having little suggestion of a sea nymph. Gilz Terera, in 2000, however, responded to the clear implication of femininity in the sea nymph by assuming a sparkling lamé dress looking, to one reviewer, 'a little too much like a maritime Shirley Bassey' (*Cahiers Elis.*, 107) (Figure 5). It is not perhaps surprising that 1974, 1993 and 1998 simply cut Prospero's request for him to don the sea-nymph disguise.

In Act 4 the implication of his line 'when I presented Ceres' (4.1.167) is that he enacted the part of the goddess in the masque. In 2000 this invitation was, for the first time, taken up – and the presence of an adult male with two other female goddesses was not entirely convincing. (In 1998 Scott Handy's voice was heard speaking Ceres' words, but he himself did not appear.) Indeed, the fact that more than one reviewer described Terera's performance as 'camp' seems to derive entirely from his two moments of cross-dressing – an indication of the difficulty for the modern adult male actor in making such gender switches. In 2002, however, Kananu Kirimi had distinctive costumes both as the 'sea nymph' (blond wig and many-coloured grass skirt), and in the masque, where she took the part of Iris rather than Ceres (a long white ballet dress). This performance for the first time really suggested something of the ease that a seventeenth-century boy actor would have brought to the transformation. The central disguise, as a harpy, has been much more successfully managed, though without a single attempt to represent the femininity of this classical avenger.

The opening exchange with Prospero sets out the two sides of Ariel, the eager servant and the 'moody' spirit. As long ago as 1951 Badel conveyed a

> really imprisoned Ariel – no tricksy elf, with none of the 'child-like simplicity' that Coleridge found in the part, but an elemental spirit

> robbed of freedom and even tortured by the loss ... who can flash
> like a winged messenger from a Blake prophetic drawing, or remain
> posed and silent like a Greek garden god.   (*Man. Guardian*)

Peter Fleming's characterization of Badel as 'a swift, agile, impersonal spirit whose longings for freedom are justly balanced against his loyalty to his master' (*Spectator*) suggests that he successfully brought together the two sides of the character. One way in which an actor can convey any particular 'take' on Ariel is through movement. Though Badel retained some of the Puckish lightness of foot of tradition as 'a spirit ever in loose-limbed gear, supply sinuous' (*Stage*), he was at the same time able to suggest invisibility and otherworldliness 'by becoming a part of his background in a trice' (*Scotsman*). In the revival the following year Margaret Leighton caught the same balance as Badel. Peter Fleming described her as 'a lithe, fleet, aloof being, bound to the earth by loyalty to her master, drawn to the air by yearning for freedom' (*Spectator*), and others saw her as 'a slender salamander' (*News Chron.*), 'a gliding, almost transparent spirit' (*Man. Guardian*), 'compounded of another element than flesh and blood' (*D. Telegraph*). Versions of this gliding swiftness might be seen in 1957, where Bedford, at least by the time of the Drury Lane transfer, had acquired 'a skimming quicksilvery fleetness' (*FT*); and in 1982, where the same doubleness which had characterized Badel's reading was to be found in the way that 'although [Rylance] is forever running nimbly up ship's masts, you detect a will of iron under the spriteliness' (*Guardian*). Both in 1988 and 1998 the Ariels were frequently to be seen 'abseil[ing] down the sides of the proscenium arch' (*SS*, 147, of 1988), and Handy, in 1998, 'achieved a style of movement that was graceful and deliberate without being too slow' (*SQ*, 197), 'impressively athletic' (*SS*, 238), whilst, like Badel, conveying at the same time 'a slightly uncanny, statuesque quality' (*Birm. Post*). In 2002 Kirimi was 'deliciously fleet' (*D. Telegraph*), scampering eagerly at Prospero's bidding.

Other actors have chosen less ambiguously to emphasize Ariel's status as Prospero's reluctant servant by refusing the text's invitation to represent an Ariel who could credibly 'drink the air before me and return / Or ere your pulse twice beat' (5.1.102–3). Kingsley, in 1970, was 'a sexless, slow-stepping Ariel' (*Birm. E. Mail*), 'a creature not of fire and air, but a slow-moving, secretive native servant' (*Guardian*). In 1978 Charleson was 'a grave, still spirit, moving and speaking deliberately' (*SS*, 203) with 'an exceedingly slow measured walk. No sprinting, even when he promises to execute a command "ere your pulse beat twice [*sic*]"' (*E. News*). And then Beale in 1993, believing that Ariel 'doesn't have to dash about because at all times he knows what he is doing' and that 'a lack of frenetic energy ... gives Ariel tremendous elegance and ease' (Symon, 143), adopted movement that was 'glacial, ponderous, even baleful' (*FT*), though achieving 'a kind of delicacy ... step[ping] lightly on bare feet, as if soundlessness were second nature' (*Observer*, Aug).

Obviously enough, at a certain point slowness of movement suggests less Ariel's ethereality than resentment of Prospero, and a detachment from the acts of magic he performs. This attitude is immediately established by the way in which at his first entrance he chooses to report on his success in raising the storm. Where Bell, Rylance, Kirimi and others delight in what they have achieved, recreating it before the eyes of the audience, the Ariels less happy in their service adopt a measured, detached delivery that indicates clearly that they have simply carried out orders as requested. The 1978 promptbook directs, beside Ariel's speech (1.2.195ff.), 'Inanimate Ariel; Prospero with facial reaction', his impassivity according with Charleson's belief that Ariel is 'a Renaissance angel, a defence of goodness. All the business of producing thunderstorms at Prospero's behest is painful for him, not his proper function' (*Glasgow Her.*). In 1993 Russell Beale appeared above the folding screen centre stage, and remained there as he delivered his report; similarly, in 2000, Gilz Terera, though demonstrating agility in the ease with which he negotiated his entrances down the steep fall at the back of the set, like 'one of Milton's Archangels sliding down beams of light' (*Cahiers Elis.*, 106), yet 'pin[ned] his arms regimentally to his sides and sp[oke] in a staccato monotone' (*Time Out*).

More difficult to reconstruct is Ian Holm's performance in 1963. Reviewers speak of a 'sinister and deliberate performance' (*S. Times*) and 'an exceedingly accomplished executant magician' (*FT*); but whereas the first felt it 'allowed no gleam ... of the ecstasies which mitigate his discontents', John Percival thought 'his bleak self-possession' was 'lightened by the glee at his own tricks' (*News Daily*). The critical reaction was perhaps complicated by the fact that this Ariel was accompanied by attendant spirits dressed almost identically, 'like skin divers with hair nets' (*E. News*). The device of these 'attendant zombies' (*Birm. Post*) representing Ariel's 'quality' was repeated in 1970 with 'sculptural spirit shapes dimly discernible behind the blue-green scrim' (*Observer*), and again in 1982 where Rylance was accompanied by five identically clad figures, memorably characterized by Robert Cushman as 'Ariel and his Full Fathom Five' (*Observer*) (see Figure 15). At Stratford they accompanied his every entrance, and mimicked his movement, gesture and reactions; but by the time the production transferred to London, their presence was much reduced – testament perhaps to the way in which, though they contributed to a sense of the strangeness of the island and ubiquity of its magic, they also diffused the focus on the central Prospero–Ariel relationship. In 1993, though similarly costumed to Beale's Ariel, the attendants were clearly relegated to the function of stagehands operating under his instruction.

It is, however, the presentation of the confrontation between Ariel and Prospero which establishes their relationship and resonates throughout the play. It is not only Ariel's attitude that is significant, but also the sense we have already been given of the nature of Prospero's feeling for his spirit. Gielgud claimed that in his four appearances as Prospero he:

was consistent in one thing – I never looked at Ariel. He was always behind me or above me, never in front of me. I tried to see him in my mind's eye, never looking at him physically. It heightened the impression of Ariel as a spirit. (Cook, 162)

It is difficult to know whether the clear contradiction of this oft-repeated statement in Figure 7 is a sign of Gielgud's overstatement, or a consequence of Angus McBean's having specially posed the photograph. But other productions have suggested that Ariel is not readily visible to Prospero. In 1988, for example, Duncan Bell delivered his first lines as he descended down the proscenium arch, and John Wood searched vainly for a while to locate the source of the sound; McCowen in 1993 did not look at Ariel at all during his impassive narrative (though this might be interpreted simply as the consequence of the fact that he had already overseen his performance in 1.1). In 1978 Michael Hordern made considerable play on the effort required to invoke Ariel, and the remote, amplified whispering in which Charleson delivered his first speech reinforced the sense of precarious control. In 1952, though Leighton was able to suggest the etheriality of Ariel, and entered with 'the kind of bogey-man laughter you hear at the fun fair' (*Time & T.*), her Prospero, Ralph Richardson, summoned her 'without raising his voice, as though Ariel was a very well-trained sheepdog' (*Spectator*). A distant whisper also marked Scott Handy's first entrance in 1998, though here the invisibility of Ariel was absolute, and crucial to the development of the Prospero–Ariel relationship throughout. Kirimi's first entrance in 2002 was prefaced by bird noises, and pained screams that seemed to be recalling Ariel's imprisonment – but once she had appeared there was no doubt of her visibility to Prospero.

The motivation of Ariel's resentment at the request for 'more work' (1.2.238) can be variously presented. Beale's haughty disdain in 1993 was continuous with the detachment he had already shown. In 1982 Derek Jacobi scarcely looked at Ariel during his narrative, not because he could not see him, but because, poring over his book, he was already moving to the next stage of his plan. Rylance seemed to be responding to his inattention, rather than expressing deep-seated resentment, and at first Jacobi responded unemphatically at 'How now? Moody?' (1.2.244), returning immediately to his book at 'No more' (246) as if thinking that was the end of the matter. Only as Ariel pursued his case did he rise to a fury, making very clear that it was the ingratitude he perceived in his spirit that truly fuelled his anger. Wood in 1988 also took some time to move from apparently incredulous amusement to anger at Ariel's insubordination. There is no record of how Ian Richardson in 1970 responded to Ben Kingsley's gesture of denial, 'sliding through Prospero's legs' at 'I do not, sir' (256), a gesture whose paradoxical nature was emphasized as it was repeated at the moment when harmony was restored and he eagerly enquired: 'What shall I do?' (301).

In the ensuing reminder of the torment from which Ariel had been freed, Gielgud spoke with 'sadistic relish' (*Punch*), David Calder circled insistently and angrily round the spotlit (but invisible) Ariel. Hordern, however, in keeping with his generally kindlier reading, was 'schoolmasterly in manner, impatiently tapping his foot as he made Ariel repeat the origin of Sycorax' (*SS*, 203). Varied, too, is the reaction of Ariel. In 1951 the promptbook places by Prospero's invocation of the memory of the cloven pine in which Sycorax had imprisoned him 'attitudinise and freeze', suggesting – though the instruction could be realized in a number of ways – that this Ariel was not cowed by the memory, painful though it might be. Badel's reaction was paralleled by Charleson in 1978, Rylance in 1982, and by Beale in 1993 who maintained his cool impassivity throughout (see Figure 16). These Ariels were not to be cowed; and indeed by their indifference picked up on the implication that this was a narrative they were compelled to endure 'Once in a month' (262) and were tired of hearing. Others, however, have reacted more violently. In 1988 Bell, who 'really had forgotten Sycorax, so that Prospero made him relive a forgotten experience' (Dymkowski, 150), as the promptbook indicates, groaned rhythmically at the recollection, and screamed and fell to the floor at Prospero's 'It was a torment / To lay upon the damned' (289–90). In 1998 Handy crouched whimpering, and in 2000 Voss's 'over-emphatic reminder to Ariel of the horrors from which he rescued him has the poor sprite scratching all over with remembered wretchedness' (*Mail Sun.*).

Exactly how an audience responds to this exchange is probably not entirely within the actors' control, however it is staged. We might see the ferocity of Prospero's account as underlining his own intemperance, and if Ariel responds painfully see that as further evidence of his excessiveness. But we might equally take such a re-enactment of the original pain as at least in part justifying Prospero's demand for service, particularly if, as in Wood's rendition in 1988, the whole builds towards 'made gape / The pine and *let thee out*' (292–3; my italics), or if, as in 1998, the moment is underlined by a striking lighting change as the spotlight which had 'frozen' Ariel dissolved. But, essentially, the dynamic of the relationship between Prospero and Ariel is fixed by this opening scene. Though his songs are important ingredients in our response to the world of the play, they are more significant to our estimation of an actor's performance than they are to our sense of Ariel as an individual character (see chapter 7). For the next part of the play, until the end of Act 4, Ariel is an executant, a function he may perform with more or less enthusiasm, and which in 1993 was much expanded, as Beale commanded scene changes and set action in motion with a wave of his hand, appearing as an inscrutable presence even in scenes where the text does not call for him. But it is only towards the play's end that Ariel's relationship with Prospero is further explored.

As Ariel answers Prospero's request to summon up the masque he asks: 'Do you love me, master? No?' (4.1.48). On the page the tinkling, trochaic line is firmly contained within the lyric by its rhyme (it was occasionally set to music in the eighteenth century). Yet on stage it is frequently a crucial moment in setting the pattern of the master–servant relationship for the rest of the play. The emphasis can fall either upon the question, or the response. So, for example, in 1978, Charleson spoke the line 'without the second note of interrogation, so that the "No" becomes a grief-stricken realisation', in 'the most effective new reading of the production' (*S. Times*). His suspicions were validated by the way in which Hordern's 'Dearly, my delicate Ariel' was 'almost a brush-off' (*FT*). In 1988, too, the question seemed more significant to Ariel than to Prospero: 'when Ariel asks, with all the poignancy possible, "Do you love me, master?", Prospero is for once perplexed, his duties in the happiness of his creations has not occurred to him' (*Independent*). In 1993, however, for the most self-contained of all Ariels, to whom the feelings of his master were of little consequence, 'Do you love me master – no' was 'a simple, flat answering of his own question rather than a wistful request for a sign of affection or even an angry rebuke' (*SQ*, 343). But the reading of this line changed during the run:

> initially a simple enquiry with the emphasis on 'love' (is that what you call the thing you feel for me?), the emphasis later became placed on 'me'; after witnessing Ferdinand and Miranda's love in the masque scene Ariel wants to know if Prospero feels that emotion for him. (Broomhead, 42)

In 1970, by contrast, the moment was of much greater significance for Prospero than for Ariel:

> The potential prig and bully is a man who can feel loss and most particularly the loss of Ariel ... For the first time, the voice hesitates and breaks. A few moments later Prospero stretches out to take his spirit's hand and finds only air. (*Times*)

Here the powerful suggestion is of a lack of reciprocity between Prospero and Ariel, a need which is the magician's not his spirit's. An interesting variation was played in 1998, where:

> Prospero could not see his Ariel and seemed merely to take him for granted as a sort of high-powered personal computer. Then, suddenly, provoked by his puzzled observation of Ferdinand and

Miranda together, Ariel asked 'Do *you* love *me*, master', and touched
him on the breast, sending a huge shock wave through him.

(*SS*, 238)

In their different ways each of these representations prepared
for the final act. At 5.1.7ff. Ariel delivers a report on his execution
of Prospero's commands, saying that the King and his followers
are 'Confined together / In the same fashion as you gave in
charge, / Just as you left them; all prisoners, sir' (7–9). (Beale, as he
had throughout, paused slightly before uttering 'sir', in the tones
of a particularly haughty head waiter.) Then, as he has so often
done before, Ariel offers a brief description that brings the picture
of the imprisoned lords to life, for the benefit of the audience as
much as for Prospero. But crucially, whereas the comic description
of Caliban, Stephano and Trinculo at 4.1.171–84 remains an
objective caricature, here the tone changes at the end of the
speech as Ariel suggests that his 'affections / would become tender
... / ... were I human' (5.1.18–20). It is a crucial line for the actor
playing Prospero, who must decide how central it is to his turn
to forgiveness (see chapter 1). But it is also of significance to the
representation of Ariel. Badel in 1951 inflected it 'with an
indescribable mixture of envy of the man's heart which *can*
"become tender" and of hope that it will' (*SA Herald*). Engstrom in
1995 had prepared for it by a softening tone as she spoke of
Gonzalo's tears, and her longing for human feeling was inflected
by her palpable affection for Prospero, and Kirimi followed the
same path in 2002. In 1998 it was the second moment at which
Calder reached out for Ariel and experienced the electric shock of
contact, and 'the path to the conclusion was immediately clear'
(*SS*, 238).

The staging of the conclusion of the play, Ariel's release 'to the
elements' (5.1.318) is capable of very different realizations,
though as Dymkowski's wide-ranging survey indicates (326–9),
Stratford has by no means explored all the possibilities. In
particular, no production seems unambiguously to have presented

an Ariel delighted by freedom and exiting in joy (though promptbook information for the earlier productions is often not clear). The only partial exceptions are Eric Crozier's ill-fated 1946 attempt to suggest Ariel's translation to the ether by having him fly out at the end, Hytner's 'final exit, disappearing over the rim of the stage in a flash of both time and light at exactly the moment that Prospero snapped his staff' (*SS*, 238), and Boyd's decision to have Ariel watch anxiously as Prospero broke his staff before slipping quickly and quietly away. Where, in Strehler's famous production in Milan, the freedom of Ariel had been symbolized by releasing the female actor from the flying rope to which she had been attached throughout, at which she ran out over the stage and through the audience exulting in liberty, most Stratford Ariels have exited much more tentatively. In 1951 the promptbook emphatically notes that Ariel exits 'VERY slowly' (though the *Leamington Spa Courier* suggests that Prospero 'followed Ariel's flight and made us "see" the spirit circle the auditorium and soar out of sight'). In 2000 'Ariel takes some time to adjust to the idea that he can in fact go and does so with some reluctance as if it takes him some time to get used to the idea' (Voss). In 1978 Ariel, according to the promptbook, 'sighs', and walked slowly offstage. In 1998, Prospero reached for the last time to touch Ariel, this time experiencing little of the 'electric shock' which had marked his earlier contacts with the invisible spirit (Figure 17), and then 'with a long intake of breath, Ariel raised himself, poised himself for flight, and then walked slowly up the aisle' (*SQ*, 197), this slowness contrasting with the speed at which he had negotiated the parados earlier. 'Now he could only struggle and limp, either because the bond between them was hard to break or because the first steps to freedom are inevitably uncertain' (*SS*, 238). In 1995 Bonnie Engstrom offered a rather different reading:

> Instead of Ariel's usual bitterness at enslavement and desperation to
> be free from Prospero's power, there seemed some reluctance to go

FIGURE 17 In 1998 David Calder's Prospero, dressed in his ducal robes, confers freedom on Ariel (Scott Handy) (5.1). He tentatively reaches out for the last time, expecting the 'electric' shock that touching Ariel has previously set off; at this moment of reconciliation it was absent.

> as with an almost idle swish of his staff Prospero dismissed the spirit and turned away from his dream world to reality.　　*(Evesham J.)*

Peter Holland suggested that:

> she turned 'Where the bee sucks' (5.1.88ff.) into a sad anticipation of parting from her beloved Prospero, before spending much of the last scene downstage, sitting with her head up, contemplating the sky with longing and loneliness intermixed ... Once released, Ariel took a yearning step towards Prospero as he turned upstage and walked away from her.　　(Holland, 229)

The indifference of Jesson's Prospero in 1995 contrasts with other performances which focus on the magician's reaction. Hordern responded, in 1978, with 'a shuddering gasp'. As Roger Warren noted, this reaction might be read either as 'relief' or as 'a sense of loss' (*SS*, 203). There was little ambiguity, however, in

1970 or in 1982, when Ariel had left the stage before Prospero's final instruction and farewell. In 1970 it fitted with the emphasis on Prospero's solitariness; in 1982 it was turned into a powerful emotional moment, as Jacobi began his instruction 'My Ariel', only to realize he was not there, pause, and deliver the endearment 'chick?' as a question, before pacing the stage and delivering his instructions to the empty air. The relationship of 'unreciprocated friendship' (*FT*) struck Michael Billington strongly:

> I have rarely been more aware of the way Ariel is subtly exploited by Prospero; yet, when he has finally been sprung, Jacobi searches the air vainly for him with a palpable sense of loss. The two-way pathos of the master–servant relationship is thus exactly caught.
>
> (*Guardian*, Sep)

In 1957 it had been possible for Gielgud simply to bless a kneeling Ariel, thus seeming 'to validate the master–servant relationship' (Dymkowski, 326); by the 1980s such an unproblematic stance was much more difficult to maintain. In 1993 its impossibility became the central focus of perhaps the most controversial of all Stratford endings. Earlier in the fifth act, McCowen had demonstrated his affection for his Ariel, touching Ariel's face at 'that's my dainty Ariel. I shall miss thee' (5.1.95). Beale's response conveyed that 'the gesture is both a presumption and at some level desired' (*Independent*). It hinted at, but scarcely prepared the audience for, the moment when, given his freedom, he paused, then spat deliberately in Prospero's face before walking, slowly as ever, offstage. To Peter Holland this was 'a superb invention, pinpointing the patronising nature of our assumption that the perfect servant enjoys serving and that Prospero's treatment of him is not in its own way as brutal and humiliating a servitude as Sycorax's' (Holland, 175). But many others did not agree. Irving Wardle wrote that: 'everyone will remember this as the production in which the liberated Ariel spits in his master's face: an effective shock, but shocks come cheap when they have no preparation and no consequences' (*Indep. Sun.*). John Peter's request that the spit should be 'cut at once' (*S. Times*), was eventually answered – it disappeared before the end of the Stratford run. After its disappearance McCowen and Beale

> experimented at length with the scene: Ariel kissing Prospero, Ariel going to speak and having nothing to say, and finally decided on simply a stare, but a stare that Russell Beale describes as 'a mixture of hatred, anger, confusion and love. Again it is up to the audience to decide precisely what Ariel is thinking at this point. I do think that's the most important thing of all, that it is so inscrutable.'
>
> (Broomhead, 41)

Even in the London transfer, however, Benedict Nightingale thought that 'the impression is of an extremely balky shop steward who, having worked overtime for Prospero Island Industries yet been denied the bonuses he merits, is flouncing off to sulk on the moral high ground' (*Times*).

But this is perhaps to refuse the significance of the production's final *coup de théâtre*. For as Beale padded offstage, he exited, as Holland noted, 'through a previously invisible door in the stage's back wall, from the stage's blue room into a world of dazzlingly white light', a moment 'poignant and enigmatic: what after all is there behind the back wall of the stage?' (Holland, 173). Powerful as it was in the context of this particular production's emphasis on the play's metatheatricality, the white emptiness into which this Ariel stepped was as anonymous as the grave to which Prospero is ineluctably heading. If Prospero depends absolutely upon Ariel as the executant of his designs, and without his 'spirits to enforce' (Epilogue 14) shrivels to the lonely figure of the Epilogue, it is equally true that without a Prospero to serve Ariel declines into nothingness. It is the troubled nature of that mutual interdependence which every production seeks to negotiate.

---------(3)---------

CALIBAN:
STEPHANO AND
TRINCULO

N o figure in *The Tempest* has been more discussed than
Caliban. Excellent studies by Alden T. Vaughan and
Virginia Mason Vaughan, Rob Nixon and others have
traced in detail the history of his transformations, alluded to
briefly in the Introduction. To simplify considerably, there are
three main perspectives which have been adopted in order to
explain the nature and function of this unique Shakespearean
creation. Coleridge articulated the once dominant view that
'Caliban ... is all earth, all condensed and gross in feelings and
images; he has the dawnings of understanding without reason or
the moral sense'. But he also noted:

> He partakes of the qualities of the brute, but is distinguished from
> brutes in two ways: by having mere understanding without moral
> reason; and by not possessing the instincts which pertain to
> absolute animals. Still, Caliban is in some respects a noble being:
> the poet has raised him far above contempt.   (Hawkes, 226, 237)

In the hierarchy of creation Caliban stands between human and
brute. Beerbohm Tree, in 1904, echoed the view that 'in his love of
music and his affinity with the unseen world, we discern in the
soul which inhabits the brutish body of this elemental man the
germs of a sense of beauty, the dawn of art'. This understanding of
the character persists well into the second half of the twentieth
century, as may be seen in the *Times* review of the 1951 Stratford

production: 'Mr Hugh Griffith kept the offending animal in Caliban vigorously alive, but in his scene with Stephano suggested a rather endearing canine devotion, and later he established the tragic yearning for humanity without which the monster is maligned.' Accommodated from the Victorian period onwards to a Darwinian concept of Caliban as 'pre-human' or a 'missing link', this view did not exclude the possibility of sympathy, even pity, for him; but even if Prospero's treatment of him might be seen as harsh, its essential legitimacy remained unchallenged.

By 1951, however, quite another view was possible. The Communist Party newspaper, the *Daily Worker*, thought Griffith's Caliban brilliant but wrongheaded, since Shakespeare was really talking about colonialism, and had more sympathy for Caliban than emerged in the production. This newspaper maintained the same perspective upon later productions – and it is important to recognize that a changing sensibility towards issues of race, empire and colonialism was apparent even before it came to dominate the literary criticism of the play from the 1970s onwards. Caliban began to appear less monstrous, more human; with the consequence that it became possible to consider the ways in which his demonization reflected Prospero's own purposes, rather than the intrinsic 'nature' of his slave.

This view of Caliban – as a human degraded by the treatment he endures – is the second main strand, and in one form or another it has been the dominant perspective at Stratford at least since 1963. The Vaughans suggest that the intertwining of an emphasis upon the injustice of Caliban's treatment with issues of colonialism, and the consequent racialization and politicization of his role, was especially strong from the 1960s to the early 1980s (Vaughan and Vaughan, 1991, 192–5). Since then the specific emphasis on racial difference has generally declined – Peter Brook, in Paris, 1990, cast a white Caliban precisely 'to bring a new vision to the part, so often presented either as a monster made up of rubber and plastic or as a Negro, exploiting the colour of his skin to illustrate in a very banal way the notion of a slave' (Brook, 107).

Caliban has been seen more widely as representing 'any group that felt itself oppressed' (Vaughan and Vaughan, 1991, 194) – Dymkowski notes, for example, a 1987 production in which he was presented as 'the trained underemployed, bored with his status, ripe for thoughtless rebellion and potentially dangerous', and another where he was 'a menacing, loud-mouthed Millwall fan, dressed in leather jacket and chains' (65). Some productions, indeed, have backtracked to the older view of Caliban. Michael Bogdanov's 1992 English Shakespeare Company production, for example, had a fur-coated Caliban with two small 'horns' which he smoothed out as he said that he would 'seek for grace' (5.1.296), accepting and underlining in a fairly obvious fashion Prospero's account of him as 'got by the devil himself' (1.2.320). The hairy, monstrous Caliban was alive and well, and living in the New Victoria Theatre, Stoke-on-Trent, in 2000. But in general it remains true that productions handle his 'monstrosity' much more warily.

There is a third potential reading of the role, in which the most important contrast is that between Caliban and Ariel, the earthy and the airy. An extension of this view is to see the two characters as embodying the two sides of Prospero's own nature. Though this has had a long run in literary criticism, it is a reading much harder to convey on stage, and it has only been hinted at in one or two productions. The Vaughans note one such production in Connecticut in 1981, where Caliban was 'an aspect of Prospero's character – the libido that cannot be controlled' (1991, 194), and Jude Kelly in Leeds in 1999 dressed Prospero, Ariel and Caliban initially in nearly identical costumes, as if to make the same point. On occasion reviewers have managed to see this in Stratford productions. Don Chapman in 1982, for example, wrote of 'the feeling you have that Mark Rylance's quicksilver spirit and Bob Peck's earthy Caliban are extensions of Prospero's own personality' (*Oxf. Mail*), and in 1998 the mirror image costuming of Ariel and Caliban in loin-cloths offered 'the suggestion that they are different aspects of Prospero's psyche' (*D. Telegraph*). But no stage production has really been able to make this allegory work – the only thoroughgoing and successful attempt is probably the film adaptation of the play, *The Forbidden Planet*, where Caliban could be represented as the 'id' of Morbius, the Prospero character, by virtue of becoming a disembodied, almost invisible shape.

Thus far it has been assumed that the prime determinants of our response to Caliban are his appearance and his relationship to Prospero. This, indeed, is the assumption of most of the academic discussions of the role; but on stage it is in the company of Stephano and Trinculo that Caliban spends the greater part of the play. It is they, even more than Prospero, who pour abuse upon him, and it is they who view him as a trophy to be taken back home and exhibited for profit. The relationships between Caliban, the drunken butler and the jester are in fact crucial to our response, and will be considered in the second half of the chapter, after a survey of the different physical representations of the part and consideration of his relationship with Prospero.

How to embody Caliban is no small challenge. Marina Warner notes the 'contradictory zoology' of his description by other characters:

> he is above all redolent of fishiness, but he is also described as 'a freckled whelp' [1.2.283], a 'tortoise' [1.2.317], and, no less than five times, a 'mooncalf' [2.2.105, 109, 132–3; 3.2.20, 21]. The word monster recurs in Trinculo and Stephano's drunken banter as its key signature, and they explicitly evoke some form of grotesque hybridity when they call Caliban 'a puppy-headed monster' [2.2.151–2] ... These shuffling, overlapping pictures have made Caliban notoriously difficult to cast and dress.   (Warner, 98–9)

In the early post-war productions it was assumed that characters speak true of Caliban's appearance, and costume designers came up with variations of monstrosity which attempted to reflect some, if not all, of the descriptions offered of him. Julian Somers's 'sonorous and shambling Caliban' (*Observer*) in 1946 looked to one reviewer 'just a little like the Demon King' (*Man. Guardian*), to another 'a clawed figure out of pantomime' (*Birm. Post*). The clawlike hands and webby feet, as well as the absurd-looking bald wig, cannot have helped Somers (Figure 2), or his successor, John Blatchley, in 1947 to suggest much of Caliban's humanity, and it is not perhaps surprising that Somers should have been judged 'a good enough symbol for the things we have to efface from our Brave New World' (*Birm. Post*). Unremarked, however, is the necklace of what appears to be fragments of bone round his neck – the gesture towards 'savagery' seems to have been so uncontentious in 1946/7 as to appear mere decoration.

Something of the same blindness characterized the response to the next production, where the part was taken successively by Hugh Griffith (1951) and Michael Hordern (1952). As Dymkowski notes, no critics mention one aspect of his appearance, the 'African caricature' of his 'blackened face, enlarged nostrils and whitened bottom lip' (159). But the fantastic elaboration of the costume, with huge webbed feet and scaly body, underlined by a first entry carrying a fish (recalling Benson's performances at the beginning of the century), explains why Alice Venezky could see him as 'a prehistoric amphibious creature newly crawled onto the land' (*SQ*, 335) (Figure 29). A number of reviewers, however, comment on the way Griffith, 'amazingly, given the costume', could yet make him 'more of man than monster ... in a performance that put the case of the slave with unusual poignancy' (*Birm. Post*). And the following year, though Ivor Brown could complacently observe that Hordern's Caliban 'is first-rate, a most human and even poignant representative of the Backward and Underprivileged Peoples' (*Observer*), the *Daily Worker* felt that Hordern, unlike Griffith, 'plays Caliban as he should be played. Mr Hordern gives us the strife, the distorted humanity, the tortured dignity of the part.' But then the reviewer, Hugh Philips, came to the play believing of Caliban: 'what is he if not the symbol of men surrounded by a gracious world, but unable to realise it, unable to enjoy it because they are allowed only such knowledge as will enable them to be slaves?' The agenda of the critic is, particularly in the case of Caliban, always an important conditioner, not merely of opinion, but of what is actually seen or deduced from a particular performance. But the sense that Hordern, more than most Calibans of his period, explored the rich potential of the character is evident in Michael Redgrave's compliment: 'Your Caliban is immensely fine, with all the pity and pathos, which last year were so heavily over-loaded that they became soggy, but with real terror and humour as well' (Hordern, 93).

If it was possible to see glimmerings of later colonial readings of the play in 1951/2, the same was not true of Alec Clunes's performance in 1957. Here the costume (Figure 18), together with the production's development of the comic scenes and Clunes's own temperament, ensured that he remained 'an ape-like monster so sympathetic that I could almost have added him to the menagerie in my home' (*Yorks. Post*). 'With a sad, vacuous, semi-human face' he reminded Muriel St Clare Byrne of Ernest Griset's 'sketches of home-life among the cannibals at the end of last century' (*SQ*, 491). Only the *Stage* could see him as 'brooding over the production like a malignant thing one would destroy, but for those moments of humbleness and simplicity that seem to redeem him'. Philip Hope-Wallace's description of him as 'more like Barrie's Nana in Peter Pan, not drawing on the strange brutish pathos some players have found in the monster' (*Man. Guardian*) was echoed in Kenneth Tynan's objection that 'Alec Clunes has domesticated Caliban too thoroughly; here is a house-trained monster who would probably enjoy a slice of plum-cake: one thought of a cross between the Abominable Snowman and some *farouche* old pantomime cat' (*Observer*). Interestingly, the production distinguished clearly between the ways in which Prospero controlled Ariel and Caliban. Where he had, in threatening Ariel (1.2. 294–300), held his magic wand above his head, before he went to summon Caliban (who entered from a downstage trap, carrying a bone, rather than the fish of 1951/2) he took out a whip from behind a rock, and threatened him with it. After the 'abhorred slave' speech (352–3, delivered by Prospero, not

FIGURE 18 A very obviously posed photograph of 2.2 in 1957. Alec Clunes's Caliban was the last of the Stratford 'monsters'. The costume of Patrick Wymark's Stephano suggested the comedian George Robey to many reviewers. Clive Revill's Trinculo hides beneath the gaberdine.

Miranda) the whip was thrown down and, apparently, not used again. The clear differentiation of the magic control of the spirit, and the intimidation of the slave with a horse-whip, emphasized Caliban's animal nature, even if his cowed posture suggested that Prospero had not much to fear from him.

This was to be the last Caliban in full-dress monster suit; thereafter he becomes more recognizably human. It is convenient to divide subsequent characterizations into those which explicitly represented Caliban as racially 'other', and those which chose to manifest his alterity in different ways. Dymkowski records the first 'blacked-up' Caliban as Roger Livesey in 1934 in a production by

Tyrone Guthrie at the Vic/Wells, and the first black actor to take the part as Canada Lee in New York in 1945. Roy Dotrice was, in 1963, the first Stratford actor to present Caliban as unmistakably racially marked. His entrance, breaking through the Perspex wall of the stage, 'snarling, slavering and gnawing upon a large bloody bone' (*Scotsman*), brought some much needed life to a very slow-moving 1.2. Physical energy marked his performance throughout; distant memory recalls him rolling and scrambling violently round the stage as he was threatened by the immobile Prospero. Alan Brien wrote that 'this naked, black insurgent, with a bald dome and tufts of hair in the most distracting places, sweats an evil energy and an aboriginal lust which would frighten Genet' (*S. Telegraph*) (Figure 19). Brien was avowedly influenced by Philip Mason's *Prospero's Magic*, one of the first critical books to develop the notion of the play as a colonialist text, just as the *Daily Worker* reflected its politics in acclaiming as the production's only outstanding success 'Roy Dotrice's interpretation of Caliban not as a monster but a Negro savage who, though taught by his masters only enough to be a slave, was yet far from lacking in appreciation of natural beauties'. Within another decade this reviewer might have winced at his use of the phrase 'Negro savage', though not perhaps as violently as Denis Blewett might have regretted his description of 'the bizarre, beastly Caliban ... a buffoon in burnt cork' (*D. Sketch*). Certainly the phallic gesture with his bone which caused the resignation of a member of the front-of-house staff might, in a more politically correct age, have been seen as unacceptably endorsing racial stereotypes.

Yet the difficulty we now have with accounts of a Caliban who is dangerous *because* he is black demonstrates clearly the ways in which too straightforward an identification of him with the colonized subject risks flattening the complexity of Shakespeare's character. In 1974, when a black actor was for the first time at Stratford cast in the part, the ambivalent reactions to Jeffrey Kissoon's performance indicated how problematic the identification of Caliban as a black native can be, especially when the actor

FIGURE 19 Roy Dotrice was the first Stratford Caliban to represent him as racially 'other' in 1963. Derek Smith's anachronistically dressed Stephano sits on his 'butt' of wine, watched by David Warner's lugubrious Trinculo (2.2). Both Stephano and Trinculo were delivered on stage on a 'travelator' set into the stage, which can just be seen disappearing into the wings behind Trinculo's raised foot.

himself is black. No photographs survive, but from the production records it seems that Caliban was naked to the waist, and clad in a loin-cloth or trunks, with some kind of 'knee bandage'. Though one reviewer noted that he twisted 'his agile frame into fantastic poses to convey the acrimony of his feelings' (*Evesham J.*), others felt that he was 'all too shapely an advertisement for black manhood' (*D. Telegraph*), who, 'though he suggests the pent-up savagery of Caliban, is much too beautiful an animal for a monster' (*Oxf. Mail*). Charles Lewson, writing that Caliban 'is no monster but the well-proportioned Jeffrey Kissoon, a slave simply because of his colour' (*Times*), seems, however, to have recognized that this is precisely the point that any fully developed anti-colonial reading of the play would want to assert; it is exactly the view taken some four years earlier by Jonathan Miller's Old Vic production, and is the axiomatic point of departure in Aimé Césaire's powerful rewriting of Shakespeare's play as *Une Tempête* which sets out to strip Prospero of all legitimacy. But Sheila Bannock, wanting to hold on to the idea of 'Caliban's innate instinct to destroy', simply denied the problem, arguing that 'connotations of racial oppression in Caliban's role ... can be very misleading' (*SA Herald*). No doubt this is in part a refusal to entertain the notion that the blessed William could possibly be a racist. The *Coventry Evening Telegraph*, however, in asserting that 'Mr Hack paints [Caliban] as a monster only in his colour, but in attempting to illustrate the white man's mental and physical cruelty to the black races ... succeeds only in being offensive to them', manifests, in this tangled logic, the embarrassment and guilt of the well-meaning member of the audience who cannot separate the fact of an actual black actor being insulted from the insults directed at Caliban within the fiction of the play.

Nonetheless, David Suchet in the next production in 1978 continued the racialized representation of Caliban, taking it as axiomatic that 'the monster was in the eyes of the beholder' (Suchet, 12). Again bare-chested and barefoot, he was dressed in a torn and dirty pair of breeches identical to Prospero's, though this seems to have been a gesture towards realism (where else would he have got clothes?) rather than making any symbolic point, neatly as one might think it underlined Prospero's colonial control (Figure 20). He wrote that 'I wanted to look like "basic man" and

FIGURE 20 Caliban (David Suchet), in 1978 made up to suggest a generalized idea of racial difference, wears breeches identical to Prospero's (see Figure 8). Ariel (Ian Charleson) prepares to imitate the voice of Richard Griffiths's pierrot Trinculo as Stephano (Paul Moriarty) attends to Caliban's suit in 3.2.

I wanted to be of a blackish hue. But I didn't want to be instantly recognizable as being obviously an African native or an Indian or an Eskimo or an Aborigine.' To this end the make-up artist, Brenda Leedham, designed 'two rubber prosthetics which covered my eyebrows and gave me a prehistoric-looking forehead', an 'African nose' and then

> made the top of my head appear bald and lumpy by placing dollops of porridge on it and covering the whole top of my head with latex ... Then I put on two layers of dark brown make-up all over my body and then sprayed it pewter-coloured. Under the stage lighting the effect was that sometimes I would look black, sometimes pewter, and sometimes I even took on a greenish hue.   (Suchet, 179)

It was, perhaps, this deliberately syncretic make-up which enabled Suchet as a white actor to put the characterization of Caliban-as-native into quotation marks, and thus to give 'the culmination of colonial interpretations' (Vaughan and Vaughan, 1991, 192) without incurring the wrath of those who would have seen 'blacking up' as intrinsically denigratory.

It was a commanding performance, and virtually all reviewers concurred in recognizing the thrust of his reading. Irving Wardle wrote: 'modern convention dictates that Caliban must be a sympathetic emblem of imperialistic exploitation, and that is how he is played here: a noble black innocent of magnificent physique speaking the language with the too-perfect precision of an alien' (*Times*). Michael Billington described

> a black-visaged, semi-naked figure with the eye-rolling fervour of Olivier's Othello [who] clearly has been unjustly dispossessed of his territory. Though hardly 'misshaped' or 'disproportioned' as the text suggests, he gives the production its chief dramatic momentum ... It is a stunning performance with both the anger and pathos of the unreasonably exploited.   (*Guardian*)

Suchet had attempted to deal with the problem that the representation of Caliban as wronged native can leach him of menace by 'playing a Caliban at times dangerous and at times childish, but at all times totally spontaneous', a character whose 'thoughts and actions are as totally instinctive as is his language, and not coloured by intelligence but by his gut feelings' (Suchet, 177), and intensified his threat by carrying, throughout the early scenes, a voodoo doll through which he clearly wished to get his own back on Prospero's magical control. But the real problem came, as Billington recognized, from the fact that this reading of the part was not 'followed through . . . by making Prospero himself a wrathful colonialist' (*Guardian*).

In the following production, in 1982, though Derek Jacobi had all the anger that Hordern lacked, and though Caliban was characterized by Bob Peck as 'a prognathous, Rasta-locked, power-hungry figure' (*Guardian*, Aug), the result, as Dymkowski suggests, was a rather 'confused interpretation' (67). The racial gesture of the Rastafarian dreadlocks and tattered loin-cloth was not fully developed, and while Ned Chaillet felt he 'could indeed be a rapist or a revolutionary' (*Times*), the *Kidderminster Shuttle* described him as 'a comic creation of half-man, half-beast loping around the stage'. In part the ambivalent reaction to this Caliban derived from the fact that Jacobi's reading centred much more on his relationship with Ariel and Miranda, and on his bitterness towards those who had usurped him, than it did on the relationship with his slave, whom he perceived not as a colonized subject but as 'the other side of man, . . . the side that is evil, and cannot be taught good' (Cook, 168). To this magus Caliban's threat was easily contained by the magic staff and book with which he warded off his lunge at Miranda on his entry. But it also followed from the simple fact that Peck chose to 'adopt a subhuman, simian crouch' (*Times*) as his characteristic posture, and this gesture towards the older view of Caliban-as-animal, coupled with the humped back covered in sores, defused any racial reading of the role.

By the time we reach Zubin Varla's performance in 2000 the colour of the actor's skin is simply unremarked by reviewers. At one level this was not surprising in a production where colour-blind

casting made it an irrelevance, yet the freedom with which
Georgina Brown could describe this coloured actor as: 'covered in
boils and sores, his posture and gait ape-like' (*Mail Sun.*)
emphatically signals the extent of change since the 1970s. Varla
chose to represent Caliban as 'clearly handicapped rather than
monstrous' (*Guardian*), adopting contorted postures and an
equally contorted vocal delivery to suggest 'a twisted, muttering,
emaciated figure whose desire for freedom is accompanied by a
psychologically persuasive relish for masochistic subservience'
(*D. Telegraph*). His posture recalled that of Peck, as he moved with
'an angular but nimble waddle, suggesting a creature who has
only recently learnt to stand upright' (*S. Times*), and so too, the
sores which covered Peck's humped back were found again
covering Varla's body. To a number of reviewers this suggested
that Caliban had long been maltreated. Patrick Marmion, for
example, described him as 'tortured and bullied by Prospero, . . . a
creature covered in weals who has been robbed not only of his
home, but also his self-respect and even his mental health'
(*E. Standard*). Philip Voss himself suggested that:

> the fury with Caliban is genuine. He is the one element in the play
> that Prospero can't control and in our production I treat him quite
> brutally, grabbing the inside of his mouth while I threaten him with
> physical pain. I use my staff on him, kick him, but then react to my
> failure and my own anger with self-disgust.   (Voss)

But he actually seemed less angry with Caliban than with Ariel.

   In 2002 Michael Boyd also cast a black actor, Geff Francis, in
the part. There was very little to suggest monstrosity; that one
shoulder was higher than the other seemed a consequence of the
harness to which, on his first entrance, he was tethered by a long
rope, rather than a deformity. But in this production, finally, the
director was offering the reading that reviewers had been demanding since the 1950s. The colour of his skin was significant; his
impressive gaberdine echoed Prospero's magic cloak, suggesting a
tribal chieftain's robe bedraggled by service (see Figure 13), and

the Caribbean inflection of his speech ensured that the colonial reading could not be missed. One reviewer, however, thought such an interpretation had missed its time by 'adhering ... to a take on *The Tempest* first popularised in the 1960s' and objected that 'Caliban has nothing of the half-man, half-fish about him' (*Time Out*). Thus do fashions take their turn. What is clear in considering these last two productions, is that we are now sufficiently familiar with the convention of colour-blind casting to interpret the colour of an actor's skin in the context of a particular production's wider emphases, to know when to register it and when not.

Throughout the period, however, Caliban's difference could be suggested in other ways than by his race. In 1970 Barry Stanton's rendition was somewhere halfway between the monstrous and the human. He was deformed, with a withered arm, and unable to stand (Figure 26). Though his appearance might have prompted the pity due to a thalidomide child, this is scarcely apparent in the reviews. One thought that 'Barry Stanton, happily, does not exaggerate a rather pathetic monster with a withered arm' (*Birm. Post*), and another characterized him as 'filthy and misshapen but markedly human' (*Birm. E. Mail*); but others continued to use animal images to convey their impressions. The *Observer* saw him as 'a memorably grotesque Caliban, flopping squatly about like a huge beached sea-elephant', and Benedict Nightingale as 'slithering, roaring, rolling in blubber, half jelly-fish, half hippo' (*New States.*). He entered, as most Calibans do, from a trap door. He was chained, and, in time-honoured style, carried a fish. As he attempted to return to his cave at 'I must eat my dinner' (1.2.331) the promptbook records: 'Prospero shuts trap / Traps Caliban's chain'; and then Caliban's response to Miranda's 'When thou didst not, savage, / Know thine own meaning' (1.2.356–7) as 'spitting "fish" mouthful' at her. The petulance of this gesture indicates the way in which Stanton, stranded by his deformity, could scarcely appear a real threat to Prospero. Equally, where Prospero correlates Caliban's misshapenness with his moral deformity in characteristic Renaissance fashion (4.1.188–92), and MacDonald's 2000 production attributed it to physical abuse, here it was simply a given, which carried little coherent symbolic weight, and was, in any case, rather undermined, as Benedict Nightingale noted, by the fact that the actor's real arm inside the costume 'could not be more visible if it was put in a sling, covered with plaster of Paris and signed in red by the entire cast' (*New States.*).

Another Caliban confined largely to crawling about the stage was encountered in 1995, when 'Dominic Letts's Caliban, wrapped in charnel house bands like an angry Lazarus' (*SA Herald*), was rarely able to rise above his knees (Figure 21). Here one might have imagined, as with Varla's performance, that his disability was the consequence of maltreatment; certainly, as one reviewer remarked, Letts 'misses the character's servility; but you can readily imagine him murdering Prospero' (*Times*). There was no attempt to play for pathos, as 'with a quixotically violent temper, he howled his way around the island' (*Cahiers Elis.*, 102). Nor was he cowed: he lunged at Miranda on his entrance, and when threatened by Prospero with cramps and aching bones, with studied insolence he nonchalantly ate the banana which he had brought on as his lunch (and employed in a phallic gesture recalling Dotrice's of thirty years earlier). Russell Jackson felt that 'he was very well spoken, having achieved complete mastery of the language he had been taught ... This linguistic facility suggested that Prospero might well have usurped one of nature's gentlemen' (*SQ*, 320), but the production video confirms that a good deal, especially in 1.2, was delivered at the shout, which robbed his protest of particularity, and of dignity.

If one tendency has been to justify Caliban's hostility to Prospero, and therefore to represent him as consumed by anger and hatred, the three final performances I consider here each attempted in a different way to deal with the problem that Caliban, for all his discontent at his enforced service to Prospero, readily subjugates himself to a 'new master'. In 1988 John Kane

FIGURE 21 This image of Dominic Letts's fearsome Caliban was taken at the 1995 production's opening at the Young Vic. Throughout, he crawled about the stage, only occasionally as here at the beginning of 2.2 struggling to his knees.

appeared to all reviewers as a 'human' Caliban 'hardly monstrous at all, apart from his skin, all pink and blue blotches, his long nails and well-studied, deep croaking voice' (*Cahiers Elis.*, 104). Robert Smallwood felt that this 'chubby, muddy, croaking Caliban ... doesn't really convince you that he does much paunching with stakes or wezand-cutting in his spare time' (*SQ*, 86), and despite an impressive first entrance, 'from behind the rock in which he was apparently immured, appearing to burst out from within it, arm first, accompanied by the sound of stone

cracking and dropping' (Dymkowski, 161), he was 'a subdued,
blotchy and uniquely subservient Caliban' (*FT*). Virginia Mason
Vaughan, in a brief piece based on interviews with the actor and
director, reveals that this was far from unintentional. She writes,
of Kane's performance:

> Caliban is no fish, hairy beast, or angry victim of colonial
> oppression. He is human in appearance except for skin like the
> underbelly of a dalmation ... On his head, hands, wrists, and feet is
> a shiny, gravelly substance, suggesting aquatic origins and the cave
> from which he appears ... Kane takes pride in his Caliban's 'unique
> servility'. This monster does not aspire to freedom or to hegemony
> over the island. Rather, he wants a master who will love him. He
> wants to return to the golden age before he was cast out from the
> family circle.   (*SB*, 11)

For at least one critic this meant that he was 'an old-style Caliban,
the savage with a soft heart, acted by a white man, and not at all
the victim of a violent colonialism the programme notes had
prepared us for' (*What's On*). But the downplaying of the colonial
was entirely deliberate. John Wood's Prospero seemed apologetic
as he told Miranda that he 'serves in offices / That profit us'
(1.2.313–14), and Hytner felt that Caliban 'is necessary to
Prospero as an object on which he can project that part of himself
he feels uncomfortable with, particularly sexual desire' (*SB*, 11).
Consistent and coherent though both Caliban and Prospero were
in this production, the absence of real tension in their relationship
caused 'a certain absence of threat' (*SQ*, 86).

A decade later, in 1998, in another production in which 'rage
at colonial exploitation is significantly absent' (*Guardian*), Robert
Glenister presented a human Caliban, this time made up in grey,
and caked with earth. The potential for a colonial reading was
there, both in David Calder's angry Prospero and in the vestigial
manacles at his wrist and ankles which were echoed in the
chained Ferdinand of 3.1, but it remained resolutely unexplored.
Instead, Glenister longingly reached up to Prospero's hand at
'then I loved thee' (1.2.337) as he crouched before him, only to

FIGURE 22 In 1998 Prospero (David Calder) winkles Caliban (Robert Glenister) out of the shell which rested on stage in 1.2. It perhaps implied his 'fishy' nature, though the shell did not reappear later. Throughout the performance Calder used his magic stick very much as a physical instrument.

have it cast aside. This was a Caliban desperate for affection, one who consequently gave 'little sense that he nurses a just grievance in having been offered linguistic education in exchange for his rightful property' (*Guardian*). In this production of rather unintegrated ideas, the oft-remarked way in which Ariel and Caliban looked 'like positive and negative photographic images of each other, both dressed in unflattering loin cloths' (*D. Telegraph*) seemed to lead no further than did the first discovery of Caliban inside a shell, from which Prospero winkled him like a stubborn sea creature (Figure 22).

But in between these two 'soft' Calibans the 1993 production saw David Troughton give the most consistently praised performance since Suchet. In appearance he was 'built like a wrestler with an alarming white body, a bald, talcumed head and a mouth full of black teeth' (*Observer*, Aug). He moved bent-kneed round the stage, 'with ape-like gait and a Hogarthian profile' (*Stage*), suggesting 'the silhouette of a Japanese wrestler' (*Cahiers Elis.*, 95). His exaggerated whiteness prevented any easy reading of him as racially 'other'. He was a human grotesque, but one who could combine threat and pathos, 'brutish and vulnerable, savage and dreamy, a creature of nature who is both dangerous and simple' (*S. Times*). Much turned on the way in which 'the rich variety of tone of his powerful voice expresses the ambiguous nature of the character – human but with the latent roar of a wild beast' (*Cahiers Elis.*, 95). Where Letts bawled his way through the part in 1995, and Kane's 'bullfrog voice seem[ed] to belch forth from the very bogs and fens' in 1988 (*D. Mail*), Troughton, like Suchet before him, used the fact of his having painfully learnt the language of his master in a self-conscious and powerful fashion. Suchet wrote that 'the voice I used was slightly stilted as I tried to make it clear that I had been taught to speak' (Suchet, 179). Troughton, 'mouthing his words with the exaggerated precision of a conscientious child learning to speak "properly"' (*Cahiers Elis.*, 95), thereby conveyed a kind of fascination with this alien speech, which could be turned to moving account as he articulated carefully the name of the 'hedgehogs' who tormented him (2.2.10), or of Prospero's 'utensils' to indicate that, as Troughton said, 'he does not understand what these things are … but he is frightened of them, whether they be magic implements or washing-up brushes' (Broomhead, 44). Even as he cursed Prospero for 'learning me your language' (1.2.366) he savoured the alliteration. This fascinated delight with words was an important ingredient in enabling him to combine 'the essential dignity and eloquence of the figure without making it incredible that newcomers to the island should think him a monster' (*SQ*, 344). Troughton's ability to suggest that he was 'less a grotesque monster than a man spiritually deformed by subjugation' (*Guardian*) was indicated at his first entry, as his powerful roar of 'this island's mine' was simultaneously undercut by being delivered still from within the wicker basket that served as symbol of his control by Prospero/Ariel, the masters of this theatrical space. He first lunged at Miranda, but then quickly cowered as she spiritedly assaulted him back.

Not the least part of Troughton's success, however, was that though Charles Spencer found it 'the funniest *Tempest* I have seen' (*D. Telegraph*), the threat of Caliban was not defused by comedy in the scenes with Stephano and Trinculo. These scenes, in fact, present a number of challenges to director and performers. In the first place, though Trinculo is a jester, he is not exactly full of jokes – as Roger Warren observes: 'Stefano's and Trinculo's humour depends much less on what they say than on what they do' (183). Inventive business is required if these scenes are to work. But at the same time, if their conspiracy is to convince us that its threat is serious enough for Prospero to break off the masque, the scenes have to carry some real menace. And this is particularly a problem in dealing with Caliban; too quickly render him the comic drunk and the darker potential of his vicious violence towards Prospero evaporates.

The first choice a production makes is how far to integrate Stephano and Trinculo visually into the period adopted for the design, and whether or not to mark their roles as butler and jester in their costuming. In 1946/7 and 1951/2 they were, albeit somewhat fantastically, clad in Elizabethanish dress, and Trinculo wore a version of a jester's costume, following the clear implication of Caliban's insulting description of him as a 'pied ninny' (3.2.61). The same was true in 1998, where Adrian Schiller's hat was a variation on the cap and bells 'with his jester's ear-flaps giving him the look of a lugubrious blood-hound' (*Guardian*), and in 1995, when Trinculo carried a fool's head on a stick. In 1978 and 1988, however, Trinculo was marked out rather differently, for though Stephano's costume belonged to the dominant period of the production, Trinculo was placed within a different theatrical vocabulary. In the first of these productions Richard Griffiths's 'endearingly funny teddy-bear Trinculo' (*S. Times*) wore a costume indebted to the pierrot, with large patches on the cheeks (Figure 20). The disjunction troubled J.W. Velz, who felt that he 'played Trinculo in the style of a modern stand-up comedian … the result was as out of keeping with the ensemble as his costume was' (*Cahiers Elis.*, 105). In 1988, Desmond Barritt, 'rouged and kiss-curled like a caricature of Oscar Wilde' (*Times*), was 'a fat, epicene Harlequin dressed in pale green and pink' (*SS*, 147), and his plaintive mournfulness was underlined by the gesture towards childhood of the gloves held round his neck on a string. His dress and his manner contrasted firmly with Campbell Morrison's Stephano, a 'bluff and hearty member of the working class', dressed in very ordinary jacket and breeches (see Figure 25).

Perhaps the most complete 'bracketing' of the characters from the surrounding theatrical world, however, was in 1993, where David Bradley's Trinculo was dressed in a check suit, with huge boots (alluding to the music-hall comic, Little Titch), and carried a ventriloquist's dummy identically clad. Stephano, played by Mark Lockyer, was presented in a ship's steward's uniform of white coat and bow tie, 'with buck teeth, a fake posh accent and a beer belly' (*SQ*, 344), which reminded reviewers of 'a loathsome cross of Oliver Reed and Terry Thomas' (*Observer*, Jul), 'Sir Les Patterson' (*D. Telegraph*) or 'a refugee from a P.G. Wodehouse novel' (*Spectator*). The distinctive identity of this group of characters was also emphasized by the way in which the theatrical skip which had earlier served as Caliban's 'cave' was consistently deployed both to bring them on and take them off stage. Stephano first appeared from out of the skip which Ariel had dragged on stage. At the end of 2.2 all three were crammed into the same basket, singing (Figure 23), and 'as Ariel pulled it off the stage, their distant voices seemed still to be coming from the basket' (*SQ*, 344). There was little doubt that the trio was firmly under control.

Bradley's allusion to a music-hall comic is a not uncommon strategy in dealing with these figures. Clive Revill's Trinculo, in 1957, reminded the *Oxford Times* of both Chico Marx and Stan Laurel, and the bowler-hatted Stephano of Patrick Wymark

FIGURE 23 In 1993, under the baleful presiding eye of Ariel (Simon Russell Beale), Trinculo (David Bradley, with his ventriloquist's dummy), Stephano (Mark Lockyer) and Caliban (David Troughton) climbed back into the theatrical skip as they sang of 'freedom' at the end of 2.2. The actors left through a trap below the basket, which was then pulled off stage by Ariel, symbolizing the illusory nature of their freedom.

occasioned frequent allusion to George Robey. The *Stage* went further in comparing them to Laurel and Hardy, though Figure 18 suggests that this particular analogy was more in the minds of the reviewers, and a consequence of the inventiveness of comic business in the production, than supported directly by costuming. In 2000, however, the analogy was unmissable (Figure 24), as Peter J. Smith remarked:

> Trinculo and Stephano were Laurel and Hardy; the former in a suit three seizes too small with hair on end and multicoloured socks, the latter in a pair of tails with dress trousers encompassing his massive waist. The benign and ignorant grins of Trinculo, and the clumsy, slapstick brutality of Stephano made the allusion all the more transparent. (*Cahiers Elis.*, 107)

FIGURE 24 Zubin Varla's Caliban, in characteristic bent posture, watches as Trinculo (Julian Kerridge) and Stephano (James Saxon) launch into the catch in 3.2. The two comics in 2000 were unmistakably versions of Laurel and Hardy.

Such allusions may help actors and audience to find their bearings in 2.2 and 3.2, but they offer no more than a starting point in negotiating the complex patterns of these scenes.

The opening of 2.2 illustrates part of the problem. Caliban enters almost always on to a darkened stage, bearing a burden of logs (notably heavy in 1982, in 1988 carried over his back in the gaberdine and emptied into a trap opened by Ariel, in 2002 made by the spirits, Figure 13). His speech, redolent of grievance, gives way to the set-piece routine of the gaberdine and the comedy of inebriation. It is essential to the play that the latter does not entirely drive out the former; and this becomes even more the case in 3.2, where the traditional *commedia del'arte* echo scene must be combined with an increasing menace as the low-life conspiracy gathers head, and real tension appears in the relationship between Trinculo and Stephano.

One way of dealing with the first transition is to recognize that Trinculo's first soliloquy (2.2.18–40) replays Caliban's speech of complaint, albeit at a very much lower level. It is also a speech that needs to take time if it is to have full effect, and Trinculo's character is to be established. Barritt in 1988 emerged slowly over the boulder on the bare stage, and perched on it, 'looking momentarily like the mermaid in Copenhagen harbour', and then, with his 'thin-voiced, querulous, petulant delivery' (*SQ*, 86–7), addressing the audience directly, milked the speech for all the sense of put-upon grievance that he could, and delivered his verdict on the meanness of the English (2.2.31–2) 'harshly' (Dymkowski, 216). A lugubrious, complaining Trinculo offers some benefits in the later development of the relationship with Stephano, and has, indeed, probably been the most frequently adopted characterization of him from Clive Revill's 'very melancholy jester, a delectably timorous zany' in 1957 (*Oxf. Times*) to Adrian Schiller's 'delightfully mournful clown' (*E. Standard*) in 1998. David Bradley's doll double in 1993, clearly to him as much of a comfort as drink to Stephano, intensified his defeated loneliness – when he reappeared in 5.1 the doll had disappeared into the pool, but he forlornly held his arm as if it were still there. It also provided a little extraneous business at 3.2, where at Trinculo's comment on a 'dead Indian' the dummy emitted a *whowho*, and, in answer to Trinculo's bafflement, remarked: 'I thought you said Red Indian.' Clifford Williams's attempts at elaboration in 1963, when the 'bombard that would shed his liquor' (21) was represented as 'dirigible with three coconuts suspended beneath it' and both Trinculo and Stephano were 'delivered by the conveyor-belt off which Stephano [was] frightened by a white rat' (*Oxf. Mail*), succeeded less well. The dividing line between the inventive and the adventitious is a narrow one. The importance of taking time, and even elaborating Trinculo's entry, however, was demonstrated when in 1995, despite picking up the idea of the ventriloquist's dummy from the previous production, Trinculo delivered his opening speech hastily in a not very well sustained northern accent and secured little response.

But then, in this production, the gaberdine sequence, played with just about the smallest cloak I have ever seen, also failed to generate much comedy. It ought to be a sure-fire success from the moment when, with evident dismay, Trinculo crawls under his shelter. In 1982, as prelude to one of the most elaborate of all renditions, 'at "gaberdine" [37], Caliban lifted his head briefly, giving the audience a startled and comic look at this new turn of events ... Trinculo lifted the gaberdine, reeled back ... put his hanky over his nose and then wrung it out' (Dymkowski, 217–18). Barritt in 1988 gave an original inflection to the moment, by pausing after announcing he would creep under the gaberdine, clocking the audience with a camp gesture, and then defensively asserting that there was no other company thereabout. As Dymkowski notes, there was no further development of this 'apparently gay subtext' (218), but it certainly got its laughs.

Stephano's drunken entrance serves to prolong the audience's pleasurable anticipation. In 1993 this was supplemented by Lockyer emerging from the basket, only to turn his back on the audience and urinate copiously; in a number of productions Stephano sits on top of the gaberdine hump – particularly painful in 2000, given Stephano's girth, already emphasized by his comic inability to lever himself up the steep fall at the back of the stage. Once Stephano spots the gaberdine, there is ample room for inventiveness. The promptbooks for 1978 and 1982, marked up with unusual care, demonstrate how much thought can go into choreographing the sequence. In the latter case a whole series of possible alignments of the two bodies under the gaberdine are described as various 'spider' positions which elevated the hidden heads and bottoms of each, and then moved into a 'swivelling spider' shuffling about the stage. When Caliban spat out the drink Stephano had poured into his mouth, 'after a pause, Trinculo's hand appeared, feeling his damp bottom'. This sequence was described as 'a brilliant bit of pantomime, which had both adults and children in fits' (*New States.*). It is unnecessary to elaborate further on the many possibilities that have been explored – of a 'pantomime horse', for example, in 1998 and 2002. Dymkowski's line-by-line commentary provides plentiful examples from a wide range of productions, and the real problem is how to negotiate what follows. For in 1982 this highly successful set piece was followed by a scene that rather lost its way. Michael Billington was complimentary, suggesting that 'the comedy scenes come off well because they mimic the main plot, with Christopher Benjamin's Stephano, a gruff, Pozzo-like tope, relishing the sway he holds over Alun Armstrong's surly, working-class Trinculo' (*Guardian*, Aug). Nicholas Shrimpton, however, was unimpressed, attributing the failure of the clowns to their being 'unsettled by their rather dignified monster' (*SS*, 155). Not for the first, or the last time, one wonders whether reviewers were at the same production, for to me it was precisely the fact that Bob Peck's Caliban became swiftly drunk, frequently falling on to his back, that robbed him prematurely of dignity, and drained his invitation to conspiracy of its potential force.

Something the same seems to have been the effect in 1957, where the malevolence of Alec Clunes's Caliban 'passes off after the first shock and he fits amiably into a fine kind of Christmas-play entertainment' with Stephano and Trinculo (*Birm. Mail*). But then, though confronted by a production which had given a notably darker reading of Prospero, audiences were still content to revel in Patrick Wymark's Stephano, who 'adroitly suggests the tippling butler's bonhomie' (*Oxf. Times*), and straightforwardly to enjoy inventive and elaborate business. We now want our Stephanos rather tougher, and the malice and threat he can embody to be more fully realized. Patrick Stewart in 1970 was 'a moustached pocket-führer from the Midlands' (*Listener*), 'more batman than butler, but aggressive enough to keep his Trinculo and Caliban ... in order' (*Times*). The 2002 production saw Roger Frost's shaven-headed Stephano, a likely recruit for the British National Party, invent extra business as he took advantage of

Caliban's offer to 'kiss thy foot' (146) by ordering him 'kiss! kneel! kiss', laughing cruelly at Caliban's indignity. In 1978 there was 'nothing funny about Paul Moriarty's Stephano, enflamed less with drink than with the ambition of repeating Antonio's coup and taking over the island' (*Times*). Moriarty was working with a Caliban whose rebellious ambition was clear. At 'the tyrant that I serve' (159) Suchet produced his voodoo effigy, at which the promptbook records 'Stephano and Trinculo start'. As the scene moved towards its close, Suchet made much of the song and dance of freedom.

> I beat my feet on the floor rather like a tribal dance – threw away my effigy of Prospero with 'Farewell master'. And then sang very loudly the song 'No more dams I'll make for fish', etc. [176ff.], and when I got to 'Freedom, high-day, high-day freedom!' I stopped singing but let those words come out of my body as though released from the depths of my soul; sometimes the words would literally lift me off the floor. And in this state of wild exuberance the scene closed with Caliban having found a new god and a new hope.
>
> (Suchet, 176)

Even in 1988, a production with a less aggressive Caliban, this final song could be given a good deal of emphasis – the stamping dance led to an exultant exit with the characters in silhouette behind the back gauze. In 2000, however, where the emphasis on Caliban's servility was dominant – he had kissed Stephano's foot with a prolonged and grotesque enthusiasm – Varla whispered his final 'freedom high day', leaving the chant to be taken over by the musicians as the characters exited.

The dynamic of Caliban's subservience and Stephano's ambition becomes more crucial still to their next scene, in 3.2. In 1951 (when 3.3 and 3.2 were reversed, and the interval placed between them) the scene opened with Caliban and Stephano asleep, and Trinculo giggling; the pencilled instructions in the promptbook seem to imply a good deal of drunken horseplay. Perhaps it was then enough for the representation of drunkenness itself to seem funny; by 1998 it needed a comic march, and

Caliban vomiting in answer to 'speak once in thy life' (3.2.20) to generate a laugh. This production, however, introduced a simple, but effective 'drunken' gag, as Trinculo spent most of the first part of the scene effortfully lowering himself to the ground, using his bottle as a prop; just as he reached the floor, Stephano issued the command 'I will stand, and so shall Trinculo' (38–9); the audience laughed at his baffled anger, as the just-entered Ariel lifted him to his feet.

But this is a scene of humiliations, and many productions in one way or another have used it to underline Stephano's propensity for cruelty. Such a reading is the more easily sustained if Trinculo is of a mournful, lugubrious mould. For in this scene the combination of Stephano and Caliban clearly excludes Trinculo, who comments sceptically from the sidelines on both of them, and Desmond Barritt, for example, disconsolately wandering at the edge of stage after being pulled up through the trap by his gloves, conveyed in 1988 a sense of pitiable isolation, which grew as the accusations of lying provoked him into childish tantrums, flapping his gloves vainly in the air, and to retreat to the rock (Figure 25). In 1993 David Bradley's attachment to his dummy was also deployed to intensify his melancholia. As Paul Taylor remarked: 'this muttering wooden creature comically contrives to make Trinculo seem all the lonelier', and especially at the moment when it appeared to betray him as Ariel provided the 'thou liest' as if in its voice, in a 'wonderful perplexed moment' (*Independent*).

Stephano may be expressly violent towards Trinculo. In 1978, for example, at 'Take thou that' (74), Stephano first gave the bottle to Trinculo but then pulled his hair. Trinculo took his hand and tried to retaliate at 'devil take your fingers' (78–9) by bending his hand back, at which Stephano stamped on his foot, and as Trinculo bent forwards, Ariel pinched his bottom. Even when offering an apparent gesture of friendship some thirty lines later, with 'Give me thy hand' he took it, only to squeeze it, forcing him to stand. (In 1988 Stephano again 'squeezed Trinculo's hand,

FIGURE 25 While Caliban (John Kane) and Stephano (Campbell Morrison) discuss the plot to murder Prospero in 3.2, Desmond Barritt's melancholy Trinculo sits forlornly on the rock which is the only feature on the bare white disc of the stage in 1988.

causing him to bend over in pain', Dymkowski, 251.) In 1998 Ariel joined Stephano in bouncing the disorientated Trinculo from one side of the stage to the other in a routine which was amusing, but further emphasized Stanton's ability to convey not merely the 'eternal boozy butler with a drinks tray secreted under his cloak' (*Guardian*), but 'a real streak of nastiness and violence ... that presented a genuine threat to Prospero' (*SS*, 239)

It is, of course, also a scene which humiliates Caliban, which some productions have chosen to underline. In 1982, for example, Stephano was carried in on Caliban's shoulders; but perhaps the most powerful gesture of all was in 1993, when, once more pulled in by Ariel in the basket, Caliban was dressed in a white jacket like Stephano's, had a large label round his neck on which 'MONSTER' had been scrawled, and huge black eyebrows drawn on his face as if to bring out the clownlike potential of his white make-up. This powerfully – and accurately – demonstrated the way in which Caliban's 'monstrosity' is very much the product of the abuse he receives from Stephano and Trinculo; the pathos that he himself did not in any way seem aware of what had been done to him further emphasized the cruelty that this Stephano – Mark Lockyer – had already begun to demonstrate in 2.2, and was to underline when, at the words 'The poor monster's my subject' (3.2.34–5), he gave him a blow which flattened him to the floor. (A rather similar gesture had been used in 1978 when Stephano had 'pinn[ed] him down by the back of the neck', *SS*, 203.) Oddly, perhaps, in 1993 David Troughton, who felt that 'the only time Caliban speaks what he really thinks is when he is drunk', also thought that this blow was 'Caliban's turning point in the play, the unexpected violence convincing him that they can succeed in the plot to murder Prospero' (Broomhead, 44).

As they had ended 2.2 with a song, so 3.2 seems headed to conclusion in the catch, 'Flout 'em and scout 'em' (121ff.), which can build into a parallel with the earlier song of freedom, but this time it is co-opted into Prospero's scheme of things, as Ariel takes it up (see chapter 7 for more on this moment). His musical transformation precipitates perhaps Caliban's most famous speech: 'The isle is full of noises' (3.2.135–43) (in 1974 transferred to the end of the scene, after Stephano and Trinculo had exited). It was no doubt their rendition of this speech above all that allowed reviewers of Hordern in 1952 or of Clunes in 1957 to compliment their verse-speaking. Though Bob Peck, in 1982, seemed so to have overplayed the drunkenness of Caliban that he could not recover sufficiently to make the speech rise above the prosaic, and Geff Francis was oddly stranded upstage in 2002, which undercut the effect, other Calibans have made it powerful and moving. Kane in 1988 and Glenister a decade later, perhaps because they had not chosen to emphasize the menace of the character, were able to give it enormous affect. Glenister paused, and seemed to weep, before 'I cried to dream again', provoking both Stephano and Trinculo to reach out to comfort him. Troughton's 1993 rendition, in which he gave rein to his powerful, but beautifully modulated voice, was hauntingly concluded as, himself lugging out the basket, he reached out at the end of the scene as if to touch Ariel, but 'felt only air' (Dymkowski, 255). In 2002, as Ariel led Stephano and Trinculo offstage, Caliban remained behind, clutching a staff with a streamer attached, and waved it as he bellowed the added line, 'This island's mine.' Unusually, the interval was placed here, so that Caliban's ambition was unambiguously emphasized.

In many productions the characters exit bemusedly following the music; in 1978, however, they exited 'dancing', underlining the irony that they are, of course, heading for the mantled pool, from which they emerge again at the end of 4.1 immediately after the masque. In 1993 and 1995 the connection between the masque and Prospero's abrupt ending of it at the recollection of Caliban's conspiracy was underlined by Caliban's presence at its conclusion. In 1946/7, the juxtaposition of masque and conspirators derived rather from practical necessity. Immediately after Ferdinand and Miranda's 'We wish your peace' (4.1.163) they entered in front of the tabs that had closed to allow the removal of the masque scenery, and continued to Stephano's 'I will fetch off my bottle' (213). The curtains then reopened, Prospero summoned Ariel to place the trumpery on the line (164–93), and the conspirators re-entered with 'This is the mouth of the cell' (216). No such rearrangement has subsequently been necessary – and in general the opening part of the scene has relied upon a comic contrast between the loud complaints of Stephano and Trinculo, and Caliban's desperate wish for silence as they approach the cell. In 1998, Barry Stanton angrily kicked Caliban at his 'Prithee, my king, be quiet' (215), further emphasizing the cruelty of his control; in 1970, however, Stephano's desperation at the loss of his bottle was underlined, as he turned and fell into a trap, to be caught by Trinculo and Caliban. But only, perhaps, in 1957 was this part of the scene afforded the elaboration of comic business that is customary in 2.2 and 3.2. The promptbook is silent, but from the faint recollections of those who saw the production, and from the reviews, it would seem that Trinculo's 'I do smell all horse piss' (4.1.199) responded to Stephano or Caliban urinating at the back of the stage. This prompted Harold Hobson's tirade:

> [Peter Brook] has emphasised, and drawn out to an interminable length, ... the disgusting comic scenes, typified by the urine of horses, with which Shakespeare has loaded a play whose theatrical weakness it would take all Sir John's genius, aided by the full cooperation of his director, to disguise. This production is dominated, not by Prospero, but by the filthiest parts of Shakespeare's text. *(S. Times)*

Most reviewers, however, were clearly delighted; the *Liverpool Daily Post* enthused about 'audacious slapstick when the magic garments suddenly appear across the cave on lines like Widow Twankey's washing-day'. The slapstick seems to have involved 'Caliban, Stephano and Trinculo, posed in close harmony, whirl[ing] up and down through trap-doors' (Trewin, 1958, 103), and 'hat-business' (*Punch*) since Trewin wondered: 'am I mistaken in thinking that towards the close of the play, in the "line and level" scene, we have Mr Brook's cheerful comment on a Samuel Beckett mime?' (*Birm. Post*). In his representation of the low-life characters Brook was content to set their unabashedly comic mode side by side with Gielgud's 'Timon of Athens fighting to regain sanity and human kindness' (*Bolton E. News*) as complementary one to the other. It was not inappropriate, then, that this production should depict 'in the best farcical vein' the 'consequence of the rash plan to murder Prospero' (*Morn. Adv.*).

Most subsequent productions have been less adventurous, and whether the 'trash' (4.1.225) has appeared on a line rising from the stage (1963), or a metal trellis 'tree' descending from above (1978), or else has been held out by the 'shapes' who also, in their duvet-cover costumes, mimed an entrance to Prospero's cell, in 1998, most have been content to intensify Caliban's distress, and to underline his subjection as more and more garments are

FIGURE 26 Trinculo (Norman Rodway) and Stephano (Patrick Stewart), having taken off their muddied clothes, are seduced by the 'trumpery' garments in 4.1 (1970). The irony of a crown for 'King' Stephano is one deployed in a number of productions. Barry Stanton's Caliban, confined to the floor and with the withered 'arm' scarcely more evident here than the actor's real arm under his costume, watches despairingly as his plot falls apart.

heaped upon him. Comedy is not helped by the accompanying dialogue, with jokes that are either incomprehensible or of stunning flatness. Understandably, lines 236–44 have often been partly or wholly cut – though strangely not in 1988, when they were particularly pointless, since the clothes were in a hamper, with nary a clothesline in view. The nature of the clothes on view, however, can have some significance. In 1970, where Stephano and Trinculo had taken off their soiled clothes, the first garment Stephano dons is a crown, and the picture underlines the futility of his ambition (Figure 26). Crowns were also in evidence in 1988 and 1993. A similar point was made a different way in 2002, when only three garments were offered – Alonso's huge, glittering cloak descended in the chair he had occupied in 1.1, to be followed by the coats of Sebastian and Antonio. This neatly underlined the parallel between the two groups of conspirators. In 1993 Sam Mendes, in perhaps the first attempt since Brook really to take advantage of this scene, effectively underlined the folly of their ambition. The 'trumpery' was brought on in a basket, opened by Ariel. There then followed 'one of the comic highlights of the production' (*Cahiers Elis.*, 96) in which 'Trinculo proceeded to dress himself in a blonde wig and purple gown, while Stephano donned a beard and crown; Trinculo, giving a royal wave and changing his voice, imitated the Queen, while Stephano sent up Prince Charles' (Dymkowski, 293). A severe critic might object that this was gratuitous amplification, but that would be to miss the point that the clowning not only made the scene funnier, it also intensified the contrast between a desperate Caliban, and the fantasy ambition of Stephano. It is but one illustration of the way that, if the Caliban/Stephano/Trinculo scenes are to work in the theatre, they need the addition of imaginative business, but at the same time, as here, and in many of the other examples cited in this chapter, must ensure that humour feeds back into a coherent view of the relationship between the low-life conspirators and of their place in the play as a whole.

Over the years the hounds which chase them out have taken many forms. The 1946 promptbook oddly speaks of 'fauns'; in 1963 the shapes of 3.3 adopted intimidating huge wickerwork heads; in 1978 they were dogs with two horns; in 1993 spirits emerging from traps in the stage floor, wearing skeletal masks. In 1988, however, the shapes retained their clothing as 'Prospero clones' (Dymkowski, 297), and in 1998 remained still rather risible pillowcases, afforded 'canine hand puppets with fangs and bright red eyes' (*SQ*, 197). Keith Hack's small-scale 1974 production made do with an abstract projected slide, while in 2000 the video projection of a wild race through undergrowth was a more successful substitute. One of the most effective representations was in 1982, where Ariel's assistants draped in black manipulated 'skeletal dogs with luminous eyes' (*Cahiers Elis.*, 117) in an extended chase.

The return of the trio, in the play's finale, offers little scope for elaboration. The humiliation of Stephano might be emphasized by the violence of Sebastian's gesture which provokes his 'O touch me not' (5.1.286) – he hit him in 1957 and kicked him in 1970 and 1998. In 1988 and 1993 the fact that the conspirators had donned crowns in the previous scene underlined their absurdity and their humiliation – though Dymkowski suggests that 'because they and Prospero were the only ones wearing crowns, Hytner [in 1988] seemed to be making a point about the worth of Prospero's regained status' (320). Whether or not Caliban is, like his companions, simply put back in his monstrous place by the comments of Antonio and Alonso depends both on the way in which Prospero articulates his forgiveness, discussed in chapter 2, and on the degree to which Caliban accepts whatever is offered him. Kane's prostration before Prospero in 1988, and Varla's ready acceptance of Voss's softened tone in 2000, suited their conceptions of the role, and allowed some warmth into this final movement. Suchet, however, declared that his suit for grace in 1978 was

> tinged with slight irony. I think that Caliban has learned that being obedient he will be safe. But when anybody else should ever come to his island again he certainly won't even try to befriend them – he will kill on sight. (Suchet, 178)

Mendes in 1993 cut the suit for grace and the pardon, in the bleakest treatment of Caliban, who was clapped howling back into the theatrical skip, but later modified its severity on the production's transfer to the Barbican. Troughton thought of Caliban as 'vicious, foul, naïve, innocent, unhappy – desperately unhappy', and therefore preferred the revised ending 'which allowed a more flexible response'. As he lowered himself through the trap door, he faced straight out at the audience, sometimes sorrowfully, sometimes aggressively; suggesting 'this way I can play his ending slightly differently every night' (Broomhead, 44–5).

In these scenes Stephano and Trinculo can be played in different ways – their potential nastiness can be more or less emphasized, their comic business be more or less successfully elaborated. The way they are realized will have an important effect on the way in which an audience responds to Caliban. He, however, is, like Prospero, a character whose complexity necessitates a performance capable of holding his multiple potential constantly before the audience. It is precisely this quality that seems to mark out the three most consistently praised Calibans, different though they were from one another – Hordern (though little detail survives) in 1952, Suchet in 1978 and Troughton in 1993. Despite the dominance of colonial readings in the literary criticism of *The Tempest*, Stratford did not see a thoroughgoing version of such a reading until 2002. To many this has seemed a fault; but perhaps the refusal of too completely allegorized a reading is precisely what allowed these particular performances to resonate and achieve a real complexity of signification.

4

FERDINAND AND MIRANDA

N either of these roles appears to offer much to the modern actor. Indeed, one might argue that to bring too much individuality to either of them risks unbalancing their central emblematic function as anti-types to the political and moral corruption of the other arrivals on the island, and as focus of the possibility of regeneration in the future. The difficulty is that in our culture, where the obedience of children to parents is not taken for granted, and premarital chastity is no longer an axiomatic good, the very virtues that they symbolize can seem pallid at best. Compared with the young lovers in Shakespeare's earlier comedies and romances, neither is given much space to develop.

For much of her first scene Miranda is the passive recipient of Prospero's narrative. Then, though she woos Ferdinand against her father's wishes, gesturing towards the familiar comic motif of the evasion of the 'blocking' father, we know that she is merely playing out Prospero's desire to seal reconciliation with his enemies by a dynastic marriage. When Miranda says 'Pity move my father / To be inclined my way' (1.2.447–8), she echoes Hermia's words: 'I would my father look'd but with my eyes' (*A Midsummer Night's Dream*, 1.1.56), but we know that Prospero, unlike Egeus, already does. The actor, then, has a problem in finding life in what seems an entirely dutiful and passive part. Her lack of individuality has often been further underlined by the ways in which she has been dressed. In the early productions she tended to be given a costume which simply labelled her as a conventional romantic female. Joy Parker was afforded an elegant ball gown decorated with a leaf motif in 1946; in 1951 Hazel Penwarden had a rich gown, and in 1957 Doreen Aris appeared in a sarong, which struck one reviewer as being 'like a South Sea beauty out of a Drury Lane musical' (*SQ*, 491). Since then most productions have attempted more realistically to dress her in something appropriate to her isolation on the island since early childhood. In Jonathan Miller's 1988 Old Vic production, narrative probability was saved by dressing Miranda in her father's hand-me-downs, and the same idea was adopted by Sarah-Jane Holm in 1995. As she explained in the programme:

> Miranda is often in a pretty dress – but where would she have got one? Gonzalo wouldn't have known what size frocks to pack! The island is a real island, a savage, not a pretty place. It's a harsh, hard life and my costume reflects that. I have some of my father's old clothes, found in a trunk.

Gonzalo had, of course, supplied 'linen, stuffs and necessaries' (1.2.164) to accompany Prospero and his daughter, and in 1982 her costume seemed to have been fashioned, rather elegantly, from brocaded fabrics that might have served as curtains or hangings, but recent Mirandas have almost always been constrained to do their best with the available bed-linen converted into a more or less designerly white nightshirt.

Nonetheless, for all that the part seems to offer little obvious opportunity, actors have suggested that they find more in Miranda than might be expected. Sarah Woodward, 1993's Miranda, in an interview in the *Hampstead and Highgate Express*, claimed:

> I love the part of Miranda because she has spirit. It gives me a chance to be a bit of a tomboy, which I like. In the past, it's been played as someone who's a little bit wimpish but I'm playing the part in quite a stubborn and aggressive way.

Sarah-Jane Holm, in 1995, thought similarly:

> Miranda is intrepid. She has to grow apart from her father, disobey
> him, just as Juliet must gain independence from Capulet ... To her,
> breaking her father's hest is something of a startling revelation but
> she trusts her intuition. She knows she loves this man. (Symon, 48)

Clearly a good deal depends on the perspective of the beholder.
Where modern actors feel they need to grasp for signs of rebellion
and self-assertion to render Miranda attractive, an early nineteenth-
century editor commented disapprovingly on Miranda's 'plain
acknowledgement of her thoughts, which in any other woman
would be disgusting forwardness' but justified it as proclaiming
'the extreme of unsuspecting innocence' (Oxberry, 10). The actor's
job is, as always, to find a way of presenting the role which
mediates between the seventeenth century and their contemporary
culture; in this case to render the lightly sketched character of
Miranda attractive, without losing the innocence which is both
the inevitable consequence of her narrative situation, and the
centre of her symbolic function in the play.

Ferdinand might be more variously dressed, his clothes
determined by the costuming of his fellows, but there is even
less obvious room for individuality. He enters droopily, led by
Ariel and grieving for his father; is quickly disarmed by Prospero,
dutifully carries logs in his fairy-tale service to get the girl and is
duly rewarded. Richard Burton, Ferdinand in 1951, later 'dismissed himself in the part ... for "tottering about, with nothing
to say of any real moment, bloodless, liverless, kidneyless, a
useless member of the human race. I found myself incapable of
playing such a role"' (Ferris, 61) (Figure 6). Many of those who
have followed him might echo his sentiments. Yet an actor
attempting to give individuality to the role is likely to run into
critical flak. Alan Rickman's 1978 attempt to give Ferdinand 'a sly
touch of self mockery' (*S. Times*), for example, did not go down
well. Gareth Lloyd Evans commented: 'I think Clifford Williams
might well reconsider why he has asked Alan Rickman to play

Ferdinand in a completely unbelievable manner ... as if he's pretending to be someone else, but who?' (*SA Herald*); and Germaine Greer, in a generally acerbic review, claimed that the audience were maddened by 'Alan Rickman's peculiar diction, which often rendered Ferdinand quite incomprehensible' (*Spectator*). Few Ferdinands attract much notice – though those that do have generally gone straightforwardly for romantic ardour. Richard Johnson, in 1957 was to one reviewer, 'impressive from the start, gripping us with his untainted ardour and shining faith' (*Stage*), and Michael Pennington in 1974 was commended as 'affectingly affectionate' (*SA Herald*) and 'a very princely Ferdinand' (*D. Telegraph*).

Yet within the architecture of the play, he is, in some respects, Caliban's brother, or at least his alter ego – like him he desires Miranda, like him he is bidden to fetch in wood; he, like Caliban, is threatened with dire consequence if he steals Miranda's chastity. The potential link between the characters can be established simply by paying attention to Prospero's threat to 'manacle thy neck and feet together' (1.2.462). In 1957 Prospero's command for Ferdinand to 'Come on, obey' (484) led to him putting his hands, as the promptbook says, 'in chains which have just come down', but this does not seem to have continued into 3.1, the point at which the potential comparison with Caliban is much stronger. Three productions have taken up this challenge. In 1970 J.C. Trewin observed that Christopher Gable was 'the only Ferdinand I have known to be duly manacled' (*Birm. Post*) (Figure 27), but the effect was considerably lessened by what, despite John Barber's approving comment that 'the handsome Christopher Gable brought vitality to that stick Ferdinand' (*D. Telegraph*), was generally regarded as an indifferently spoken and underpowered performance. In 1998 the device was repeated, with the black actor, Evroy Deer, similarly shackled. The parallel was further hinted at in the detail noted by Symon, that 'when Caliban tries to lure Stephano and Trinculo away from the clothes line, they simply deck him out in clothes like those worn by Ferdinand in 1.2,

FIGURE 27 In 1970 Ferdinand (Christopher Gable) was manacled as he performed his labours in 3.1, interrupted by Estelle Kohler's Miranda.

a purple silk cloak and large white ruff' (Symon, 167), and clarified by the fact that Caliban also wore a collar around his neck. Here the chaining of a black actor might have led to a suggestion of a political reading, were it not, as Robert Smallwood observed, that 'in a theatre rightly committed to blind casting, and in a production not (for a change) offering the modern cliché colonialist reading' there did not 'seem much relevance in the sudden appearance of a log-bearing Ferdinand in chains that invited us to equate Prospero with a Confederate slave-master' (SS, 239). Only in 2002 was the parallel fully developed and clearly part of an overall conception. Ferdinand's logs were the spirits Caliban had carried in 2.2, and he was held in check by a rope attached to a harness round his chest identical to that worn by Caliban. The parallel, however, focused on the fact that it was Ferdinand's sexual desire for Miranda that was being restrained. It recalled the vengeful way in which Prospero had responded to Caliban's 'Would't had been done!' (1.2.350) with a bang of his staff which caused Caliban to clutch his genitals in anguish. The parallel between the two might be more lightly drawn by having Ferdinand pick up logs Caliban has left behind, as he did in 2000, when 'he also began to resemble him physically – stripped to the waist, his body discolored by the labor and his posture lowered to a crouch by his burden' (SQ, 114). But this symbolic potential in Ferdinand's role, though it might enrich a production's analysis of power and subordination, or of sexuality, gives little help to the actor in establishing Ferdinand's individuality.

On the surface, then, neither of these are grateful roles, and it is frequently impossible to glean from the brief notices they attract very much sense of how the lovers were played, especially in the earlier post-war productions. It is to a consideration of some of the ways in which actors have dealt with their few opportunities that we now turn.

Throughout the first part of 1.2 Miranda has little to do but respond with attention and sympathy to her father's narrative. How far she is permitted to do so will very much depend on the degree to which her Prospero in fact directs his story to her, rather than focusing his, and the audience's, attention on the tide of remembered emotion. But for the audience it is absolutely crucial that Prospero's apparent suspicions that she is not listening be unfounded, for through her response theirs can be significantly directed. So, for example, in 1982 'Alice Krige's wide-eyed Miranda really does listen to her father's story' (Oxf. Mail), and the horror she clearly felt and expressed supported and underscored the intensity of Derek Jacobi's recollection. In 1978 Sheridan Fitzgerald's 'intelligent' Miranda, was 'curious about the family

FIGURE 28 In 2000 Prospero (Philip Voss) sat beside a rapt Miranda (Nikki Amuka-Bird) throughout most of his long narrative in 1.2. His magic cloak and book are by his side.

history her father thinks must bore her' (*FT*). Her support is important, too, to the actor playing Prospero. Philip Voss, discussing the difficulty of the opening scene, felt that Nikki Amuka-Bird's support was a 'lynch pin' in enabling him to find a way through it, describing a rehearsal process for the 2000 production in which 'we work so wonderfully together and, in the process, establish a very recognisable father/daughter relationship ... we go agonising step by step from incomprehension to a scene of pain, exposition and revelation' (Figure 28). Curiously, in 1951, the promptbook indicates that a line or two before each of Prospero's requests for Miranda's attention, he 'makes sign and Miranda grows sleepy'; indeed she seems to have been charmed to sleep for the whole of his account of his brother's treachery (1.2.90–105) with her 'head on his knee'. What purpose this was intended to serve, and what effect it had on the narrative and the audience's reception of it, is an open question. Not surprisingly, perhaps, the business was cut in the revival the following year.

But if careful attention to her father is the main focus for Miranda in this part of the scene, she nonetheless has an opportunity in her opening speech to establish something of the character that will later emerge. It is not a straightforward speech; in it Miranda is both recreating in verbal terms the violence of the storm – a function rather less necessary on the modern stage than perhaps it was in its original performance – and at the same time registering the 'very virtue of compassion' (1.2.27) that Prospero notes in her. It is often, then, played as a virtual soliloquy, with Miranda looking out at the audience and viewing the wreck now situated, as it were, at the back of the stalls. She might emphasize the heartbreak more or less violently. In 1957, Doreen Aris was praised for 'allowing herself a much greater range of passion than the part is traditionally supposed to bear: when did a Miranda make her first entrance in so violent a storm of tears' (*Leam. Spa Cour.*); whereas in 1993 Sarah Woodward (in an otherwise fairly unrestrained performance) spoke quietly, emphasizing her pity. In 1988 Melanie Thaw delivered a high-octane, 'frantically emotional' speech (*Independent*). In such a torrent of feeling, however, there is a potential in this speech which is generally underplayed. Miranda begins with a question: '*If* by your art, my dearest father, you have / Put the wild waters in this roar' (my italics). There is here an anxiety about the extent of her father's power, and even a critique of his deployment of it. Alice Krige, in 1982, certainly gave full vent to the emotion she felt, with a long-drawn-out 'Ohhhhh, I have suffered'; but her rather more restrained delivery allowed a sense of her bafflement at her father's part in the generation of the storm to emerge, and thereby explained Derek Jacobi's angry tone in his first address to her as a response to her implied criticism of him. The volcanic entry of Penny Layden in 1998, 'sprinting down the aisle walkway, from among us, desperately demanding what's going on' was 'a fine, bold picture' (*SS*, 238), but her delivery did not, to my ear at least, quite provoke the same questions. In 2002, however, Sirine Saba entered first, looking out as her father approached through the audience. Here, in a slowly delivered rendition, her anxiety was clearly directed at him, and her fear of the extent of his power was then underlined by her refusal to take his magic cloak from him, at 1.2.23–4. This bolshy teenager really had to be won over by her father's explanation.

After this opening Miranda has to wait a considerable time for her next opportunity, as she is woken to confront Caliban, the creature that, since he had (presumably fairly recently) attempted to rape her, she is understandably reluctant to 'look on' (1.2.311). Crucial to this section of the play, however, is the director's decision whether or not to afford Miranda the 'Abhorred slave' speech (352–63). Unambiguously given to Miranda in the 1623 Folio, in the eighteenth century it was considered altogether too gross and indelicate for an idealized young girl to utter and reascribed to Prospero. Whilst Eric Crozier changed his prompt-book to afford Miranda the speech in 1946, in 1951 it was restored again to Redgrave's Prospero, retained by Gielgud, but returned to Miranda in 1963. It has remained with her since, with the notable exception of 1982, where it suited both Jacobi's emphasis on Prospero's volatile anger, and Krige's convincing playing of Miranda as a fifteen-year-old girl. Nonetheless, in most productions where Miranda is entrusted with the speech, it is a moment of anger quickly defused by Caliban's response, often a physical lunge which forces her back across the stage to retreat behind her father who stays Caliban with his staff (or his book, in 1982 – giving point to Caliban's later request to Stephano and Trinculo to 'Burn but his books', 3.2.95) (Figure 29). A very different approach was that of Sam Mendes's Miranda in 1993, Sarah Woodward, who energetically strode across to David Troughton's Caliban, forcing him to retreat submissively. This (though it might make one wonder, in retrospect, how he had plucked up the courage to attempt rape) enabled her to endow the speech with regret, even to convey a moving tenderness towards her errant former pupil

FIGURE 29 Miranda (Zena Walker) cowers behind her father in fear at Caliban's first entrance in 1.2. The 1952 production used the same set as in 1951 (see Figure 3), but Ralph Richardson's costume was much simpler than Michael Redgrave's the previous year (see Figure 6). The Caliban costume, worn here by Michael Hordern, remained the same.

(Figure 30). The same aggression was conveyed by Sirine Saba in 2002, and Miranda's energetic protest was underlined by Prospero's immediate infliction of genital agony on Geff Francis's Caliban.

The final movement of 1.2, Miranda's first encounter with Ferdinand, is prefaced by a minor theatrical problem, in that for some thirty lines and two songs, Miranda must not see her destined spouse. Some directors have solved the problem by having Prospero and Miranda simply exit from the stage after the Caliban scene (for example in 1946, 1978 and 1982). In the last of these Prospero and Miranda re-entered both clutching the magic wand, and Jacobi was 'holding his hand in front of her eyes'. Others (for example 1951, 1995, 1998) have had Prospero with a

FIGURE 30 In complete contrast to Figure 29, Sarah Woodward's 1993 Miranda vigorously assaults the 'abhorred slave' Caliban (David Troughton), watched by Alec McCowen's Prospero. Caliban had entered from the ubiquitous basket in 1.2, and behind Prospero is a screen set in front of a trap door from behind which characters appeared 'magically'.

gesture charm Miranda into suspended animation until she is invited to open her eyes and say what she sees. The promptbook suggests that in 1970 Ian Richardson, having taken Miranda to him at the end of the exchange with Caliban, 'holding, comforting' her, then wrapped her in his cloak, opening it on cue at 'The fringed curtains of thine eye advance' (1.2.409). Miranda has little to do except look in amazement; though in 1988 Melanie Thaw's 'ingenuous, impulsive Miranda' (*Int. Her. Trib.*) responded by walking slowly across and touching Ferdinand's shoulder to gain his attention.

But if the actor playing Ferdinand wishes to make him something other than the 'stick' he is so often expected to be, he is not helped by this entrance, bemusedly following Ariel's music and gently lamenting his father's death. There is little room for emotional expression here, since he tells us that his grief has already been mollified by the music itself. Nor is there much space in what follows for anything but romantic ardour, though his miscategorization of Miranda as a goddess provoked Sheridan Fitzgerald's 'enchanting Miranda' (*S. Times*) in 1978 to 'giggle', as the promptbook instructs, in response to 'How I may bear me here' (426). In 1988 and again in 1993, Ferdinand extracted some comedy from his first address to Miranda by adopting the slow, careful elocution of a foreign traveller, amplified in the latter production by Mark Lewis Jones with sign language and a doubletake of astonishment when Miranda answered. '"My language! heavens" he exclaimed … as though he had found a local who knew what an American Express card looks like' (*SQ*, 344). Sadly, this was probably the high point of this Ferdinand's evening, for many reviewers echoed Angela Maguin's feeling that 'it was difficult to imagine the fiery-spirited, independent young woman who is Sarah Woodward's Miranda, falling for this brawny stranger' (*Cahiers Elis.*, 95). This scene, however, demands only that the audience accept the convention of love at first sight. Some mild amusement can be derived from Ferdinand's inability to hear Prospero's repeated 'one word more' as he besottedly gazes at Miranda (John Wood, with tolerant exasperation, stamped his foot on the floor to regain Ferdinand's attention at 'I charge thee / That thou attend me', 453–4).

Miranda customarily reacts with simple bafflement to her father's treatment of Ferdinand, though in 1982 Alice Krige's protest made Jacobi 'turn around and look at her with clear amazement' (Dymkowski, 179). Slightly earlier Miranda questions her father's conduct directly at 'Why speaks my father so ungently' (445–8). Many modern editors add an 'aside' to this speech, thinking (probably rightly) that a direct challenge to paternal authority would have been extremely indecorous in the seventeenth century, and actors do indeed customarily speak these lines to themselves or to the audience. But in 1998 Penny Layden developed her spirited characterization by addressing it directly to her father, and Sirine Saba in 2002 positively pushed Prospero backwards. Whatever the details, most couples manage to stand the test of this first scene – but it is in their next, 3.1, that the challenges for them both really begin.

Coleridge considered this scene 'a masterpiece', in which 'the first dawn of disobedience in the mind of Miranda to the command of her father is very finely drawn', and executed with 'exquisite purity' (Hawkes, 227). Crucially, it relies upon a ceremonious rhetoric delightfully to postpone the moment when Miranda utters her show-stopping line 'I am your wife' (3.1.83), which achieves its force precisely through delay, and its contrast with the formal language that surrounds it. This is the climax of the scene, for, in the handfasting and present-tense promises that follow, Ferdinand and Miranda actually enact a clandestine marriage ceremony. The architecture of 3.1 is clear, and beautifully executed in the writing, but the pitfalls in apparently so simple a scene are many, and they are problems deriving from the fact that a modern audience is less educated than their seventeenth-century forbears in taking pleasure in formal language, and more accustomed to assessing realistically the representation of a couple in love. Robert Speaight commented of the 1963 performance that 'the scenes between Ferdinand and Miranda fell sadly short of the lyrical and almost liturgical simplicity they demand. Reality was sacrificed to realism' (*SQ*, 425). The balance between naturalism and rhetorical formality is a precarious and difficult thing to achieve.

The problem is posed right at the start of the scene. Ferdinand's log-carrying is a very 'real' activity, whether his log(s) are very large (as in 1970), or small (as in 1982); Ferdinand might also emphasize the reality of toil, as in 1988, by beginning to carry logs before the end of the interval. Then he made several trips across the stage, emptying the logs into the same trap that Caliban had used earlier, until finally he could not make it and sat down, apparently genuinely wearied by the task. In 1995 David Thacker represented the logs symbolically by Ariel and attendant spirits; as fast as Ferdinand carried them across the stage they revived and ran back to where they had started, so that his task seemed endless, a device again used in 2002 (Figure 31). But once he begins his speech Ferdinand must move at once into a formal rhetoric of paradox, and cope with that most awkward of modes of speech for the modern actor, the direct address to the audience. If, like Evroy Deer in 1998, or Alan Turkington in 2002, he strains for realistic complaint (neither of them ceased carrying their logs during the speech), the effect is hectic and overstated. Much more effective was David Fahm's quietness in 1995, which allowed the speech to build towards the moment when, without self-congratulation, he could think of Miranda weeping over him.

In the text, Miranda is followed on stage by Prospero. His presence, watching over the scene that follows, can have considerable effect on the way in which an audience is encouraged to respond (though in 1947 he entered only at the last moment for his final speech, his earlier comments being cut). In 1957, if Angus McBean's photograph is to be believed, Prospero entered above, looking somewhat severely down upon the lovers beneath, 'papa, as it were tapping the telephone wire' of their conversation (*Liv. D. Post*). (On the transfer to Drury Lane, the promptbook suggests he stood downstage.) This might well have cast something of a damper on the exchange; visually it certainly suggested how much this is a wooing controlled by Prospero. Michael Hordern, in 1978, altogether more benevolently, entered downstage, and, the promptbook tells us, 'clock[ed] audience' as Miranda said that her father was 'hard at study' (3.1.20). This business was elaborated in 1988, when John Wood entered from below the front of the stage, stopped when he saw Miranda and turned to go, only to be halted by his daughter's line. Thereafter he stood leaning on the front of the stage contemplating the action with amusement and evident pleasure, though turning away when the couple kissed. In 1982 Jacobi was rather less benign, 'anxious to see Miranda mated but peering round the leaning mast ... in case she goes too far' (*Guardian*, Sep). His

FIGURE 31 The logs that David Fahm's Ferdinand bears across the stage were spirits in 1995. Here he carries Bonnie Engstrom's bird-like Ariel, with make-up and unblinking stare, and Sarah-Jane Holm's Miranda struggles to assist him. (3.1)

reaction to their kiss was more pained than Wood's, as, later, his release of Miranda to Alonso was fraught with a sense of loss. In 2002 Prospero's effort to control Ferdinand's sexuality was emphasized by the way in which spirits hung on to a rope attached to his harness, and, as his ardour rose, so more spirits joined the tug of war. Malcolm Storry's asides, not surprisingly, were less than entirely convincing.

A real difficulty with this scene is that it is driven by Miranda. Despite her anxiety at breaking her father's commands, despite her confession of her own ignorance of men, it is she who takes the initiative in demanding a declaration of love, and a commitment to marriage. It is perhaps this which accounts for Burton's distaste for the 'unmanly' Ferdinand, even as it helps to explain the problems many actors have had with a part that allows them so little to control the action (the vestigial sense that the man ought to be the initiator in a love encounter seems never far from their minds, no matter how well educated they may be in contemporary attitudes). But it also sets Miranda a problem, since the text makes it obvious that she is perfectly well aware of 'What I desire to give' and 'What I shall die to want' (3.1.78–9); her innocence is not sexual ignorance. Representing an 'innocent' sexuality does not come easily to modern Mirandas. Debbie Bowen seems to have been successful in 1974, adopting 'animal crouches' to 'well suggest a girl brought up in the wilds' (*Times*), and offering a 'naive ... but intelligent Miranda' (*SA Herald*) in a 'performance of rare quality and originality ... credible and convincing' (*Coventry E. Tel.*). Sheridan Fitzgerald, too, persuaded Bernard Levin in 1978 that she was 'full of the true vernal innocence that is so often falsely cloyed' (*S. Times*). In 3.1 she expressed her tenderness towards Ferdinand by mopping his brow as she spoke of taking his logs from him. The force of her question 'Do you love me?' (67) was emphasized as Ferdinand, hitherto kneeling opposite her, and then rising to make his declaration of love, 'Hear my soul speak' (63), had turned back to his log-carrying at 'Am I this patient log-man'. They embraced at line 73. By coming to physical contact at this point, however, they pre-empted the climax of the scene in the handfasting and decorated it instead with comic business, as Ferdinand offered his hand, only to realize it was dirty and brush the dirt off, prompting Miranda to laugh.

Compared to some recent productions, however, this embrace was fairly restrained. Several have tried to inject a realistic 'life' into the scene by making Ferdinand and Miranda an enthusiastic, rather contemporary teenage couple and explicitly emphasizing her control of the scene. Sarah Woodward in 1993 was praised by Michael Billington as 'an unusually randy Miranda' (*Guardian*). Her Ferdinand whisked her off her feet in an embrace as she delivered 'I do not know / One of my sex' (48–9), and she kissed him enthusiastically immediately after 'I prattle / Something too wildly' (57–8). Hers was not the innocence of a girl who has never seen a man, but the enthusiasm of one let out of a restrictive boarding school, only too aware of what she was after. There was little possibility, therefore, of giving any sense of solemnity or ritual to their coming together.

In 1982 Alice Krige contrived a rather more delicate balance, for though Billington spoke of 'a Miranda and Ferdinand ... so keen to make it in the sand that Prospero's restraining paternal hand has some point' (*Guardian*, Aug), Ned Chaillet's description of her as 'innocent and yet emotionally wise' (*Times*) is endorsed by David Nokes's view that she played Miranda

> with a credible gawky innocence that nevertheless admits rather more than a few blushes of desire. While attending to her father she is a schoolgirl in pigtails, but when she moves through the island she is the wild thing of Caliban's dreams. (*TLS*)

The delicacy of her playing, in which restraint and uncertainty relaxed into a long kiss once vows were exchanged, explained Desmond Pratt's enthusiasm: 'for the first time in my memory, the young lover pair makes the centrepiece of the play with the wonderment of sudden self-revelation and maturity in Alice Krige's lovely virginal girl and Michael Maloney's handsome, honest Ferdinand' (*Yorks. Post*). The scene was only marred by a gratuitous comic effect at its end, when Miranda piled logs on Ferdinand and kissed him over the top. It suggested that she had rather too quickly turned from innocence to a housewifely determination to see hubby do the chores. For this is a scene in which comic effects must be extremely carefully handled if they are introduced at all – and the unconvincing and unnecessary elaboration in 1993 which had Miranda carry easily the log with which her Ferdinand had struggled, suggesting that 'she had kept up a better training regime' (*SQ*, 344), was a further blemish in a generally unconvincing rendition.

Even if physical contact is restrained, it is still possible for the scene not to work – in 1995, despite David Fahm's eloquence, Sarah-Jane Holm's determination to project a feisty and independent Miranda led her both to press too naturalistically upon her speeches, and to refuse any real gesture of affection at the end of the scene. In 2002, where a 'fabulously sensual and untamed Miranda' (*D. Telegraph*) was only prevented by the spirits tugging on Ferdinand's harness from making the physical contact she fairly obviously desired, there was little sense of ritual in the scene. Perhaps the simplest playing of all was to be found in 2000, where Nikki Amuka-Bird's 'sweet and innocent Miranda' (*Mail Sun.*) (who was yet capable, with real effort, of carrying one of Ferdinand's logs offstage) and Oliver Dimsdale's Ferdinand delightfully hesitated towards one another throughout the scene, with the handfasting their first physical contact. But precisely, perhaps, because their playing was so straightforward it was scarcely remarked by reviewers.

This scene of just over ninety lines is all that Ferdinand and Miranda have to make their mark in a production. Though most of the next act is given over to the celebration of their betrothal, they have little to do, once it has been decided how physical their embrace should be in order to provoke Prospero's stern warnings to Ferdinand not to anticipate his wedding night. Here, perhaps, there is some measure of changing cultural attitudes – in 1951 the promptbook suggests that the couple were only 'laughing' together; by 1974 Michael Pennington exhibited 'a youthful impatience with the old man's strictures and a healthy desire for the flesh and the fleshpots' (*Coventry E. Tel.*). By 1993, the audience on the video recording seemed to be laughing at Prospero's strictures themselves, rather than, as in 1978 or 1988, at the irony that both Hordern and Wood introduced into the 'Well' (4.1.56) with which Prospero responds to Ferdinand's protestations, suggesting that they'd heard that one before. In 2000, though the embrace was fairly restrained, Voss's 'Well' was positively indulgent.

Since it has occasioned acres of academic controversy, it is perhaps worth remarking in parenthesis that the question whether Ferdinand expresses his delight at the masque by speaking of 'so rare a wondered father, and a *wise*', or 'so rare a wondered father, and a *wife*' (4.1.123), is, on stage, one that barely registers. The reading 'wife' was resurrected in Orgel's Oxford text in 1987, rejected in the Arden of 1999, but retained in my New Cambridge edition of 2002. 'Wife' was used in 1988, 1993 and 1995, but only in the last of these productions was it underlined by a fond look from Ferdinand to Miranda; thereafter 'wise' returned again – and none except the most anorakish of editors probably noticed. The only important thing is that Ferdinand and Miranda's delight be rendered credible to the audience by the staging of the masque itself – which is by no means an aim always achieved (see chapter 6). Their disappointment at its sudden end can be intensified if, as in 1982, they themselves participate in the dance of nymphs and reapers; even more in 2000 where they themselves were the dance. But the focus is clearly on Prospero, and they are simply pushed offstage in a rather bemused state.

Their last entry returns Ferdinand and Miranda firmly to an emblematic status. They are revealed by Prospero as his concluding 'wonder' to 'content' Alonso (5.1.170). There is the practical problem of how this revelation of Ferdinand and Miranda playing at chess is to be achieved. In the older productions, where Prospero's cell was a physical reality on stage, there was no difficulty in drawing a curtain to reveal the lovers. In 1982 they were also disclosed by drawing a curtain; in 1978 they rose on one of the traps; in 1993 the screen that frequently stood in the middle of the stage fell flat. Where the setting is barer, then other devices might be used. In 1963 they walked on stage with Ariel carrying the chessboard; in 2000 they simply had to get themselves on to the bare white stage whilst the lords were looking the other way, setting their chessboard down and beginning to play; in 2002 they were somewhat unceremoniously wheeled in on a trolley by Ariel.

Chess was a game associated both with courtly society and with love from the middle ages onwards. To a modern audience it might seem a rather tame occupation for lovers, and to one reviewer Michael Pennington in 1974 suggested 'not for him a game of chess with Miranda, whatever the text may say' (*Coventry E. Tel.*) – though no Stratford production (thankfully) has gone as far as Pip Symmons at the Riverside Studios, London, 1978, who had them 'engaged in intercourse' (Dymkowski, 315). Indeed almost all productions have skimmed over the problem that Miranda's first line accuses Ferdinand of cheating, treating it as a little harmless lovers' banter. The exception was 1988. Here Prospero's cell was below stage; the lovers could not therefore be 'revealed' within it. The solution was to have Ferdinand erupt on stage, using the chessboard as a shield to defend himself from the chess pieces hurled at him by a pursuing Miranda shouting 'Sweet lord, you play me false' (5.1.172). Whilst her vigour implied that she was 'a chip off the old block' (*Guardian*, Jul), 'marital harmony is hardly what comes to mind' (*Times*, Jul) at this explosive entrance. It also led to practical problems. The production records note an occasion on which a flying chess piece went into the audience hitting a woman who 'reported with cuts around her nose and eyes, blood and a little shocked', prompting the memorable instruction: 'Mr Purefoy and Miss Thaw have been asked to re-route their pawns.'

Even though one reviewer thought it 'pleasantly imaginative' (*Cahiers Elis.*, 105), so decided an undermining of the moment too violently threatened the precarious balance of the scene – there are enough problems to come without exaggerating this one. For the game of chess is immediately followed by Miranda's 'O wonder! / How many goodly creatures are there here!' (181–2) which also needs careful negotiation. (In 1988, not surprisingly, it frequently merely roused laughter.) Prospero himself undercuts her enthusiasm with his ''Tis new to thee' (184), a line which can be delivered in very different tones – with a light irony (as in 1951, 1970, 1988 and 1995), or with considerably more bitter emphasis, as in 1982. A number of productions have chosen further to underline her naiveté by having her direct the words to Antonio and Sebastian (see chapter 5), though in 1978 she addressed Gonzalo, who knelt to her, kissed her hand, and then stood and talked to her during the ensuing dialogue. The association between her innocence and the benevolently disposed Gonzalo left the optimism of both in question, but movingly suggested that it was not contemptible. In 1993, however, Mendes chose to sabotage her words completely, as Miranda's 'stress on "*wonder!*" made one of the lesser lords back away in alarm' (Dymkowski, 316), and her emphasis on the 'man' in 'mankind' suggested that she was not long to remain content with Ferdinand. It was the culmination of this production's comic undercutting of the Ferdinand/Miranda relationship; its devaluation of the lovers perhaps took a step too far. For in any production poor Ferdinand's job in getting some real warmth out of his discovery that his father is not dead is difficult enough; so thoroughly to demolish his hopes for his marriage even before he has introduced his wife rendered it impossible. In 2002 Sirine Saba's procession round the lords completely took attention away from Ferdinand. Though her enthusiastic embrace of Adrian suggested to one reviewer that she was a 'fledgling nymphomaniac' (*D. Telegraph*), by the time the production came to Stratford her pause before kissing Antonio chastely on the cheek, precipitating his weeping, was nicely judged.

The brief interlude of Ferdinand's exchange with his father and introduction of Miranda is almost always straightforwardly played. The reconciliation with Alonso might be suggested, as in 1957, by a kiss, or, as in 1988, by a reduplication of Prospero's gesture in 4.1 of joining hands; in 1970 particular emphasis was placed on Alonso's kneeling to Miranda at 'I am hers' (196), to which she responded by prostrating herself before him. But even this moment is barely allowed to expand, since Prospero cuts in on Alonso's desire to ask forgiveness of his daughter-in-law with 'There, sir, stop' (5.1.198). In most productions, and perhaps especially in Wood's 1988 performance, Prospero's injunction is kindly meant; his subsequent instruction not to 'burden our remembrances' becomes a purposeful renunciation of the fierce injunction of Ariel in 3.3 to 'remember', and preparation for healing. It accorded with the way Wood clearly hoped for, and expected, reconciliation. In 1982, however, Jacobi, who had earlier reacted with visible pain as Ferdinand led Miranda towards Alonso, positively shouted the line, implying that it was the danger of awakening his own bitter 'remembrance' so recently and narrowly overcome that he wished to avoid. It was an idiosyncratic reading, though entirely concordant with his overall view of the role, and one at the opposite end of the scale from Philip Voss's satisfaction, in 2000, at seeing his plans come to fruition. For, as John Peter suggested:

> when he arranges for Miranda and Ferdinand to fall in love, you sense that this is not so much to be benevolent as to sort out the dynastic complications between the ruling houses of Milan and Naples. Exiled and humiliated, Prospero is not so humbled: he is still a statesman who can play the long game. (*S. Times*)

After this, Ferdinand and Miranda retreat to the play's margins. Though their exquisitely written love scene comes at the centre of the play, the tonal complexities surrounding their appearance in the fifth act signal clearly that they are not central to its ending. It is entirely typical that though Prospero speaks of his 'hope to see the nuptial / Of these our dear beloved solemnized' (309–10), the lines which follow redirect our attention back to himself, and to his retirement. It is his assertion that 'Every third thought shall be my grave' (312) which sticks in the memory, not the affirmation of hope in the next generation.

5

THE LORDS

Within the design of *The Tempest* the lords parallel the low-life figures of Stephano, Trinculo and Caliban. Each trio is involved in a conspiracy which functions as an analogical re-enactment of Antonio's usurpation of Prospero's dukedom twelve years earlier. Each of their conspiracies is foiled by Ariel, and the illusory banquet which leads to Ariel's castigation of the lords in the form of a harpy is analogous to the sidetracking of Caliban and his co-conspirators by the 'trumpery' which acts as 'stale to catch these thieves' (4.1.186–7), leading to their being hounded by spirit-dogs. Intellectually, then, one can appreciate their integration into the play's tightknit construction, as they refract its concern with power, usurpation, repentance and punishment in serious and comic modes. In the theatre, however, it has never proved easy to make the lords any more than ciphers. They are sketchily represented, providing little of substance for actors to work on. In the opening storm scene, even if the text is given in full and is not obliterated by thunder and lightning, we are scarcely aware of who is who (no names are given), and though Gonzalo is set apart from his fellows in a fashion we later come to recognize as indicative of his position in the courtly group, what matters at this stage is the generalized confrontation of upper-class characters with the desperately working Boatswain and crew, and the way in which the disruption of social hierarchy on board ship prefigures the play's concern with the nature of authority.

Faced with the anonymity of characters in the opening scene, directors have attempted to clarify matters for the audience by introducing the lords on stage during Prospero's retrospective narrative in 1.2. Declan Donellan's Cheek by Jowl production at the Donmar Theatre, London, 1988, is the first which Dymkowski notes as adopting this strategy (130). It was imitated by Sam Mendes, whose lords in 1993 appeared from behind a central folding screen on cue, as if called up by the very act of Prospero's recollection, while David Thacker in 1995 initially attempted a rather more complicated miming of the events of the conspiracy to accompany Prospero's words (though this business was cut after the production transferred to Stratford). Michael Boyd's introduction of the lords in 2002 is discussed in chapter 1. The lords' third scene, the banquet and the appearance of the harpy in 3.3, is powerful on stage, but offers very little opportunity for them to do anything but react to the strangeness of the spectacle and then to respond to Ariel's reminder of their usurpation of Prospero's dukedom. It is an episode derived from Virgil's *Aeneid*, and functions morally and emblematically, with little space for individuated personality (see chapter 6).

The lack of particularity in 1.1 and 3.3 would not necessarily be a problem, were it not that 2.1, the lords' principal scene (and the second longest in the play), contains in its first part arguably one of the worst-written passages in Shakespeare's work. One can understand at an abstract level what seems to be intended – we are introduced to those of whom Prospero has informed us, and we see Alonso grieving for the apparent drowning of his son. Sebastian and Antonio are clearly contrasted with Gonzalo in their cynical habit of mind, preparing us for the scene's second part, in which Antonio persuades Sebastian to re-stage his own successful usurpation, and thus confirm Prospero's description of him as a man who could 'set all hearts i'th' state / To what tune pleased his ear' (1.2.84–5). But in its execution there are several real difficulties. In the first place, the grief of Alonso has to be established almost entirely by the actor's reaction to the attempts of others to comfort him – he has barely fifteen lines to speak. Secondly, Shakespeare chooses to manifest the corrosive scepticism of Antonio and Sebastian by an habitual destructive punning, but their puns are generally feeble, and not infrequently incomprehensible to a modern audience. Finally, the dynamic of the first part of the scene turns on the way in which Gonzalo is presented, and the text sends out contradictory signals. He might be, as Antonio suggests, a pedantic, well-meaning but irritatingly verbose purveyor of platitudes. Yet in his oddly unmotivated 'Golden Age' speech (2.1.148–69) he offers a utopian vision that connects with other visionary moments in the play, one that we, if not the onstage audience, should listen to seriously. If he is taken to be an ineffectual proser, the cousin of Polonius, then not only is Alonso's impatience with the words he crams into his ears justified, but at the same time the jibes of Antonio and Sebastian are validated, and our sense of their malignity diminished.

Roger Warren, in his account of the staging of 2.1 in Peter Hall's 1988 National Theatre production, noting that this scene 'is one of the most difficult for actors to perform and for audiences to concentrate upon', argues that 'when reviewers complain – as they usually do, . . . – that the court scenes are slow or dull or that their jokes are stale, they blame actors for providing what is plainly required by the text' (Warren, 174–5). This is a dangerously circular argument – it is inherently unlikely that a dramatist would set out to bore his audience – and, in fact, as he goes on to describe the actors' efforts to give life to the jokes, we find that they saw the attempted witticisms as 'the remarks of sophisticated but very frightened men who are under great pressure as a result of their ordeal', and used this to inject life into the exchanges. Faced with the scene's problems, many Stratford directors have chosen to cut it more or less severely. Large chunks of the first part, in particular, have been discarded, with 1946, 1982, 1988, 2000 and 2002 being exceptions in choosing to play virtually the whole text. The utterly obscure references to 'widow Dido' (77ff.), over which editors have laboured, but upon which recent literary critics such as Hamilton and James have ingeniously built arguments about the relationship of *The Tempest* to Virgil's *Aeneid*, almost entirely disappeared in 1947, 1951/2, 1963, 1970, 1974 and 1995, and others of Antonio and Sebastian's opaque puns were severely pruned in 1978, 1993 and 1998. It is entirely understandable that actors should be keen to avoid the embarrassment of Antonio and Sebastian in 1988, desperately trying to persuade an audience that they were indeed cracking jokes by laughing at their own witticisms, but, as the video confirms, eliciting, at least on that occasion, no answering laughter from the audience. In vain do actors clutch at comic business on 'Foul weather?' 'Very foul' (143), with flapping elbows or an added 'cluck, cluck' (as in 1993 and 2002) to underline the possible foul/fowl pun, and there can be few lines in Shakespeare that can seem so helpless as Antonio's in this exchange with Gonzalo:

GONZALO

>   You rub the sore
>   When you should bring the plaster.

SEBASTIAN

>   Very well.

ANTONIO

>   And most chirurgeonly!

>   (2.1.139–41)

I have yet to see an Antonio whose eyes did not glaze over as he launched this (surprisingly rarely cut) line into the void, having neither a sense of how the continuation of Gonzalo's medical image is supposed to mock him, nor any hope that the audience might understand it. Yet if the earlier part of the scene is ruthlessly pruned, it makes its second half problematic. Warren cites E.M.W. Tillyard's suggestion that 'Antonio's transformation from the cynical and lazy badgerer of Gonzalo's loquacity to the brilliantly swift and unscrupulous man of action is a thrilling affair' (178); but if the 'badgering' is cut there is no springboard into the second half – and few of the Stratford productions have got anywhere near achieving such a 'thrill'.

It is not only excess verbiage that makes the scene difficult, for it also contains, in Adrian and Francisco, two of the bittiest of bit parts in the canon. In 1957 Peter Brook simply excised Francisco, giving his lines to Gonzalo, while John Barton in 1970 hoped to build a more persuasive picture of the three lords fruitlessly attempting to console Alonso by redistributing small parts of Gonzalo's speeches to these attendants. The smaller-scale productions, for practical reasons, have also combined these parts: in 2000 Francisco was cut; in 1995 the parts were merged into a single female role, the Lady Adriana, while in 1974 they were cut completely. (In 2002, when James Garnon, the Francisco, was called to play his understudy role of Trinculo at the performances I saw, the fusion of the two roles of Adrian and Francisco into one, played by Dylan Charles, was accomplished effortlessly.)

In the Blackfriars Theatre of the original performance it is likely that there was a break between the end of the first act and the beginning of the second, to allow time to trim candles. In more recent productions, the tendency has been to emphasize continuity. Mendes's omnipresent Ariel, for example, stayed on stage at the end of 1.2 to direct the stagehands, his attendant spirits, in fixing huge sunflowers in place; once they had done so a handclap summoned Alonso, followed by the rest of the lords, on to the stage. Earlier, in 1982, as David Nokes puts it: 'the shipwrecked nobles at first appear like beached crustaceans, clambering awkwardly ashore beneath the weight of their heavy sea-green armour' (*TLS*). In some ways, perhaps, it was easier when scene breaks were more complete. In 1946, the promptbook tells us that after a new set had been introduced behind the curtain, Alonso was 'discovered, laying on his cloak by R[ight] rock', and Crozier amplified the opening of the scene. Offstage voices were heard calling out 'Prince Ferdinand, Halloo'. Antonio and Sebastian entered first, Alonso looked up, but they moved silently apart and sat down; Adrian crossed the stage, calling 'Prince Ferdinand', before returning and joining Gonzalo. At each entry Alonso hoped for good news, only to sink down disconsolate; Francisco remained offstage, and was to be heard still calling for Ferdinand just before his entry to deliver his speech to Alonso. In this arrangement several ends were served simultaneously: space was given to establish Alonso's distress, the distinction between the groups of lords was clearly made, and the delayed entrance of Francisco gave a little impetus to the scene. In 1951 Michael Benthall followed the same idea – introducing a new set, and again beginning with voices off calling 'My Lord Ferdinand' (Alonso observed his paternal role by shouting 'Ferdinand, Ferdinand'). Adrian and Francisco entered first, going downstage one each side, calling as they went, to be followed by the others.

However the lords make their way on stage, there is a good deal of similarity in the grouping they adopt. The 1978 promptbook, for example, notes that Gonzalo enters separated from the rest and 'backing in', while Alonso, downstage, 'falls to the ground distraught'. Gonzalo then moved to join him, while Antonio and Sebastian took up their positions downstage left where, lying down, they conducted their satiric commentary on Gonzalo's efforts at consolation. This grouping is entirely typical of almost all productions, as can be seen in Figure 32, a photograph of the 1982 rendition. Donald Sinden, however, records that Clifford Williams in 1963 at first tried to get away from this conventional pattern.

> If there is one irrefutable fact of the lords' scenes, it is that the two villains ... are a 'double act'. They are always conspiring together. They attempt the murder as a twosome and they share their come-uppance. When the lords gathered ... Clifford Williams addressed us saying, 'In every production of *The Tempest* I have seen, Antonio and Sebastian always seem to be played as a double act. We must get

FIGURE 32 (*opposite*) On 1982's permanent set of a wrecked ship Alonso (Paul Webster) ignores Adrian (William Haden) and Gonzalo (Edward Jewesbury) disputing about widow Dido (2.1). Francisco (Raymond Llewellyn) stands at the back, whilst Sebastian (Jeffery Dench) and Antonio (Robert O'Mahoney) cynically watch from the side.

away from that – it is a cliché – so old-fashioned, so I want Antonio on one side of the stage and Sebastian on the other'.

(Sinden, 1985, 87)

He records the problems he and his Antonio had with this arrangement, and then gleefully narrates how Peter Brook, finally appearing to observe a rehearsal, countermanded his associate's direction. And, by and large, it is as a double act that they have continued – though, as Roger Warren observes, in the National Theatre performance of 1988 the actors themselves chose to deliver 'their mockery of Adrian and Gonzalo provocatively, flinging their remarks back and forth from either side of the stage' (176); and during Gonzalo's 'Golden Age' speech, Antonio and Sebastian at Stratford in 1993 sat at either side of the stage, ironically, as it were, 'framing' his efforts and distinguishing themselves from Francisco and Adrian, who sat on the floor, listened intently and applauded at its end.

It is the relationship and balance between Gonzalo and the evil lords which is crucial to the scene's first part, and most difficult to achieve. It seems to have been the earlier productions which had greatest success: reviewers in 1946, 1951 and 1957 all find something to praise in the handling of this scene. It is not easy from the scant evidence of photographs and promptbooks to be confident in establishing why this should be, but perhaps it was the readiness of these earlier productions to give time to establishing Alonso's bewildered grief which helped; in part, too, it may have been a readiness wholeheartedly to play Antonio and Sebastian for comic effect. In 1951, Ruth Ellis commented on 'an excellent pair of villains from William Fox and William Squire who turn the "sleepy language" of the King and courtier scenes into sparkling comedy' (*SA Herald*). The promptbook records that they began the scene laughing at Gonzalo early, at line 6, and rarely let up thereafter. As they sat down on a rock to observe and ridicule, Sebastian shoved Antonio along to make room; Antonio parodied Adrian's intake of breath on 'The air breathes upon us here most sweetly' (49), and they engaged in some further parodic business after Gonzalo reacted with a surprised 'Huh?' to Sebastian's line 'he doth but mistake the truth totally' (59), and with 'yawn business' throughout the 'Golden Age' speech (148–69). Finally, Sebastian's line 'An it had not fallen flat-long' (181) was literalized, as Gonzalo tripped over one of the shells on stage. In the terse record of the promptbook this scarcely appears as rivetingly imaginative, but others apart from the ever-enthusiastic Ellis were persuaded, including Harold Hobson who praised William Fox for making 'Prospero's usurping brother sarcastically worthy of his relative' (*Theatre*).

Peter Brook, too, was ready to be expansive in developing business for Antonio and Sebastian in 1957 – though the promptbook in this case is extremely difficult to read with any certainty, since it was used both at Stratford and in the Drury Lane transfer, where a good deal was changed, including much more aggressive cutting of the first part of the scene. So, for example, where the promptbook notes that Antonio and Sebastian 'share a bottle', passing it from hand to hand to indicate their boredom with Gonzalo's major speech (for which Sebastian has 'put up his feet on rock'), the Angus McBean photograph – looking distinctly 'posed' – has them playing cards in front of Gonzalo, though such business is not mentioned in the promptbook (Figure 33). If they did indeed share a bottle, it would have linked them in an interesting fashion with Stephano and Trinculo, their low-life alter egos. What is clear, however, in Figure 33 is their rather pantomimically 'evil' mustachios, perhaps signalling a fairly full-blooded performance which could persuade the *Morning Advertiser* that 'Mark Dignam adds to his Stratford honours by memorably revealing the sardonic streak in the character of Prospero's usurping brother'. But what, above all, seems to have made the scene work was Cyril Luckham's Gonzalo. J.C. Trewin in a number of reviews consistently praised the scene, and his playing in particular. In the *Birmingham Post* he wrote:

> With ease the actor established [Gonzalo]: kindly, generous, hopeful, shrewd enough to know the exact value of Sebastian and

Antonio. The director had timed the scene, as I wrote on the first
night, with a care almost Chekovian. Its pattern, its flow, became
curiously exciting ... Antonio and Sebastian had a menacing quality
these petty villains usually lack. And, over all, Gonzalo's vision of
the Utopian commonwealth rang in the mind as if new.

Muriel St Claire Byrne similarly praised this 'delightfully sympathetic, alert, humorous and rounded concept of a far-from-actor-
proof part' (*SQ*, 491). It was almost certainly because of the success
of Gonzalo that the 'petty villains' emerged more strongly; they
need a worthy adversary for us to be able to register their foolery as
a corrupt indecorum and selfish preoccupation, rather than as a
justifiable deflation of a prosy windbag. This was the case in 2002,
where Jerome Willis (who had played a mariner in 1952) gave a
strong reading of the part, expressing a believable contempt for
Antonio and Sebastian. This helped them 'instead of the usual
ciphers ... to become savage political plotters' (*Guardian*).
Whereas, in 1998, though Peter J. Smith praised Alfred Burke for
a 'wonderfully twittering Gonzalo' (*Cahiers Elis.*, 123), virtually
every other reviewer echoed Charles Spencer's verdict that 'neither
Antonio nor Sebastian has sufficiently caught the slick wickedness
of the men of sin' (*D. Telegraph*), and the fact that all the lords were
represented as utterly bored by his ideal commonwealth did not
encourage an audience to take him seriously. When Burke played
the part ten years earlier, Nicholas Hytner attempted to underline
the casual, petty contempt of the lords by having Antonio lob
pebbles at him; an analogous piece of business in 2000 had
Sebastian contemptuously throw money at Gonzalo to underline
his derisive 'a dollar' (20). (In this production, too, Sebastian took

FIGURE 33 (*opposite*) At the front of the stage the very obviously
'villainous' Sebastian (Robin Lloyd) and Antonio (Mark Dignam) are
watched by Cyril Luckham's Gonzalo as they play cards. At the back Robert
Harris's Alonso talks to Toby Robertson's Adrian, with Ariel (Brian Bedford)
keeping a watching eye. How accurately this represents the stage action of
2.1 in 1957 is a matter of doubt, but the casual contempt of the lords was
undoubtedly strongly presented in this production.

off a shoe and made a glove puppet out of his sock as if to ridicule Gonzalo's prosing.) So long as Gonzalo is, as John Peter described Clifford Rose, a 'kindly, waffly' character (*S. Times*, 1993) the first part of the scene will inevitably lack real pointedness.

But Burke in 1998 also had to deal with an Alonso who seemed to show very little sense of grief at his loss, resolutely standing downstage and apart from the others, yet sounding indignant rather than overwhelmed. In such a rendition Gonzalo's solicitude seems, precisely, to be unnecessary fussing. To find the right balance, however, is no easy matter. In 1951/2 the promptbook records that after 'It is foul weather' (142) Alonso crossed downstage 'pursued by Gonzalo'; yet the positive reviews, especially of Raymond Westwell in 1952, commended for 'making a thoroughly charming character of the sometimes boring though worthy courtier' (*Stage*) and for giving the part 'exceptionally humorous point' (*News Chronicle*), suggest that he managed to convey real solicitude despite the raillery to which he was subjected. In 2000 Robert Langdon Lloyd (a younger Gonzalo than is usual) similarly pursued Paul McLeary's Alonso to the front of the stage, and addressed 'Had I plantation of this isle' (144) to his indifferent back, as if trying to get his attention. He ran his hands through his hair repeatedly, giving the impression that he was desperately improvising this speech as he went, rather than making it a formal, set-piece oration. This Gonzalo played the part as 'consistently vexed, rather than the conventional amiable old buffer' (*FT*). In somewhat similar fashion, in 1995, and again in 2002, Gonzalo paused anxiously before launching into the speech, as if attempting to hit on something that would penetrate Alonso's self-absorption. These attempts to motivate this speech are, however, also symptomatic of the real awkwardness of it. There is no obvious reason for a long-time royal servant suddenly to slip into a utopian vision of sovereign-less equality, and even less for him to think that it will prove appropriate as consolation for a king. But it does require that, as in 2002, Gonzalo really sounds as if he is himself intoxicated by the vision he has created.

The second part of the scene, Antonio's attempt to whip up Sebastian to murder, on the face of it ought to be much more straightforward; though the transition, in which the other lords are charmed to sleep, itself offers choices to the director. The text directs 'Enter ARIEL *playing solemn music*' (184.1), and in many productions it is simply the presence of sound that makes the lords suddenly feel sleepiness come over them. Mark Rylance's entrance in 1982, playing pan pipes, worked particularly effectively, whilst, at least for me, a similar entry by Scott Handy in 1998, ostensibly blowing a prop pipe, was rather undermined by the fact that the music we heard was a mismatched clarinet with instrumental accompaniment. In performances such as these, the unresponsiveness of Antonio and Sebastian becomes a symptom of their essential moral turpitude, marking them out as 'fit for treasons, stratagems, and spoils' (*The Merchant of Venice*, 5.1.85), according to standard thinking about music's effects. But in a number of productions, especially the more recent, Ariel has specifically charmed each individual to sleep. In the blue light which signified the presence of magic in 1993, Simon Russell Beale moved gravely among the lords, passing his hands before the eyes of each in turn to precipitate their collapse. A similar strategy was deployed in 1995 and 2000. The effect is to emphasize the deliberateness of Prospero's plan – he sets up the situation, knowing how Antonio and Sebastian are going to react. One or two productions have given an ironic twist to this moment of transition. In 1970, for example, Antonio and Sebastian actually helped Alonso to the floor, while in 1988 'Antonio crossed to Alonso and started to drape a cloak gently over him; when the king fell asleep before he had finished, he tossed it carelessly down' (Dymkowski, 201). This gesture gave a springboard into the scene's next section, where Antonio immediately recognizes the possibility of turning the situation to advantage – in 2002 Brian Protheroe picked up Alonso's crown and peered through it at Tom Beard's Sebastian.

The basic pattern of the scene's second section is clearly delineated: like other villains earlier in Shakespeare's career,

Antonio uses indirection as a means of gradually stirring Sebastian to thoughts of murder. Whereas in the first part of the scene it was Sebastian who spoke more, and arrogated to himself his familial right to berate his brother Alonso for arranging the marriage of Claribel, the second part is Antonio's to control. The wordiness of his persuasion has prompted some directors to make significant cuts – especially of the obscure lines on ambition (240–5), the elaboration of Claribel's distance from Naples (246ff.), and the image of a chilblain (277–9). But essentially the section is given its dynamism by juxtaposing Antonio's mental activity and urgent ambition with Sebastian's self-avowed slothfulness. In 1951 the contrast was made by having Sebastian remain seated for some considerable time; in 1978 he lay down at Antonio's 'I am more serious than my custom' (219), and there is no promptbook instruction for him to move until he rose to his knees at 'But for your conscience?' (276), standing only at 'I'll come by Naples' (293). In 1988 Antonio 'stood on Caliban's rock as he broached his plot, during which the actors emphasized Antonio's cleverness and Sebastian's slow wit' (Dymkowski, 201).

It is possible to play this relationship for comedy – Dymkowski quotes a review of Jonathan Miller's Old Vic production, 1988, in which

> Peter Wear's saturnine, effete Antonio trie[d] to nudge Sebastian's thoughts to crime with the quietly exasperated, ironic patience of a don coaching one of nature's Lower Seconds. In a pointedly witty touch, Peter Guiness's slit-eyed Sebastian fiddle[d] throughout with an obviously marked and rigged pack of cards, beautifully distinguishing his mundane small-time crookedness with Antonio's sweeping, incorrigible evil.   (Dymkowksi, 201)

At the Globe in 2000 this was taken even further, with Antonio exasperatedly beating his brow and eyeing the audience, inviting them to laugh at Sebastian's dimness. No Stratford production except, perhaps, 1988 has really gone in this direction; the general effort has been rather more straightforwardly to chart the success of Antonio's persuasion. The 1982 production was one of the most successful in this attempt, to some reviewers. Roger Warren, after noting that the rest of the lords had discarded the armour in which they first appeared, continued:

> the chief advantage of the armor was to bring real substance to Sebastian and Antonio's plot against Alonso. It has been argued that the function of this scene is to re-enact for the audience the original conspiracy against Prospero, but this is the first time I have known the scene to have any such effect, thanks largely to Jeffery Dench's remarkable Sebastian. With his pale face, surrounded by curled hair set back from a receding hairline, and his blue and gold armor, this Sebastian was a resplendent Elizabethan grandee, as it were a conflation of Leicester, Essex, and Southampton [see Figure 32]. He effected a marvelous transition from tired, sarcastic witticism to murderous conspiracy – and even to a touch of grandeur at 'I *the King* shall love thee' [295] as Antonio knelt and kissed his hand … The world of political power was presented with exceptional conviction.
> (SQ, 85)

It is notable, however, that in the small-scale productions of 1974, 1995 and 2000, a number of reviewers, often with some surprise, comment on the unusual effectiveness of this whole scene. Charles Lewson commented in 1974 on the 'icy' Antonio of Jonathan Kent, and suggested that under his persuasion 'James Aubrey's Sebastian makes something genuinely depraved of the plot to kill Alonso' (*Times*). In 1995, Russell Jackson noted that 'on the Swan's platform stage the first scene of the court party, with the by-play of asides and interruptions and the conspirators' plotting, engaged the audience to a degree rare in the greater distances and spaces of larger proscenium theatres' (*SQ*, 321) (a verdict borne out by the production video, where the audience is actually to be heard laughing during the first part). In 2000 Ian Shuttleworth commented that 'Prospero's usurping brother Antonio pulls off the feat of making all those tiresome witticisms sound natural' (*FT*). In the spaces in which it was performed (I saw it myself in a leisure centre in Northallerton) the malevolence of

Antonio and Sebastian's empty-headed, malleable vanity emerged with clarity.

But this intensely difficult scene offers one more challenge to the director. As Antonio and Sebastian prepare to carry out their murders Sebastian hesitates, and asks for 'but one word' (297). At this point, in the text, Ariel enters and wakes Gonzalo in time to interrupt the renewed assault of the villainous pair. It is a particularly 'stagy' moment, and not at all easy for actors to suggest why Sebastian should draw back, or convincingly to fill the time of Ariel's song with byplay. Not surprisingly, a number of productions have chosen to have Ariel enter earlier, to cut the 'O, but one word', and to 'freeze' the conspirators while the song is sung or chanted, usually with a change of lighting to indicate that magic is at work (1970, 1974, 1993, 1995, 2002). The scene is then quickly wrapped up. Sebastian and Antonio's wildly improvised explanation of their drawn swords – that they heard a noise of 'bulls, or rather lions' (313) – can sometimes raise laughter, and Benthall and Mendes chose to bring us back to Alonso's grief at the very end – the former by having the courtiers pick up again the cry of 'Prince Ferdinand' with which the scene opened, the latter by keeping Alonso alone on stage as Ariel spoke his final words 'So, King, go safely on to seek thy son' (328).

The lords' next scene, 3.3, is discussed principally in the next chapter, but the variation played by Boyd in 2002 is worth noting here. His lords actually ate the banquet they were offered, and, as they did so, they turned it 'into a hideous orgy of blood and greed' (*D. Telegraph*), 'a demonstration of debased character' (*Independent*), confirming the picture of their evil natures that had been built up more convincingly than is often the case in 2.1, and, in particular, suggesting that Alonso is no different from the others. But the confrontation of the 'three men of sin' (3.3.53) with the reality of their guilt is not worked through until the final act. This scene has already been considered in chapter 2, from Prospero's point of view. For the actors playing the lords, however, the central question is what attitude they will each present when finally confronted with the erstwhile Duke of Milan – once it has been decided how they make their way on to the stage. In 1970 their subjection to Prospero was emphasized as they crawled up from the trap door; in 1995 a distinction was offered between Alonso who walked on bemused, and Antonio and Sebastian who crawled in a fashion which seemed deliberately to recall Caliban's characteristic dragging of himself across the stage. The oddest entry was in 1963, when the characters were brought on stage on a conveyor belt or 'travelator'. Donald Sinden recalled the actors' introduction to this device at the dress rehearsal:

> Then came the conveyor belt. It was there all right, but instead of extending into the wings it began only a couple of feet off-stage, so that only one lord could mount it and had practically no time to make a frantic gesture before being propelled, 'standing charm'd' in front of the audience, allowing the next lord to jump on. However, six lords one by one succeeded and were moved, like targets at a funfair shooting-booth, across the front of the stage – and straight off the other side! Somebody had failed to turn off the switch ... We had to begin our entrance all over again. Six lords were for the second time conveyed 'standing charm'd' across the stage. Somebody turned off the switch: the belt stopped dead and six lords fell over. That was to herald the end of the conveyor-belt. (Sinden, 1985, 86)

It makes a good story – but is imperfectly remembered, since the travelator remained in use; it is, indeed, one of the few things that I remember from attending this production in my youth. Unfortunately memory extends no further than to my having found this entrance highly (if inappropriately) amusing, and in the absence of a promptbook it is impossible to say quite what happened next. In most productions the lords enter the magic circle in varying degrees of attitudinal distress. In 1951 Prospero, standing within the circle on a small rostrum, pointed with his staff as he named each of the lords (5.1.62–79) and they fell to their knees. In 1993, as Dymkowski notes, 'a distinction was made between the lords: all had lost their jackets, but only the guilty were filthy. Once they had entered the magic circle, Ariel raised his hands, causing them to cover their faces in a penitent gesture' (305). In 1982, the distinction was made more obviously by having Antonio alone remain standing within the circle, all the other lords having collapsed to the floor. Boyd essayed a more obviously symbolic staging in 2002: Sebastian's hands were covered in blood, whilst Antonio stood like a figure from a Renaissance emblem book, pushing his dagger into his hand.

Once Prospero declares himself, there is almost always a distinction made between the reaction of Antonio and Sebastian and the others. Alonso, as had been intimated at the end of 3.3, has repented, and makes immediate restoration of Prospero's dukedom. In 1993 Paul Greenwood's wonder was well conveyed by the hesitant gesture with which he reached out to touch Prospero's cheek at 'Thy pulse / Beats as of flesh and blood' (5.1.113–14). In 1982 a similar gesture, reaching out to Prospero's temple on this line, carried more intense effect because it seemed to echo Ariel's earlier action of appearing to listen to the pulse in Prospero's wrist at 103, and suited with the emphasis in this production upon Prospero's precarious abdication of magic in favour of his human(e) side.

The crucial figure is Antonio. In older performance traditions the desire for a comprehensive reconciliation at the end of the play had led to various attempts to suggest that he too was penitent. In 1934 William Bridges-Adams delayed this moment until the very end, when Prospero addressed 'Please you, draw near' (319) directly and only to his brother, the single figure left on stage, who then crossed it, kissed his hand and entered the cell. In 1946 Alonso knelt as he requested Prospero to 'pardon me my wrongs' (119), followed by all the lords except Antonio who was left standing – a differentiation which is commonplace. But Crozier clearly wanted to achieve a full restoration of harmony. He therefore cut the whole of Prospero's vicious condemnation from 'But you, my brace of lords' to 'Thou must restore' (126–34), and simply had Antonio finally cross to join the others in kneeling to him. (The cut is particularly noticeable in a production which otherwise gave almost the full text.) In 1951, where the prompt-book indicates that Antonio first knelt and then sank to the floor as Prospero berated him, it might have been intended that the audience should think he was included in a general reconciliation; the promptbook for 1957 gives no clear sense of Antonio's attitude in a conclusion which, as we have seen, was optimistic. In 2002 Malcolm Storry's hard-won, if rather contemptuous, forgiveness was underlined by the gesture of offering Antonio a handkerchief to staunch his self-inflicted wound, but this was an exception among more recent performances.

In 1978 'Paul Brooke, as the usurping Antonio, goes smugly through the play, a venomous sneer on his lips, and is left facing the audience in the final scene, as malignant as ever' (*Times*). The promptbook notes that he 'reacted' to the first mention of Prospero's daughter (147) – though whether with guilt or anger is not stated – and photographs show him sitting in the seat downstage left which Prospero himself had occupied for much of 1.2 (Figure 4). J.W. Velz felt that this

> truly sinister Antonio was the energy centre of an otherwise undistinguished court party. His hard exchange of glances with his brother Prospero in the general exeunt of Act V was one of the morally tense moments of the play – this Antonio was unregenerate, a descendant of Cain, and it was appropriately ironic when Miss Fitzgerald timed her *how beauteous mankind is* so that it became a response to seeing him loitering at the edge of the group.
>
> (*Cahiers Elis.*, 105)

This ironic underlining of Miranda's *naïveté* and Antonio's villainy becomes something of a commonplace – used again in 1982, 1988 and 1998. In none of these did Antonio react; but at Leeds in 1999 the device was taken one step further as Miranda's address to Antonio actually precipitated a final repentance, as, perhaps, did Miranda's kiss of Brian Protheroe in 2002. In 1982 'Antonio knelt and brushed Prospero's hand with lips that were twisted in hatred

FIGURE 34 In 1988 John Wood's Prospero attempted to signal his reconciliation with Antonio (Richard Haddon Haines) with a kiss (5.1), but Antonio rigidly refused his embrace.

as he found himself compelled to restore the dukedom' (*SQ*, 85), a gesture all the more powerful in its revision of the willing submission Antonio had offered Sebastian in 2.1. Even more pointed was the rendition in 1988, where John Wood 'was very much the family man, unqualified in his forgiveness of Antonio: voicing it, he embraced and kissed him. Antonio remained implacably stern' (*SS*, 147) (Figure 34). Alex Renton described the way 'his magic abjured, and facing the Neapolitan court, Wood is almost unendurably pathetic: they accept his kisses with the mild embarrassment they'd reserve for the harmlessly simple-minded' (*Independent*). Similar business was used in 1998, after Prospero had earlier stripped the ducal emblem from his brother's chest, but, for Russell Jackson, 'little was done with Antonio, who certainly did not respond to Prospero's uncomfortable attempt to embrace him but merely looked slightly vexed as he left the stage at the end' (*SQ*, 199). In 1995, after surrendering his dukedom, 'Antonio walked aside, sat on a packing case, moved up to Alonso to make his cynical remark about Caliban, and finally remained there, aloof' (*SQ*, 321). As a final emblem of disruption Antonio functions powerfully to establish the limits of Prospero's power to command the minds as well as the bodies of his enemies.

6

STAGING THE
SPECTACULAR

T̲he tradition of staging *The Tempest* as a spectacular show has a long history. And though modern directors might want to focus our attention upon the human, the individual and/or the political, and certainly would not wish to slow down the action by interminable scene changes, they yet have to deal with the fact that in the storm scene at the play's opening Shakespeare was attempting, in his own time, a theatrical tour de force, as Andrew Gurr has demonstrated, and that in the masque of Act 4 he provided the longest and least obviously dramatically motivated 'play within the play' of his career. Between these two comes the moral interlude of 3.3, where, at Ariel's entry clad as a harpy, the stage direction '*with a quaint device the banquet vanishes*' (3.3.52.2–3) draws specific attention to theatrical trickery. Each of these scenes poses particular challenges – how does one stage a convincing theatrical storm in the age of film? what shape are the '*shapes*' (3.3.17.2)? what dramatic vocabulary can one employ to make the lost conventions of the court masque speak? The larger challenge is to ensure that each of these scenes contributes to the overall direction of the production, and is properly balanced within the movement of the play.

The storm scene was, throughout the nineteenth century, one of the most potent selling points for a production, and endless ingenuity was expended in rendering it as realistic as possible. The tradition persisted well into the twentieth century, and the convincing rolling, tossing ship in Bridges-Adams's 1934 Stratford production was its highlight. In 1946/7 something similar was attempted, but without success. 'Eric Crozier . . . gave us a well-built ship that was supposed to be tossing violently on the destroying waves. Actually it looked as if it was merely rocking on a children's sea-saw in a suburban park' (*Birm. Sun. Mer.*). By 1951, though a reasonably realistic ship's prow was in evidence, Michael Benthall was attempting a more self-consciously symbolic rendering (Figure 35). The enormous company included ten nymphs whose function was to lie around the bottom of the boat, then to spring into movement to suggest the surging seas which surrounded it. Their sequence of movements was choreographed in great detail as the production records show. One sequence, for example, as the storm builds, reads: 'Front flail and back on two knees; do two rocks and a right, left flail with right arm over (crawl) drop to left knee.' One reviewer politely found it 'a trifle fussy' (*Scotsman*), many others became quickly tired of what had seemed at first a 'strikingly imaginative idea' (*Times*). This production also chose to have Prospero on stage from the beginning, his hand raised to begin the tempest, and Ariel entering briefly at the opening to a 'bird-cry', and then returning at the end on the prow of the ship in a sheet of flame to signal its wreck. In a further elaboration, Ferdinand pushed past Ariel and jumped overboard, to be taken off stage by nymphs 'as though dashing him against the rocks'. The point is an obvious one: we are made to see that this is a 'magical' storm by the self-evident staginess of the flailing nymphs, and left in no doubt as to whose magic it is by the presence of Prospero and Ariel.

The idea of having Prospero's agency evident from the beginning had plenty of precedent – going back at least to Frank Benson's production in 1891. But the decision whether or not to show the magician or the spirit during the storm is one which divides subsequent Stratford productions. Prospero appeared again in 1963 when the shaking of his staff precipitated the play's opening. In 1978 Michael Hordern stood downstage left holding

his staff and looking at his magic book. In the small-scale productions of 1974 and 1995 Prospero and Ariel not only appeared, but actually took over the words of the Master and Boatswain. (Somewhat surprisingly, Eric Shorter in 1974 thought 'placing Michael Aldridge's noble and weary Prospero in the middle of the opening storm – as if to let us watch him willing it' was 'fresh and imaginative', *D. Telegraph*.) In 1995, as in 1951, Ariel shot flame into the air at the storm's climax. The most complete assertion of magical control, however, came in 1993, as we have seen in the Introduction, when Ariel not only initiated the action, but directed it throughout – as, for example, when he stilled the swinging lantern as a signal to halt the sound effects and allow Gonzalo's speeches to ring out in the silence. His absolute control was emphasized at the scene's end as he stood impassively, looking out at the audience. Not all reviewers were happy with the device. Irving Wardle thought it 'a thrilling spectacle, but it occupies an undefined zone between stage trickery and natural magic' (*Indep. Sun.*); more firmly Peter Holland labelled it 'a mistake ... for there are few effects in Shakespeare quite as thrilling as the realisation that the hyper-realism of the opening scene is really only a trick of the play's magician' (Holland, 172). This is a crucial interpretative decision; for whilst one might argue that displaying openly the magic of the storm helps to integrate it into the narrative – especially, as in 1951 and 1993, when that magical control is central to the larger reading of the play – Holland and others are surely right to emphasize the way in which it not only wastes a theatrical effect, but, more importantly perhaps, sucks the force out of Miranda's interrogative 'If'' in her opening speech, and with it the questioning of the proper limits to the exercise of magical power.

FIGURE 35 (*opposite*) Michael Benthall's symbolic storm in 1951 was indicated by nymphs performing energetic movements round the bottom of the boat on which stand the Master (David Orr) and Boatswain (Duncan Lamont). Alan Badel's scantly clad Ariel presides. (Prospero was also on stage from the beginning, but does not appear in this photograph.) (1.1)

FIGURE 36 In 1970, with an undulating ceiling and floor, the storm was suggested by ropes and a ladder, with entrances from 'below deck' through a front-stage trap. (1.1)

Whether or not Prospero appears, however, the 'hyper-realism' of the storm is generally suggested by visual synecdoche as some part(s) of a recognizable vessel stand in for the whole. In 1957 the 'whole stage was set as the deck of the ship, with railings running the width of the stage at front and back, ropes and rigging rising from the stage floor' (Dymkowski, 78). In 1970, in a minimalist version, a rope and ladder were suspended from the top of the stage up and down which the actors pursued their 'excellent if nautically garbled acrobatics' (*Observer*) (Figure 36). Nicholas Hytner in 1988 had his Master in a crow's-nest hanging above the stage; in 1982 a huge flapping sail reached into the audience with the prow of the ship jutting out of the forestage. These 'realistic' tokens are then supplemented by more self-consciously symbolic elements. So Peter Brook's 1957 production had a huge lamp, which when the play began was:

lying flat on the stage, and then it rises to describe a huge semi-circle, and falls extinguished on the other side. As soon as it has drawn its great arc, another lamp, much smaller, at the back of the stage, behind the sinking mariners, gives a faint reflection of its tremendous span. Thus can the waste of waters put out the life of man.   (*Times*)

John Barton's 1970 production had both floor and ceiling of the tunnel-like set undulating and flapping; in 1988 huge silks stood in for sails. Adrian Noble in 1998 emphasized further the theatricality of his storm by representing the sea as a billowing silken floor-cloth. Here there was a self-conscious gesture to one of the most famous of all *Tempest* productions – Strehler's in Milan, 1978 – in the model galleon that was first seen bobbing in the distance (or else to Greenaway's *Prospero's Books*, 1991, which borrowed the same idea). In 1934 Bridges-Adams had intensified the realism of his storm by projecting film of crashing waves on to the backcloth; in 2000

we began with a small circular projection (as if at the end of a telescope) of tiny wavelets which were projected onto a square sail which hung vertically downstage of the biggest curve. As the storm gathered so a wind machine billowed this sail and it fell to cover the stage and ruffled over its surface. The projection then covered the whole set with scudding clouds and crashing seas.

(*Cahiers Elis.*, 106)

The effect in 2002 was quite contrary to that of 1934, for the 'realism' of the video projection emphasized the non-naturalistic way the Mariners and passengers were crowded on to the narrow walkway at the top of the set. At the storm's end some of the characters were precipitated off the walkway, sliding down, as it were, into the sea (though the production records note 'if Matthew plays Master or Bosun, has vertigo – can't slide').

A production must also choose whether to 'have the usual half-dozen actors writhing and reeling to indicate that the ship is tossing dangerously' (*Times*, 1957), or to essay something rather more stylized. Most productions play variations on the familiar bustling confusion, often with the lords emerging from trap doors. But in 1963

> the people of the imperilled vessel entered on a moving strip as if they were bound from Waterloo to the Bank. While the house was still laughing uneasily at this mobile strip cartoon, passengers and crew reappeared in the well of the forestage where they were duly swept under in the least persuasive wreck I can recall.   (*Birm. Post*)

In 1978, when 'a glowing orange sun fades out and the curtain changes to a transparent silk, riven with flashes of lighting, ... the blanched faces of the ship's company are picked out in the darkness' (*Times*). They then stood 'absolutely stock-still' (*SS*, 202). Hytner in 1988 also offered a stylized rendering. Underneath the swinging crow's-nest 'a line of mariners ranged horizontally across the stage mov[ed] in the same rhythm' (Dymkowski, 80); the lords were confined to a number of traps through which they poked their heads. In 2002 Michael Boyd arranged a striking variation. His storm was presided over not by Prospero, but by Alonso, let down from above on a throne, with his huge robe trailing near to the level of the stage. His Mariners clambered up and down steel ladders, and only gradually did the stylization of movement, as two of the company shinned up ropes to disappear above the stage, begin to suggest that this was no 'natural' tempest (an impression confirmed as Mariners transformed into 'shapes' in later scenes). The scene, uniquely, began in silence, with Master and Boatswain looking anxiously out at the oncoming storm. As it progressed the storm was represented, rather as in a seventeenth-century production, almost entirely by the occasional noise of drums. This meant that the exchanges between Mariners and lords were never lost, and that one did begin to get some sense of the unpleasantness of aristocratic self-preoccupation, and the contrasting kindliness of Gonzalo. Some earlier productions had also kept sound effects to a minimum. Hytner in 1988 had very sporadic thunderclaps, 'otherworldly' noises and high-pitched screams punctuating the speeches, so that the production achieved 'startling success [by] playing the usually chaotic storm scene in deathly quiet, as though one false move or raised voice would sink the ship' (*Times*, May). Brook had, in 1957, also punctuated the noise in deliberate fashion, especially in 'a spell-stopped, ominous quiet before the final split' (Trewin, 101). But not all productions have managed the 'good refereeing of the usual competition between the dialogue and the sound effects' that Robert Smallwood found in 1998 (*SS*, 238). However much a director may back away from realistic representation of the wreck itself, few can resist turning up the volume control on the wind, waves and thunder effects, as, indeed, few have helped the visual differentiation of characters by the half-light and blazing light-ning that they all too rarely refuse.

The next question is how to end the storm. In 1946/7 and 1951/2 it was simple: the tabs were drawn to allow the ship to be removed (in 1947 the promptbook records an 'Ariel mime in front of tabs' to cover the delay – a reaction, presumably, to the difficulties experienced the previous year with getting the ship off). Subsequently a quick darkening of the stage has been sufficient to transform the set to Prospero's island. In three productions this moment of transition has been handled with especial force and point. In 1982, as the lights went up after the final 'split', Derek Jacobi was revealed at the rear of the stage on the gaunt wreck, back towards the audience, arms stretched out, holding staff and book, and trembling, 'convulsed in a magical orgasm' (*Times*, Sep). In 1998 the shipwreck had taken place before a transparent curtain, which became opaque when front-lit; at its end it flew out to reveal Prospero standing with huge blue curtains draped round his shoulders 'suggesting a magic cloak directly connected to the skies' (*SQ*, 196). In a not dissimilar fashion the silks which had served for sails in 1988 were released and pulled down into the central trap, revealing Prospero standing on stage alone – though in this case with less assertion of magic potency. In all three, the agency of Prospero was made evident, but in a way which underlined, rather than violated, the text's implication that we, like the characters on board the ship, believe the shipwreck, while it is happening, to be a natural occurrence however symbolically it is staged.

The next spectacular scene, 3.3, is much more straightforward in its implication. The lords, bemused by their wanderings, are offered a banquet by some 'people of the island' (3.3.30), which is snatched away as Ariel appears as the classical figure of the harpy, traditionally seen as Jupiter's scourge upon the greedy, to remind them of their usurpation and terrify them into repentance. But the text is evasive in its descriptions; the figures that bring on the banquet and solicit the lords to eat are '*strange shapes*' (3.3.17.2) a 'living drollery' (21), 'monstrous' (31), yet mannerly, provoking ambivalent reaction in the lords. Productions have represented them very differently. In 1951 they were the barnacles, hedgehogs and apes that had accompanied Prospero from the beginning; in 1963 Clifford Williams provided surreal wickerwork masks and figures. Subsequent productions have emphasized strangeness, rather than monstrosity. In 1982 the 'shapes' were Ariel's doubles; in 1988, wearing 'grey balaclavas at Stratford ... blue face-masks in London', they were dressed in the same 'contemporary brown baggy trousers, white shirts and wide belts' as Prospero (Dymkowski, 258), but moved with jerky gestures and a curious, pattering walk. In 1998 the actors were encased in duvet covers (Figure 37). In 1993 they were simply the same human figures in suits matching Ariel's who had already functioned as scene-shifters; in 2000 they were the musicians in black sweaters and trousers, in 2002 they were distinguished only by their green faces from the Mariners of 1.1. In these three last-mentioned productions the audience were required in their imaginations to supply the monstrosity of which the lords spoke, in defiance of what they actually saw, just as in a number of productions, including 1957, 1963 and 1988, they had, despite their ears, to believe that the sounds which accompanied their entrance were 'Marvellous sweet music' (19).

FIGURE 37 Scott Handy's Ariel was provided with huge red wings in 1998 for his entrance as a harpy (3.3). His performance is here commended by Prospero (David Calder), while at either side of the stage stand the 'shapes', looking like animated tea bags.

The banquet itself could be numinous and strange – in 1982 an orb contained a Star of David, with candles set between its points – or completely imaginary (1974, 1995). In 1993 it was more elaborately staged, as, compensating for the lack of mystery in the shapes themselves, a long cloth laid out on the stage miraculously transformed itself into a table capable of supporting a substantial spread (a magic-consultant is credited in the programme). But in 2000 the 'banquet' was a rather sorry single heaped plate, which reminded Russell Jackson of a 'baked Alaska' (*SQ*, 113). Sometimes the banquet is offered in individual portions. In 1970 a cloth was laid out with six dishes upon it; in 1988 each spirit carried a 'plastic sea-food display' (*FT*, Jul), and eagerly solicited an individual lord to taste of what lay inside the globes. In 2002 the shapes balletically held pumpkins above their heads, which the lords seized, sliced in half with their swords and ate ravenously.

The scene's big moment is, of course, the entry of Ariel-as-harpy. He can walk in, covered by flashing light (1970), simply pop up from behind the table (1963, 1982) or rise more impressively on a telescopic lift (1957) (this last reminded Trewin of 'the growing and shrinking Alice', 102). Simon Russell Beale in 1993 emerged through the table itself (more illusionist magic). Or else Ariel can fly in from above (1951, 1978, 1988, 1998). His most frequent dress is as a winged creature. In 1952 Margaret Leighton wore a 'half-mask from the top of which protruded two long plumes ... [with] extremely long feathery wings' (Dymkowski, 261). Mark Rylance had impressive, scaly, multicoloured wings in 1982. In 1988 Duncan Bell's entrance was one of the strongest visual moments in a generally austere production as he descended 'bewinged, white-faced, brilliant blood staining his mouth, the ghost of bloody revenge' (*Cahiers Elis.*, 104) (Figure 38). Scott Handy's descent in 1998 was very similar, except that his wings were blood-red, rather than the white of Duncan Bell, suggesting 'some dangerous angel breathing fire and brimstone' (*E. Standard*). A new variation was played in 2002, where Ariel had been invisibly bent forward in a downstage trap, with a swan on his back; the lords attacked it, thinking it part of the banquet, severed the neck and drank blood from it, only for Ariel to stand, with swan's wings extended, and begin the speech.

The winged harpy is not, however, inevitable. In 1978 Ian Charleson was flown in, but 'enclosed within a circle, arms and legs outstretched, after Leonardo's famous illustration of Vitruvius's "Proportions of the Human Figure"' (*SS*, 203). Quite what was the emblematic point of this learned recollection is not clear to me – but this Ariel also wore a beaked mask, and cawed ferociously, so that the *Times* saw him as 'a luridly illuminated bird of prey on a blood-red trapeze'. In 1963 the table tipped forward to reveal Ian Holm in an enormous wig, straw hair reaching to floor level, standing on (or behind) a huge tarantula. Simon Russell Beale erupted wearing a blood-stained white version of his customary dress, suggesting either a 'blood-stained Banquo'

FIGURE 38 Duncan Bell's white-winged Ariel (with John Wood's Prospero standing beneath) intimidates Sebastian (Colin McCormack), Alonso (Nicholas Selby) and Antonio (Richard Haddon Haines) in 3.3 (1988). In the foreground stand two of the orbs containing the 'banquet'. On Ariel's entry they were supposed to flip over, converting food into a pile of sand – but where the right-hand orb has performed its task, that on the left still displays the food. This malfunction was not infrequent.

(*Observer*, Jul) or 'a waiter who had eaten one of the diners' (Holland, 172). It is at this moment that the banquet is supposed to disappear '*with a quaint device*' (3.3.52.2). In fact by far the majority of productions do very little with this instruction – the dramatic appearance of the harpy being enough of itself to stifle the lords' appetites. In 1970, for example, though the tablecloth was whisked away through Ariel's legs, the lords, who had already picked up their bowls, simply dropped them like 'hot plates', according to the promptbook. In 1951 monsters just carried everything off at the end of the scene; in 1982 the banquet descended with Ariel after his speech. In 2000 Ariel did make the exiguous feast disappear with the very unquaint device of stamping on it, leaving the shapes to clear it up with dustpan and brush, and in 2002, though Ariel had, as we have seen, been part of the banquet itself, he then had to sweep away the remains of the food before carrying out Prospero's next instruction. Only in 1988 was much effort made to derive symbolic significance from the disappearance. 'The bottoms of Hytner's individual banquet-globes were opaque and the tops see-through glass: as the lords tried to get at the food, the fruit inside suddenly flipped over, revealing in its place a little pile of sand' (Dymkowski, 262) (Figure 38).

The end of this scene is a good deal less precarious than its beginning. Ariel's sombre speech, with its elevated and angular syntax, is clear in its moral purpose, and even without the electronic amplification which (to my mind regrettably) seems to have become de rigueur in recent performances, can scarcely fail. In a number of productions the speech is enlivened by the lords' efforts to raise their swords against Ariel, and in 1993 his freezing of their efforts was effectively underlined as blood-red kabuki streamers erupted from his talons at 'You fools!' (60). In 1951, as Ariel speaks of 'all the creatures' who are 'Incensed ... / Against your peace' (74–5) the promptbook contains the memorable instruction, 'monsters begin to appear again and fantasticate', and as the lords attempted to stab Ariel at the end of the speech they 'appear from hiding places and laugh'. The guilt of the lords is generally conveyed in postures of anguish and disbelief. In 1970 a distinction of response was made as Antonio and Sebastian remained in a frozen crouch as Alonso spoke, and cried out as he mentioned 'Prosper' (99). The Folio stage direction indicates that Prospero watches the proceedings '*on the top*' (3.3.17.1). In 1998 an interesting variation was played as Prospero, who had stood, invisible, underneath the suspended Ariel, responded to Sebastian and Antonio's determination to fight by himself moving among them, lashing them offstage with his staff.

Though representing the 'shapes' can be awkward, this scene presents nothing like the difficulties that attend the masque in 4.1. Prospero's 'vanity' of his art (40) gestures towards a generic vocabulary for which there is no real modern equivalent. It is not just that we encounter three classical goddesses, but that the style of their verse, the habit of iconographic reading that they imply and the dramatic shape of the inset scene they perform, all allude to the most period-bound of literary forms, the court masque. The masque was deeply implicated in the culture of the Stuart court, and Shakespeare's text engages in a complex negotiation with the form and the debates that surrounded it. Masques were almost always performed on one night only; the transience that Prospero speaks of in 'Our revels now are ended' (4.1.146–63) was therefore a central issue to those who wrote them. To discuss these issues would take us far beyond the frame of this study – they can be followed up in Orgel (1975) and Lindley (1984) – but the basic fact is that whereas many among a seventeenth-century audience would have been able to 'place' Prospero's betrothal masque very precisely in a specific cultural context, a modern director must attempt to find a kind of dramatic translation in the staging of this scene in order to convey some equivalent sense of a shift of generic gears without losing the essential didactic function of the masque, which is to convey the vision of plenitude that awaits Ferdinand and Miranda if they respect the rites of Hymen.

It is a challenge which has defeated many directors. Indeed, in many twentieth-century productions the episode has been drastically abbreviated or entirely cut. Only in 1974, however, where nothing but the song 'Honour, riches' (4.1.106–17) was retained, and the goddesses suggested by a projected slide, has anything like this tactic been adopted at Stratford. The earliest productions, oddly enough, perhaps had the easiest task, in that their audience was happy to accept spectacle for what it was, and the designers responded by direct invocation of the historical scenic practices of the Stuart masque. In 1946 'when the Masque of the Reapers brought in the attendant spirits, the presiding goddesses seemed to move in a cloud suffused with light; and their golden vesture shone in shooting rays of colour' (*Birm. Post*). The photograph of the set shows at the back of the stage a rainbow above receding halos of clouds that recall directly Inigo Jones's seventeenth-century masque settings. In 1951 Loudon Sainthill's goddesses were attired in virtual copies of Jones's costume designs. Ceres and Iris both entered on chariots attended by nymphs, and then 'Juno rose triumphantly on her throne in the background and garlands descended from the skies to frame her', attracting a 'spontaneous burst of applause' from the audience (*New States.*). Though the promptbook suggests that monsters were substituted for the reapers to dance with 'garland nymphs', this does not seem to have been intended to imply any darker note. The *Manchester Guardian* praised the 'unspared profusion of a tremendous transformation scene' which elevated 'that nuptial Masque which can fall so flat in plainer versions'. The terms here suggest that one reason for its success was precisely that its dramatic vocabulary was familiar to an audience at a time when even the most provincial of theatres celebrated Christmas with a pantomime incorporating a spectacular 'transformation' at its end.

By 1957 it seems to have been much more difficult to satisfy the audience. W.A. Darlington felt that

> it is characteristic of Peter Brook's production ... that the masque of spirits which celebrates the betrothal of Ferdinand and Miranda should become the crown and climax of the play. Many producers

> make little of this masque; they either turn it into a perfunctory short scene or even cut it altogether. Mr Brook throws into it all his resources, making the figures of the goddesses and the dancers seem to be silhouetted in fire and floating in air.   (*D. Telegraph*)

But others were much less complimentary. It was not the masque itself, with its three goddesses in gauzy costume, which caused the problem, but the dance that followed. Kenneth Tynan called the dance the production's 'one big visual gaffe ... in which men dressed as stooks wave plastic sickles and are surrounded by chanting vegetables' (*Observer*) (Figure 39). This 'embarrassed absentee from an international folk dance festival' (*Birm. E. Desp.*) may have suffered from the fact that Brook accompanied it, not with straightforward music, but with a 'choral iteration of "barns, garners, vines, flowers"' (*Birm. Post*). He also introduced at its end the symbolic figure of Father Time, 'interrupting the proceedings far too late' for Milton Shulman (*E. Standard*). Despite Darlington's praise, Brook succumbed to the hostility, and when the production transferred to Drury Lane 'the whole Masque scene [was] re-arranged and designed; with Juno descending from gilded clouds in a golden litter, it is certainly as dreamily gorgeous as anything ever contained in a Drury Lane pantomime' (*FT*). Brook's experiment seems to have been folded back into the world of the 1951 production.

After this, however, there was a failure of nerve in confronting the masque. In the first place, it seemed that directors felt that the goddesses themselves needed to be represented in some symbolic fashion. In 1963 Clifford Williams had them appear first as huge 'corn-dolly' figures at least ten feet high, from behind which the human actors emerged, and by which they were diminished. (The designer defensively claimed in the programme that it was 'deliberately not in the style of Inigo Jones ... we want to see Ariel set free, not watch a lot of nymphs and shepherds come away. So I created ethereal marionettes.') In 1970 'the masque conjured up by this poor Prospero was appropriately frugal and low in key.

Near-naked bodies hovered on the black stage. When the three goddesses appeared they too were naked and played by men' (*D. Telegraph*). The *Birmingham Post* reported that 'in spite of the haunting incantation ... I was not happy about these shapes of Iris, Ceres and Juno in the darkness; and I really see no reason why the trinity of goddesses should be a male-voice choir'. In 1998, too, the amplified voices of the masque were male – one of them provided by Ariel. The goddesses were similarly rather dimly perceived behind a gauze, with the billowing silks of the storm returning for no very obvious reason. (Perhaps it was an attempt to suggest a relationship between the imaginary storm and the imaginary masque as products of Prospero's magic.) The goddesses were represented in 'plain white masks with finely sculpted eyebrows and open mouths' (*SQ*, 197); the text was cut more heavily than usual, and the dance was brief. Robert Smallwood found a nice touch in 'the masquers who wouldn't go away immediately when Prospero changed his mind, spirits who'd learned their lines and put on the play he'd asked for, and who didn't see why they should give it all up at his whim' (*SS*, 239), but it is hard not to concur with Peter J. Smith's condemnation of the 'ludicrous ... masque of the goddesses in which they appeared in Greek masks and bounced up and down waving rainbow flags while their lines were rendered as disembodied voice-overs' (*Cahiers Elis.*, 125).

In other productions the first part of the masque might more or less be negotiated only for the dance of nymphs and reapers to fail. In 1978 there was a determined effort to give the masque some kind of splendour and amplitude. In common with the rest of the production, set on Koltai's black stage, the goddesses' costumes were bright: 'cartwheels of chromatic fabric matching their green and orange and aquamarine hair' (*Spectator*), seen by

FIGURE 39 (*opposite*) Peter Brook's extravagant masque (4.1), here being brought to an end by the entrance of the unscripted Father Time, provoked some approval, but far more ridicule, in 1957.

B.A. Young as 'colourful goddesses making patterns like living blossoms' (*FT*). Ceres and Iris entered from a trap door, and Juno stood on the curled 'wave' at the back of the stage, with, the promptbook tells us, 'characteristic arm movements', before joining her colleagues. Though some attempt was made to characterize them allegorically (Iris, for example, had 'heavy rainbow-striped make-up', *Cahiers Elis.*, 106), the impression was one of uniformity – of 'overdressed country matrons with plush auburn hair-dos' (*New States.*). Perhaps more important was the fact that they could not, vocally, carry the music Guy Woolfenden had written for them and later in the run they mimed their song of blessing to a pre-recorded tape. But the real failure seems to have been in the dance, where first the nymphs danced on their own, and then, after Ariel reprised 'Foot it featly' (1.2.380) from his first song, the reapers entered, performing their own dance before joining their partners. The music director's score carries the acerbic title 'The bloody DANCE', and a memorable variation on the Folio stage direction where 'certain Reapers' is transformed to 'uncertain reapers'. Germaine Greer castigated 'clumsy nymphs whose awkwardness was only half-hidden by crumpled synthetic cloths which could never be described as draperies, for drape they would not' (*Spectator*). It is, with hindsight, ironic that this unsuccessful masque included Juliet Stevenson and Ruby Wax as two of the nymphs.

In 1988 Nicholas Hytner attempted an even more ambitious strategy. His three 'blue-faced, blue-clad, blue-lit goddesses' were flown in from above, whilst three children who were 'miniature versions of themselves' presented gifts to Ferdinand and Miranda (*SQ*, 87). As they descended the goddesses performed mannered, puppet-like gestures 'paddling away like flippers on a clockwork dolphin' (*Int. Her. Trib.*). The dance prompted a shift into a completely different mode as there unfolded 'a hyper-realistic scene showing a sun-bathed, undulating cornfield in front of which white-behatted and white-dressed reapers [were] engaged in a slow dance' (*Cahiers Elis.*, 104). This 'collection of evidently embarrassed actors dancing upstage' (*SQ*, 87) prompted Kate Kellaway to object that 'the rich and strange is briefly overtaken by the rich and kitsch' (*Observer*), and Jean-Marie Maguin to find it an effect 'sudden and nauseating, like discovering *The Tempest* on the back of a packet of Weetabix' (*Cahiers Elis.*, 104). Throughout the masque Prospero lay before it, apparently asleep. The rationale offered by the director was that 'the tableau was intended as an ironic undercutting of what is evidently cheap and "kitsch" in Prospero's projected yearnings' (*Cahiers Elis.*, 104). There are a number of obvious problems with such a strategy. It requires an audience to make a self-conscious leap both of the imagination and of the intellect to say to themselves, 'this masque looks silly; perhaps that's intentional; perhaps it's connected with Prospero's lying on the floor'. But the attempt to psychologize it betrays a complete lack of confidence in the audience's capacity to respond to the masque in and for itself.

In 2002 Michael Boyd also sent up the first part of the masque. Ariel entered as Iris, and danced with two of the shapes in mannered fashion; but then Ceres and Juno were played by the Boatswain and Master in drag, the former looking to Benedict Nightingale like 'a blend of Chiquita Banana and Lily Savage' (*Times*). Iconographically their dress was not inappropriate, at one level, but the camp humour of their appearances (and the 'joke' of the huge fish offered by the shapes to Ferdinand and two pumpkins rather obviously placed in Miranda's arms) sat uneasily with the fact that they sang their 'Honour, riches' (106–17) with considerable skill. The dance, however, prefaced by the bounding of somewhat menacing reapers on to the stage, was quite another thing, a trapeze ballet in which the aerial nymph and reaper ended by giving every indication of a determination to join the 'thirty-foot-high club' (Figure 40). It was their simulated sex which proved too much for Malcolm Storry's puritanical Prospero and precipitated the dissolution of the masque. This conformed to the production's insistent underlining of the significance of desire. Charles Spencer thought 'the usually tedious marriage

FIGURE 40 In 2002 the 'dance' of nymphs and reapers (4.1) became a spectacular, highly erotic aerial duet. Jami Quarrell and Fiona Lait are watched by James Hyland, Gracy G. Goldman and Dan Crute.

masque ... a blast, half camp drag ball and half superb trapeze act' (*D. Telegraph*), but to me it failed to cohere.

Only three productions since 1951 have really found a satisfactory means of persuading a modern audience of the importance of the masque. In 2000 the masque itself got by through the use of video projection both to underline the emblematic significance of each of the goddesses – a rainbow for Iris, a harvest field for Ceres and peacock's feathers for Juno – and to assist the actors in negotiating the highly stylized verse. This was certainly more effective than the earlier touring production in 1995. There 'the divine masque, which should be visually stunning, [was] performed in white sheets' (*TLS*). But what gave a truly celebratory feel to the 2000 betrothal masque was the dance, despite the fact that no actors were available to perform as nymphs and reapers. Instead, Orlando Gough's music was

> endowed with a kinetic energy in the manner of a poltergeist. Miranda and Ferdinand were given gold spangled shoes to wear. A spirit on either side of the stage crouched down with their hands in identical pairs of shoes. As the spirits choreographed the steps of the dance by moving their hands, so the shoes of the couple empathically followed them: the effect was of Ferdinand and Miranda being danced from the feet up. (*Cahiers Elis.*, 108)

The physicality of the music, generated entirely by the singers, combined with the abandoned exuberance of the lovers to make this one of the high points of the production.

In 1993 Sam Mendes fixed the masque within his overall emphasis on metatheatricality, by having Prospero produce, as he invited Ariel to go and prepare the masque, a Victorian pop-up theatre book. Ariel tucked it under his arm like a head waiter with a menu, and then proceeded to summon from the heavens an exact, magnified replica, within which the three 'crinolined goddesses ... move[d] with the stiff movements of the figures on traditional musical boxes'. Angela Maguin concluded that 'its stylization ma[de] the most of the stilted accents of the dramatic insert'

(*Cahiers Elis.*, 96). It was certainly possible to believe that it was 'Harmonious charmingly', even if not quite the 'most majestic vision' of which Ferdinand speaks (4.1.118–19). There were no nymphs in the dance, only straw-hatted reapers who continued the stylized movement to tinkly music, before the revelation of Caliban as one of them brought the masque to its abrupt end. It stands out as a convincing attempt to find a distinct, novel equivalent for the artificiality and self-consciousness of the Stuart masque. But at the same time, it did, inevitably, suggest that the masque was merely a 'trick', a 'vanity of mine art' as Prospero calls it (37, 40). Though many in the seventeenth century might have agreed with this valuation of the genre, it is possible to represent it as a more serious celebration of art's high power to instruct and celebrate.

And this was precisely what was achieved in 1982, in the most completely successful of all Stratford renditions. The masque was turned into a through-composed mini-opera, with goddesses 'all glitter and light, all colour and hooped skirts with collars of shining wire and air' (*Times*, Aug). The decision to distinguish the episode generically by its music seemed to me one that worked admirably (it is discussed further in chapter 7). It established the celebration of marriage and fertility as a genuinely positive counterweight to the anger and darkness elsewhere evident in the production. There was no straining after symbolism in the representation of the goddesses – they were simply finely dressed singers giving the performance their all. And in this context, the movement to the elegant dance of nymphs and reapers worked, as it was supposed to in the seventeenth century, as confirmation of the harmony achieved in the masque itself (Figure 41). This was further emphasized as, in imitation of the customary practice in the Stuart masque, Ferdinand and Miranda joined the dance. They, and the audience, were caught up in the mood of celebration, so that the masque's sudden dissolution had an extremely powerful effect. Or so, at least, it seemed to me.

The *Leamington Morning News*, however, spoke for a number of reviewers when complaining that 'the only incongruous note in

FIGURE 41 In 1982 the masque (4.1) was a through-composed opera, leading to a graceful baroque dance. Here the singing goddesses on the right, Angela Kazimierczuk and Christine Botes, summon the nymphs and reapers to the dance, watched by Juno (Theresa Lister) on the left, Ariel (Mark Rylance) at the back and Prospero (Derek Jacobi) on the right.

an imaginative production came during the wedding scene, when lengthy opera-type singing and ceremonial dancing did not blend in at all'. The choice of a fully musical realization was, inevitably, a risky strategy; and this comment betokens the inability of the particular reviewer to accept and enjoy its musical language. *The Tempest* is Shakespeare's most musical play – and yet an audience's response to music is perhaps less predictable and less controllable than to almost any other element in a production. And it is to the music that we finally turn.

7

MUSIC AND SONG

The King's Men acquired the Blackfriars Theatre in 1608, and with it new, enlarged musical resources. This might explain why Shakespeare in 1610–11 felt able to call for more music than he had ever done before. More importantly, it might also have been the stimulus to undertake a profound exploration of music's nature and function in the theatre. For though the worlds of Illyria and Arden, in *Twelfth Night* and *As You Like It*, are characterized by music, in *The Tempest* the sounds of the island are not merely part of its character or nature; they also – and crucially – function as a spring of dramatic action. Ferdinand, Caliban, Stephano and Trinculo are moved about the island by the lure of Prospero's music; the lords are lulled to sleep by Ariel, and woken again by his song to thwart the assassination of Alonso and Gonzalo; it is music which cures the frantic fit of the lords, and the music and dance of the masque which tempts Ferdinand to 'live here ever' (4.1.122).

Music, therefore, has a practical function in the play. But it is important to recognize that the seventeenth-century view of the nature and function of music was very different from that which a modern audience brings to its experience of the play. When Prospero speaks of 'heavenly music' (5.1.52), or when Ferdinand remarks upon the power of Ariel's song to calm the tempest, and to allay his passion (1.2.393), they are each drawing upon the conventional neo-Platonic belief that earthly music imitated divine harmony and acquired its power to affect human actions and feelings through its reflection of the cosmic music of the moving spheres of the heavens. Such an understanding of the source of music's potency affords the island's sounds a more powerful symbolic potential than they can ever have in modern theatre, film or television, where 'incidental music' simply characterizes and underlines mood and atmosphere. Indeed it may be doubted whether music was ever 'incidental' in the modern sense in Shakespeare's theatre, since the music called for in the plays is always assumed to be heard by the characters themselves. It might be thought that Caliban's famous assertion that the isle is 'full of noises, / Sounds and sweet airs' (3.2.135–6) gives full licence to the addition of musical cues, but in the symbolic architecture of the play it is crucial to note that music is only possible because Prospero had released Ariel from the cloven pine in which he was imprisoned by Sycorax. The only 'music' the young Caliban can have heard was the groaning of the spirit which 'Did make wolves howl' (1.2.288). At the same time, however, the origin of the island's music in Prospero's action emphasizes the way in which throughout the play it is at his command, and for his purposes, that music is generated. If Antonio, according to Prospero, could 'set all hearts i'th' state / To what tune pleased his ear' (1.2.84–5), then Prospero himself, in a much less metaphorical sense, performs exactly the same trick to pursue his own political ends. After all, the song 'Full fathom five' (1.2.397ff.), exquisitely though it calms Ferdinand's grief, is at the same time telling him lies. Alonso is not dead, but it is important to Prospero's purposes that Ferdinand should think him so. Music represents magic and is an emblem of moral harmony, but it is also a means of manipulative control. In the modern theatre the prevalence of 'incidental' music dilutes its specific dramatic function.

This crucial dimension of the music in the play was ignored throughout the eighteenth and nineteenth centuries, which preferred instead simply to elaborate the play's musical set pieces. Not only were songs added to the play, but even the storm itself might be replaced by a musical opening – as in Thomas Linley's 'storm chorus' for Sheridan's redaction of the play in 1777, surely one of the finest pieces of music ever composed for a Shakespeare performance. The songs were frequently given elaborate settings with substantial choruses, and treated as separable from the continuity of the play's action. In 1867, for example, the rendition of 'Where the bee sucks' (5.1.88ff.) by Julia St George in Charles Calvert's Manchester production was encored three times before the play was allowed to continue. She had, furthermore, deliberately countermanded the director's decision to employ the new score by a young Arthur Sullivan, and performed instead the familiar setting by Thomas Arne, which dates back to 1746 (Lindley, 2002). The songs functioned, indeed, very much as actorly 'points'. Russell Jackson notes that 'the Victorian performer expected an audience to acknowledge each "point" with a round of applause', and that 'many of these "points" became customary, so that actors were praised according to their ability to fulfil expectations in some, and surprise in others' (Jackson, 120–1). It is precisely that mixture of the familiar and the new that audiences expected in the music, and their expectations were satisfied well into the twentieth century. Sullivan's music was still to be heard in Regent's Park productions of the play in the 1930s and the *Daily Mail* nostalgically commented on Anthony Bernard's music for Bridges-Adams's 1934 production that it 'sounds too much like diluted Purcell to give much pleasure. If Purcell's music alone were used we should have nothing but praise for a brilliant opening' (17 Apr 1934).

Nothing could be further from the practice of post-war production. Every new staging is supplied with a new score, and the composer is expected to shape and revise the music in the course of rehearsal to suit precise practical needs. The musical director's score is always full of optional repeats, cuts and crossings out, arrows indicating points in the dialogue which must match moments in the music and so on. But yet, subservient though the music may seem to be to practical necessity, it makes a contribution which is capable of profoundly conditioning an audience's response to a production as a whole. There are many decisions which director and composer have to make. They must choose a musical vocabulary, or code, which suits with the overall setting and interpretation of the play. They must decide how far the music is to be represented as a sign of Prospero's magic control and a product of his willed intention, and therefore to be motivated by the action, rather than standing outside the play as a parallel commentary on it. They need to consider how far Ariel's songs should characterize the spirit, as well as the island. An appropriate music must also be found for Caliban, Stephano and Trinculo, for the apparition of the shapes and harpy in 3.3, and for the masque and dance of 4.1.

Conveniently, the first two productions for which substantial evidence survives, 1951 and 1957, occupy the extreme ends of the spectrum of styles that have been adopted since the war, and provide an introduction to the range of possibilities explored and varied in other settings. (There is no trace of Lennox Berkeley's score for the 1946/7 production, nor of the recording of it which was used in the theatre.) John Wooldridge provided the music in 1951, scored for a small symphony orchestra of strings, woodwind, brass and harp, restoring the live music abandoned in the previous production. There was a reassuring familiarity in this arrangement, which extended to the musical vocabulary – palely pastoral, in the style of much English art music of the 1940s and 1950s – and also to the uses of that music. It covered the transitions from scene to scene, so, for example, tempering the rebelliousness of the ending of 2.2 as it introduced a 'romantic' motif for Ferdinand and Miranda. This motif appeared again at the beginning of 4.1, and at the appearance of Ferdinand and Miranda in 5.1 – an example of the way in which music can bring its own thematic organization to bear on the audience's experience of the play as a whole. At many points there was 'incidental' music, uncalled for in the text, and not associated with any specific manifestation of Prospero's magic. So, for example, Miranda's approving comment on

Ferdinand, 'nothing natural / I ever saw so noble' (1.2.419–20), was underlined by a sustained string chord, and virtually the whole of Prospero's 'Ye elves' speech (5.1.33 –57) was accompanied by quiet, rather indeterminate sound, giving a halo to his words. One might see this as music 'symbolizing' magic, but its effect was rather to rob Prospero's speech of its dangerous near-blasphemy, to contain, even to sentimentalize, its perilousness. The continuation of the 'solemn air' which is a 'comforter' to the lords (58) underneath the whole of Prospero's speech as he considers each of his 'enemies' in succession, and as their consciousness begins to return, was more obviously justified by the text, and its modulation without pause into 'Where the bee sucks' integrated that problematic song effectively into the continuing action. But it still sat on the borderline between music as the dramatic medium of Prospero's magic, and an incidental music which persuades the audience to a particular response to a 'magical' moment. It is this borderline which all productions negotiate in their deployment of music additional to the cues specified in the text.

The composer thought well enough of his settings of Ariel's songs to publish them independently (like Tippett's wonderful *Three Ariel Songs*, deriving from his score for the 1962 Old Vic production, they are slightly adapted in the published version). Yet, despite the almost universal praise for Badel's Ariel, no reviewer commented on his singing. It would certainly seem that the songs were written for an actor not necessarily vocally expert, since they have a limited vocal range and make few technical demands. They are, indeed, rather bland, if 'Harmonious charmingly' (4.1.119), and would, one imagines, have served well enough to persuade an audience that Ferdinand might be led by them to Prospero's cell. The absence of direct comment is not, however, particularly unusual – theatre critics are frequently inattentive to music. In general, Wooldridge's score operated within the conventional assumptions of its period, both in terms of the way it was deployed, and in its musical style. It is inevitable that incidental music will rely on conventional language – for codes such as 'tremolando strings = emotional tension' depend upon their widespread familiarity in order to be comprehensible. And yet *The Tempest*'s island is a strange and otherworldly place – and music can be called upon to create an alien quality.

That, emphatically, was what Peter Brook attempted in 1957. He put together recorded *musique concrète* which sounded to Kenneth Tynan 'like a combination of glockenspiel, thundersheet, Malayan nose-flute and discreetly tortured Sistine choirboy' (*Observer*). Brook told John Barber:

> I use the guzzler – a tiny, one-stringed fiddle which I bought in Belgrade, I use Yugoslav pipes. And I play the piano in curious ways. I play the strings with a violin bow. Or I just stamp on the pedals ... marvellous effects. My favourite is the pure sound you get when a record of choirboys singing is played very slowly.   (*D. Express*)

Brook himself explained the philosophy which persuaded him to devise such music:

> It is no longer the ideal to go to an eminent composer ... and ask him to write a score to accompany a play ... A good incidental score nowadays is more a matter of timbre and tone colour than of harmony or even of rhythm; it has to appeal to a mind which has at least one and three-quarter ears fully occupied with following the dramatic narrative; it is, in fact, quarter-ear music.
>
> (*S. Times*, 22 Sep 1957)

Music to Brook functions primarily as a directorial instrument, like set and costume, to generate a view of, and response to, the play as a whole. In this case it created, by the oddity and novelty of its musical 'language', a soundscape which represented the strangeness and fearfulness of Prospero's island, rather than its capacity for harmony. Nothing more divided reviewers than their reactions to this sound world. Where Barber felt 'the music is superb: it fills the isle with remote, terrible plonks, and a tolling like bells from a cathedral under the sea' (*D. Express*), Robert Wainwright in the *Star* complained at Brook's 'deliberate rejection of the power of music to create magic. The plinks and plonks and grunts and groans of his own "Musique concrete", so effective in *Titus Andronicus*, are meaningless on Prospero's island.' In part this was simply a reaction to unfamiliar musical language, but other critics recognized that the abandonment of any conventional musical syntax posed particular problems in this play, where music cannot merely be a creator of mood. Tynan made a crucial distinction in observing that it 'twangles just as dreamily as Caliban said it would, though it fails to supply even passable settings for the songs' (*Observer*), a verdict echoed by the *Liverpool Daily Post*, suggesting that 'it seems incredible that lyrics so enchanting and faultless could inspire Mr Brook to nothing better than a sort of eight-note recitative. Perhaps that is one reason why Ariel is so earth-bound.'

No trace of Ariel's songs seems to survive. Recordings of Brook's musical assembly, however, are still to be found in the archive, on 78 rpm discs. They are confusingly labelled, and it proved impossible for me to match them with any confidence to the music cues specified in the promptbook. But what actually strikes the ear most strongly is not something alien but the impression of amateurishness. These fragments sound like something that any half-competent teenager might nowadays assemble on a computer on a wet Wednesday afternoon. What was once controversially avant-garde has been completely overtaken by advances in technology. Nonetheless, only partially recoverable though it is, Peter Brook's 'score' contradicts many of the assumptions on which Wooldridge's music is founded. These are noises that, precisely because they contradict expectations about what constitutes 'music', belong exclusively to the island of the play; or, rather, to the island in this production of the play. They disorientate an audience by refusing to supply the conventional matches of music and emotion. And yet Brook shares with Wooldridge the acceptance of incidental music to illustrate the text at various moments, and the tape-recorded effects engineered by the director, just as much as the symphony orchestra placed in the pit, stand at the same time both within and outside the action of the play itself.

If Wooldridge and Brook represent two poles of the musical spectrum, the scores for subsequent productions occupy different positions between them – and interact in varied ways with the overall tendency of the productions in which they figure. Guy Woolfenden's 1978 score used the Stratford wind band, rather than the theatre orchestra of 1951, but stylistically was closer to the earlier score, in its lightly 'spiked' but accessible vocabulary. Irving Wardle thought his 'drugged lullabies and ethereal dances memorably transmit the island's poetry' (*Times*), and Robert Cushman praised 'the most haunting songs Guy Woolfenden has ever composed' (*Observer*). His music certainly softened, even contradicted, the hard, black world of Ralph Koltai's set. In 1988, however, the bare white disk and bright lighting of the production were supported by Jeremy Sams's much more edgy, modernist music language. As is usual for music of this kind, it was objected to by some reviewers, Jeremy Kingston, for example, remarking (of the masque particularly) that 'it is foolish to obscure the language with harsh, plinky-plunk music' (*Times*, Jul). Martin Hoyle, however, felt that 'Sams's elusive music does indeed create an isle full of noises, sounds and sweet airs' (*FT*, May). It certainly generated something of a contradiction between the approving comments of the onstage audience on the 'Marvellous sweet music' (3.3.19) at the entry of the shapes and the discordant lurching march that Sams provided for them.

Shaun Davey, in 1993, adopted a softer musical style, with substantial use of (synthesized) piano sound ensuring that, like many Stratford productions in the late 1980s and early 1990s, its aural palette was aimed at an audience accustomed to 'easy listening'. As Angela Maguin observed, it was 'in the *South Pacific* tradition, bland, tuneful, pleasant. There is nothing strange or disturbing about it; it is light and popular and asks no questions.' For her 'the music – colourless and totally without invention – was the weak element of the production' (*Cahiers Elis.*, 95–6). Few reviewers thought it worth comment, and in its use of ostinato figures on glockenspiel and harp to signify 'magic' it went for the easily recognizable gesture. Equally unremarkable was the music in 1995, a combination of principally synthesized sound with a lugubrious cor anglais that at least complemented the rather downbeat atmosphere of the whole, with the songs, though 'composed', being delivered in half-speech, half-song. In 1998 Stephen Warbeck provided a much more complex score, in which the dividing line between sound effects, pre-recorded and 'live' music was not easy to note. (The score has not yet become available in the archive.) Perhaps the composer was encouraged by the fact that Scott Handy was 'a spirit with an unusually fine singing voice ... to arrange subtle and technically complex versions of the songs' (*Cahiers Elis.*, 124). Alistair Macaulay was less complimentary, observing that

> Warbeck has composed Ariel's songs each in a different idiom, and the melancholy/sinister note of 'Full fathom five' is good in a Brittenesque vein: from then on, unfortunately, each sounds more strained than the one before, and less vocally congenial.   (*FT*)

There was a good deal of underlining of text with instrumental music and effects; vibes and ostinato phrases again figured as signs of magic in the air, but, unlike Davey's music, there was an urgency and musical complexity that made a richer and more ambivalent contribution to the island setting, by turns mellifluous and threatening.

The production of 2002 saw just about the most restrained musical accompaniment of any of those under review. An occasional harp ostinato functioned to suggest magic; flute, trumpet, violin and a single high soprano briefly appeared at appropriate moments, and a battery of drums (visible, like the other musicians, just offstage) supplied the tempest. Continuity was provided by the Boatswain's whistle, which moved from the instrument of command on board ship, to the instrument with which Ariel summoned Ferdinand and then others on stage. It substituted, indeed, for the song 'Come unto these yellow sands' (1.2.376ff.), which was cut. This was an island of sounds and noises, rather than of continuous music.

Of Stephen Oliver's music for 1974 nothing seems to survive; it was played by a small 'baroque' ensemble, and, as the music director, Michael Tubbs, tells me, manifested Oliver's characteristic skill at writing pastiche. But in 1982 the composer returned to provide one of the most ambitious and richest scores for any of the productions under review. He moved effortlessly through a range of musical styles, each purposefully deployed, climaxing in the through-composed setting of the masque. Of this score I shall have more to say, but for the moment it is enough to observe that, though it did not challenge the ear in the way that Sams and Warbeck did, it provoked perhaps more comment than any music since Brook, and received an equally varied critical reception – especially of the operatic masque. But this was, emphatically, not 'quarter-ear' music; it demanded and commanded attention in its own right.

Brook's use of electronically generated music looked forward to what is now commonplace. In almost every recent score the line between music performed by human players and singers, and sound effects electronically generated is blurred; one slips into the other. A particularly imaginative use of electronics was offered by Nancy Meckler's Shared Experience Company touring production in 1996, where all the noises of the island were generated by computerized manipulation of sounds emanating from Ariel – breathing, moaning, whispering, as well as singing. In many ways the logical extension of Brook's thesis, as well as his technology, this dramatic solution also answered Ferdinand's question about the origin of the music – 'Where should this music be?' (1.2.388) – unambiguously. It came not from an orchestra pit, nor from pre-prepared tapes, but was generated in 'real time' by the play's central musical character.

Ferdinand's enquiry is a key question about the music in the play in several ways. As well as pointing us to important issues concerning Prospero's power, it gestures towards a more straight-forward ambiguity in all theatrical music – is this music 'in' or 'out' of the stage world of the play? The location of the music within rather than outside the action has been attempted by several productions. In 1963 Raymond Leppard followed Brook in providing an electronic score (of which virtually nothing survives), but added to it vocal parts for Ariel's onstage attendant spirits that were half-speech, half-song. They did not go down particularly well; Colin Frame, for example, complained that 'the enchanting songs ... were delivered in a rock 'n' roll chant by sprites dressed like skin divers with hair nets ... No wonder poor Ferdinand got an unasked laugh with his opening lines "Where should this music be"' (*E. News*). J.W. Lambert was slightly less negative in characterizing the score as 'unearthly hums and skirling, pinched ritualistic chants like embittered children's playsongs for Ariel' (*S. Times*), and Philip Hope-Wallace became positively enthusiastic about 'an astonishingly original piece of work – the enchantments of the island are those of abstract art and musique concrète, and those to whom such things are a matter for sniggering will not much like them' (*Man. Guardian*). Significantly, he praises the music for its match to the other elements of the production, but his patrician put-down also seizes on one of the problems that is particularly marked when the musical vocabulary is difficult, and is devoted primarily to the creation of an alien atmosphere. For at several crucial points the text insists on the harmoniousness of the music – in 3.3 and 4.1 in particular – and, narratively, it is important that we should believe in its power to charm its hearers. Every member of the audience will have a different view of what constitutes 'harmonious' music. Oddly enough, the same Hope-Wallace who enthusiastically endorsed Leppard's music, had commented acerbically on Brook's score that 'we do not necessarily want to "come unto these yellow sands" in the manner of Roger Quilter. But so much twangling is like a restless radio next door; it breaks up and disperses the speech rhythms instead of supporting them' (*Man. Guardian*, 1957).

Two other productions have attempted to generate the bulk of the music explicitly on stage. It may have been the rushed preparation that meant that the music in 1970 was provided by 'members of the cast', with Ben Kingsley writing his own songs, and singing to a disguised autoharp. Unfortunately there is little trace in the archive of what this music might have been. Not all of it was vocal, since Michael Tubbs's music director's book refers to a harpsichord, and to a 'raga'; the promptbook itself, however, suggests that the 'spirits' underlined considerable portions of speech with motivically linked sound. So, for example, there is the instruction for 'spirit crescendo' under Prospero's castigation of Ariel at 1.2.269ff., which modulates to 'spirits light, happy' once Ariel has submitted and asks 'What shall I do?' (301). Later, at the end of 3.3, 'Full fathom five' is reprised by the spirits as Alonso speaks of Ferdinand in the oozy depths of the sea (100). But however thought out the accompaniment might have been, it left little mark on the reviews.

Quite different is the final example of music performed, as it were, 'in view', Orlando Gough's score for the 2000 touring production. Here almost all the sounds were vocal, and provided by figures classed in the programme as 'spirits', but dressed, not in costume, like the extra 'Ariels' of 1957 and 1982, but in the black sweaters and trousers of stage hands. Their liminal position, visibly part of the performance yet detached from it, placed their music exactly. It might function as commentary, but could also, persuasively, cause action to happen – especially in the masque's dance. Its musical vocabulary was 'strange' in the nonsense syllables out of which the 'mouth-music' was built, and sometimes in its harmonic astringency, coupled with jazz-type syncopation, but it did not have the impersonal, alienating effect of electronic music precisely because it was made by human voices, pushed to their limits in the huge demands the composer made for singers to range over at least two octaves. The first act, for example, was rounded out by the 'mermaid' motif, where the top soprano rises to a very high F. This simultaneously suggested otherworldliness in its pure, ethereal sound floating over held, hummed chords, and yet at the same time created in its audience an astonishment that a real human voice could possibly be reaching such stratospheric heights, and a sense of the perilousness of the performer's effort. Both 'inside' and 'outside' the world of the play itself, strange but not alienating, Gough's score seemed to me (and to many reviewers) one of the highlights of this particular production, although even here dissentient voices can be found (see Introduction).

One thing that is true of all these scores, however, is that virtually none attempted to employ a musical vocabulary that was historically consistent with the visual world created on stage. Whether that was more or less Tudor–Stuart (1951, 1957, 1978, 1988, 2002), Napoleonic (1993) or high Victorian (2000) the music, however varied, belonged to the twentieth century. The partial exception is Oliver's score in 1982 (and perhaps earlier in 1974), which did employ self-conscious gestures towards historical musical styles, though as a whole clearly belonging in the present – the allusions were always, as it were, in quotation marks. To someone like myself, interested in the revival and 'authentic' performance of early music, this aural mismatch is always a challenge. William Poel in his 1897 performance, which attempted to recover 'original' staging, commissioned Arnold Dolmetsch, the early music pioneer, to provide 'authentic' music, or to compose new in strictly Elizabethan style; the 1951 production at the Mermaid Theatre, London, again employed an early music specialist to supply the sound. But the toleration of anachronism, that during the nineteenth century allowed minutely accurate historical visual sets to be accompanied by a compost of music from the previous 150 years, still persists in the twenty-first century. Though we now achieve consistency by entrusting the music to a single composer, we are perfectly content for it to be an entirely modern soundscape. Music, therefore, becomes inescapably distinct from the onstage world, however powerfully it solicits the feelings and emotions of the audience.

We turn now to consider more specifically some of the crucial ways in which it may shape an audience's perception of, and response to, the play. The possibility of deploying musical motifs, identified with 'magic', or with individual characters, to bring together different moments in the play has already been noted. Music can also create larger patterns within the play as a whole. Guy Woolfenden provided for the 1978 production a short 'overture', a formal, marchlike fanfare whose ceremoniousness suggested the world of Italian courts from which the various characters came to Prospero's island. This fanfare was then picked up once more as a prelude to 'Honour, riches', in Act 4, and reintroduced as a play-out at the end. It suggested a world very different from the bleak island of the play's setting – and by its return at the end implied Prospero's triumph in recovering the dukedom of Milan. In the course of the performance, however, it was set against the haunting phrase which initiates Ariel's song, 'Come unto these yellow sands', and which itself recurred throughout the play, a signature, as it were, of the island world itself. This motif returned underneath Prospero's 'Ye elves' speech, where, like Wooldridge's earlier score, it softened the force of the magic which it symbolized.

Like Woolfenden, Orlando Gough 'framed' the play with a musical motif. But where, in 1978, music implied the world of Milan as the point of departure and return, in 2000 it was human breath which opened and closed the play, and a haunting brief setting of the phrase 'calm seas, auspicious gales' (5.1.315), sung over sustained dissonant chords, that foregrounded the island's mysteriousness and the dominance of the elements. Out of musical calm came the tempest at the play's opening, and as the island was folded up at the end, so it returned to this unearthly, lulling peace. It was a musical version of the return of the ship setting in Brook's 1957 performance. Stephen Oliver took a rather different direction in 1982, when the final play-out picked up the music of the Act 4 dance of nymphs and reapers. This jaunty, but graceful music had formed the climax of the triumphant setting of the masque, but, of course, had been fractured by Prospero's recollection of Caliban's conspiracy. Returning to it at the end seemed to affirm once more the optimistic possibility that the masque embodied, and to confirm Derek Jacobi's hard-won victory over his passions.

The masque and its dance obviously require music. In the text it is only the final song, 'Honour, riches, marriage-blessing' (4.1.106ff.), that must be set, and in almost all productions its ceremonious, ritual function is underlined by providing for it a chordal, hymnlike setting, a musical code readily recognizable to the audience. But in 2002 the male Ceres and Juno were given a baroque duet, which sat rather oddly with their camp, pantomime-dame appearance, and whose effect was undermined by the comic business which surrounded it – well sung though it was. Some productions have extended the musical accompaniment further. In 1978, 1998 and 2002 the words of Iris and Ceres were haloed with sound. In 1988 the musical score indicates that there was an intention to have the actors speak the preliminary dialogue rhythmically to the music. Its discordant, severe character, however, not only threatened to drown speech, but scarcely helped to create any atmosphere of celebration. In 1982, as has already been noted, Stephen Oliver set the whole masque (with some judicious cutting of the text) as a through-composed opera, with alternation of arioso and recitative leading to a triumphant trio for the goddesses. Over rushing, upward scales the voices rose to ecstatic climax. It was not surprising that the audience on the production video burst into applause at its end. The musical vocabulary was deliberately eclectic, hinting at Monteverdi, Purcell and the high baroque. David Nokes objected, calling it 'a glittering set-piece in the baroque manner of Purcell, which teeters on the brink of parody' (*TLS*). But that was precisely the finely calculated point. The self-conscious pastiche underlined and acknowledged the artificiality of the genre of the masque itself, and yet demanded that we be drawn emotionally into its celebration of marriage. Similarly, the anachronism of the 'baroque' dance music which followed acknowledged the fragility of the harmony it celebrated, even as its elegant jauntiness made one smile with pleasure and experience the masque's dissolution as a painful shock.

But in the play 'high art' music is contrasted with the 'low' music of Stephano, Caliban and Trinculo. Composers have had much less of a problem with finding an appropriate musical vocabulary for the latter. Almost always their songs have been unaccompanied, and, where settings are provided for Stephano's songs, or Caliban's song of freedom, they are of an emphatically rhythmic, vaguely 'folkish' kind. Often no setting survives – which suggests that Stephano in particular might be left to improvise his drunken airs. In 2002, in a nicely comic variation, onstage spirits anticipated the ends of some lines of Stephano's 'The master, the swabber, the boatswain and I' (2.2.45ff.), much to his bafflement. As we have seen, the song which ends 2.2, 'No more dams I'll make for fish', can build to a defiant assertion of freedom. Perhaps the most interesting of the 'low' songs is the catch which Caliban requests Stephano to sing at the end of 3.2. A 'catch' is a musical round, where the same music is taken up in succession by each singer. In *Twelfth Night* Feste, Andrew Aguecheek and Sir Toby Belch employ the same musical form to 'make the welkin dance' (2.3.58), and provoke the wrath of Malvolio. In both plays the close intertwining of voices seems an appropriate embodiment of a rebellious energy. Most composers have, indeed, provided a round – and most productions have given sufficient space for it to begin to develop some sense of momentum. The problem is how to bring it to an end. The text is not particularly clear, as Caliban's 'That's not the tune' (3.2.124) can be taken as a criticism of the performance of his compeers, or else as acknowledging the presence of Ariel taking over the music. In many productions Ariel does indeed lead the conspirators away with a variation on the tune of the catch itself, played on an instrument (pan pipes in 1982, the iconographically appropriate bagpipes in 2002) or, in 2000, taken over by the spirit chorus. But in 1988 there was a witty comic elaboration as, after the catch had been worked round a couple of times, Trinculo, standing apart, improvised a little descant in piping falsetto as the others continued with the round, provoking Caliban's 'That's not the tune'.

There is, obviously, much more variety in the setting of Ariel's songs. Until the final song, 'Where the bee sucks', Ariel is singing for a purpose, to manipulate characters at Prospero's behest. The songs therefore function not as direct expressions of his own 'personality', but as embodiments of the nature of the island itself. The first of them, 'Come unto these yellow sands' (1.2.376ff.), is a curious lyric, where the opening invitation is followed by the sound of dogs and of 'strutting Chanticleer'. The potential menace of the second half must be balanced against the summons of the first. In 1988 and again in 1998, where the dominant musical vocabulary was modernist, the astringency of the setting suggested perhaps more easily the strange threat than the warm invitation. In 1978, however, Woolfenden opened his setting with an unaccompanied flute playing the motif which began the song, a haunting phrase which, once heard, sticks in the mind. Ruby Wax movingly recalled how Ian Charleson, Woolfenden's singer, was 'lowered from the ceiling and he sang. For those few minutes he created something brilliant. For a year, every night the chills would go up my back' (57–8). But even in this setting, though the dogs were simply taped noises, 'cock a diddle dow' prompted an increasingly urgent vocal cadenza with aleatoric effects in the instruments, before order was restored by the return of the opening motif. The mood of 'Full fathom five' (1.2.397ff.) is more straightforward – Gough instructed his singers in 2000: 'Funky, dark and soothing'. Oliver with typical musical wit built his song over a ground bass, recalling Purcell's well-known songs of grief in *Dido and Aeneas*, though superimposing distinctly modern harmonies.

In all such fully composed songs the power that music may have can only be released by an Ariel who can really sing. In many productions over the centuries the songs have been performed by someone other than Ariel – and in 1946 the young David O'Brien was not called upon, since all the songs were pre-recorded by the BBC Singers. In 1988, I found myself that the exposure of Duncan Bell's vocal limitations in attempting Sams's difficult vocal writing was a continuous source of discomfort. For though the songs do not directly express Ariel's character, the actor is not helped in his portrayal if he cannot sing adequately, or if the music that is given him allows for little expressiveness. Ian Holm, in 1963, may have sung 'like a sergeant major' (*E. News*), but then it would seem that he had little chance with Leppard's settings, which required him to 'declaim ... after the style of Edith Sitwell in full fathom "Façade"' (*SA Herald*). Ian Charleson certainly could cope admirably with Woolfenden's songs; so well, indeed, that a recording was made at the time and sold in the theatre. But the warmth of the singing contrasted with his generally detached portrait of the character. And the same was true again in 1993 when the singing of the apogee of resentful Ariels, Simon Russell Beale, was 'a joy' (*D. Mail*). The disjunction between expressive singing and impassive presence struck Paul Taylor: 'only when he sings in a beautiful tenor does he seem to understand anything about human feeling' (*Independent*). Somehow we cannot help believing that a singer is in some way involved in the song itself; like Feste, he must 'take pleasure in singing' (*Twelfth Night*, 2.4.68).

One way of suggesting that Ariel is a 'disembodied' voice is to place the songs high in the tenor range, or else to employ falsetto. Perhaps influenced by Benjamin Britten's opera, *A Midsummer Night's Dream*, where the part of Oberon was written for a male alto, a number of composers have used the 'unnatural' quality of the falsetto for Ariel's songs. Kingsley in 1970, according to reviewers, sang in 'a childish, sexless chant' (*Times*), using 'a weird falsetto voice to some effect' (*Guardian*) (though Michael Tubbs recalled him as a high baritone). Rylance in 1982 sang at the top of the tenor range (alternative parts a minor third lower were provided for his understudy); in 1998 Scott Handy sang in 'a beautiful counter-tenor' (*E. Standard*); and in 2000 Gilz Terera also moved into a heady high alto – though his voice was generally surrounded by the voices of the spirits themselves, so that he was less an individual singing, more part of a collective vocal sound.

Only in Ariel's final song does he sing as himself. As he dresses Prospero in his ducal robes he sings his own song of freedom. There is a disjunction between the two activities which, one might argue, is purposeful – Ariel looks forward to a life of indolence even as he loads Prospero with the careful robes of office. But this awkward match of song and action has led, in a number of productions over the centuries, to a re-siting of the final song, often as an optimistic finale to the play. In 1982 at Stratford, where the uneasy relationship between Prospero and Ariel was to be highlighted at the end (see chapter 2), Ariel pointedly sang to himself, in a wiry duet with bassoon, leaving Prospero's robing to his attendant clones. On the transfer to Newcastle the song was moved to the beginning of Act 5, and recomposed in a rather more conventional style. Quite why this was felt necessary is not clear. In 1978 Woolfenden provided a lilting, 6/8 melody for Charleson's final song. But in many productions this paean to freedom is less than full-hearted. In 1995 it was half spoken, and the melancholy cor anglais emphasized Ariel's sadness at parting. In 2000 Gough gave extended melismata on 'fly', rather as in Arne's most famous of all settings of the song, but in a minor tonality which undermined any simple sense of release. In 2002 the difference of this final song was suggested by the way that, really for the first time, Ariel sang 'properly'. ('Come unto these yellow sands' was cut, and 'Full fathom five' delivered almost on a monotone.) The actor's voice was picked up electronically, so that each strain of the song was echoed, as it were, in the air. In 1998 Warbeck produced an interesting variation, as Scott Handy, whose earlier songs had been in the alto register, suddenly sang in his 'natural' baritone voice. If the music was wistful, rather than celebratory, the suggestion that, for the first time, Ariel could use his own voice was powerfully made, and then poignantly elaborated as Prospero briefly picked up the tune of 'Merrily, merrily' himself, before breaking his staff (see chapter 1).

Music, then, contributes in essential and powerful ways to the character – and to the success – of a production. It is, however, true that recent theatrical scores, unlike those of earlier periods, are so embedded in the particularity of the productions they serve that they are unlikely to have, as once they might, an independent life. Even when recordings are made (as in 1978 and 2000) and excellent though Woolfenden's and Gough's scores were, they seem mementos of a theatrical experience rather than free-standing objects. But this does not justify the neglect that has commonly overtaken the contribution of music to the history of productions. *The Tempest* is set upon a bare isle indeed without the noises, sounds and sweet airs which animate it.

PRODUCTION CREDITS AND CAST LISTS

Unless otherwise stated, all productions were staged at the Royal Shakespeare Theatre (known as the Shakespeare Memorial Theatre until 1961). The cast list follows the order of the First Folio – though the programmes for productions vary this order – but reflects, where distinctions are made, the categorizations of additional parts made in individual productions.

1946

Director	Eric Crozier
Designer	Paul Shelving
Music	Lennox Berkeley
Choreography	June Rouselle
ALONSO	James Raglan
SEBASTIAN	Myles Eason
PROSPERO	Robert Harris
ANTONIO	Paul Stephenson
FERDINAND	John Harrison
GONZALO	Christian Morrow
ADRIAN	Donald Sinden
FRANCISCO	Duncan Ross
CALIBAN	Julian Somers
TRINCULO	Hugh Griffith
STEPHANO	Robert Vernon
MASTER OF A SHIP	Antony Groser
BOATSWAIN	Patrick Ross
MIRANDA	Joy Parker
ARIEL	David O'Brien
IRIS	Muriel Davidson

CERES   Nancy Nevinson
JUNO   Jenifer Coverdale

MARINERS, NYMPHS, REAPERS:
William Avenell, Trevor Barker, Frances Brette, Pat Brewer, Eileen
Clark, Robin Griffin, David Hobman, Anthony Hooper, Pamela
Leatherland, Sulwen Morgan, Barbara Ormerod, Michael Rose, June
Rousselle, Leonard White

Number in company   32
Press night   20 April 1946

1947

Director	Norman Wright
Designer	Paul Shelving
Music	Lennox Berkeley

ALONSO	Paul Stephenson
SEBASTIAN	Donald Sinden
PROSPERO	Robert Harris
ANTONIO	William Avenell
FERDINAND	John Harrison
GONZALO	John Ruddock
ADRIAN	David Oxley
FRANCISCO	Julian Aymes
CALIBAN	John Blatchley
TRINCULO	Douglas Seale
STEPHANO	Duncan Ross
MASTER OF A SHIP	Leigh Crutchley
BOATSWAIN	Antony Groser
MIRANDA	Daphne Slater
ARIEL	Joy Parker
IRIS	Muriel Davidson
CERES	Irene Sutcliffe
JUNO	Margaret Courtenay

MARINERS, NYMPHS, REAPERS:
Anne Daniels, Elizabeth Ewbank, Margaret Godwin, David Hobman, Pamela Leatherland, Joanna Mackie, Lennard Pearce, John Randall, Herbert Roland, John Warner, Beryl Wright, Kenneth Wynne

Number in company	30
Press night	9 May 1947

1951

Director	Michael Benthall
Designer	Loudon Sainthill
Music	John Wooldridge
Choreography	Pauline Grant
ALONSO	Jack Gwillim
SEBASTIAN	William Squire
PROSPERO	Michael Redgrave
ANTONIO	William Fox
FERDINAND	Richard Burton
GONZALO	Geoffrey Bayldon
ADRIAN	Brendon Barry
FRANCISCO	Alan Townsend
CALIBAN	Hugh Griffith
TRINCULO	Michael Gwynn
STEPHANO	Alexander Gauge
MASTER OF A SHIP	David Orr
BOATSWAIN	Duncan Lamont
MIRANDA	Hazel Penwarden
ARIEL	Alan Badel
IRIS	Heather Stannard
CERES	Rachel Roberts
JUNO	Barbara Jefford
MARINERS	John Foster, Michael Hayes, James Moss

SHAPES:
Ian Bannen, Leo Ciceri, Keith Faulkner, Ralph Hallett, Timothy
Harley, Clifford Parrish, Robert Sandford, Kenneth Wynne

WATER NYMPHS:
Wendy Barker, Karen Beattie, Mary Chester, Eileen Elton, Christine
Hearne, Patricia Kerry, June Konopasek, Audrey Seed, Sybil Williams

Number in company	38
Press night	26 June 1951

1952

Director	Michael Benthall
Designer	Loudon Sainthill
Music	John Wooldridge
Choreography	Pauline Grant

ALONSO	Jack Gwillim
SEBASTIAN	David Dodimead
PROSPERO	Ralph Richardson
ANTONIO	Ronald Hines
FERDINAND	Alexander Davion
GONZALO	Raymond Westwell
ADRIAN	Brendon Barry (Eric Evans from 22 September)
FRANCISCO	Alan Townsend
CALIBAN	Michael Hordern
TRINCULO	Michael Bates
STEPHANO	Lyn Evans (Brendon Barry from 22 September)
MASTER OF A SHIP	John Turner
BOATSWAIN	Mervyn Blake
MIRANDA	Zena Walker
ARIEL	Margaret Leighton
IRIS	Alison Petrie (Jill Showell from 23 June)
CERES	Margaret Chisholm
JUNO	Veronica Wells

MARINERS:
William Peacock, James Vowden (until 5 June), John Nettleton (from 5 June), Jerome Willis

SHAPES:
Ian Bannen, Eric Evans (until 22 September), Michael Hayes, Derek Hodgson, Charles Howard, Peter Johnson, Richard Martin, Thomas Moore, Kenneth Wynne (from 22 September)

WATER NYMPHS:
Jocelyn Britton, Mary Chester, Hilary Hardiman, Patricia Salonika, Monica Kirton, Phyllida Porter, Maureen Quinney, Audrey Seed, Jill Showell, Judy Storm

Number in company	39
Press night	25 March 1952

1957

Director	Peter Brook
Designer	Peter Brook
Music	Peter Brook
Choreography	Raimonda Orselli

ALONSO	Robert Harris
SEBASTIAN	Robin Lloyd
PROSPERO	John Gielgud
ANTONIO	Mark Dignam
FERDINAND	Richard Johnson
GONZALO	Cyril Luckham
ADRIAN	Toby Robertson
CALIBAN	Alec Clunes
TRINCULO	Clive Revill
STEPHANO	Patrick Wymark
MASTER OF A SHIP	Peter Palmer
BOATSWAIN	Ron Haddrick
MIRANDA	Doreen Aris
ARIEL	Brian Bedford
IRIS	Jane Wenham
CERES	Stephanie Bidmead
JUNO	Joan Miller

MARINERS, NYMPHS, REAPERS:
Robert Arnold, Eileen Atkins, Thane Bettany, Antony Brown, Edward Caddick, Simon Carter, John Davidson, Henry Davies, Mavis Edwards, William Elmhirst, Elizabeth Evans, Kenneth Gilbert, Julian Glover, John Grayson, Derek Mayhe, Norman Miller, Rex Robinson, John Salway, John Murray Scott, Gordon Souter, Roy Spencer, Pamela Taylor, Barry Warren, Gordon Wright

Number in company	41
Press night	13 August 1957
London venue	Theatre Royal, Drury Lane, 5 December 1957

1963

Directors	Clifford Williams, Peter Brook
Designer	Farrah
Music	Raymond Leppard

ALONSO	John Welsh
SEBASTIAN	Donald Sinden
PROSPERO	Tom Fleming
ANTONIO	Nicholas Selby
FERDINAND	Ian McCulloch
GONZALO	Ken Wynne
ADRIAN	John Corvin
FRANCISCO	Roy Marsden
CALIBAN	Roy Dotrice
TRINCULO	David Warner
STEPHANO	Derek Smith
MASTER OF A SHIP	Marshall Jones
BOATSWAIN	Brian Jackson
MIRANDA	Philippa Urquhart
ARIEL	Ian Holm
IRIS	Janet Suzman
CERES	Cherry Morris
JUNO	Susan Engel

MARINERS, NYMPHS, REAPERS:
Barbara Barnett, Shaun Curry, Valerie Cutts, Peter Geddis, Brian Harrison, James Hunter, Robert Jennings, Penelope Keith, Henry Knowles, Caroline Maud, Rhys McConnochie, Tim Wylton

Number in company	30
Press night	2 April 1963

1970

Director	John Barton
Designer	Christopher Morley, Ann Curtis
Music	Ben Kingsley, members of the cast
Lighting	John Bradley

ALONSO	Patrick Barr
SEBASTIAN	Clement McCallin
PROSPERO	Ian Richardson
ANTONIO	William Russell
FERDINAND	Christopher Gable
GONZALO	Philip Locke
CALIBAN	Barry Stanton
TRINCULO	Norman Rodway
STEPHANO	Patrick Stewart
MASTER OF A SHIP	Hugh Keays Byrne
MIRANDA	Estelle Kohler
ARIEL	Ben Kingsley
IRIS	John York
CERES	Alan Howard
JUNO	Terence Taplin
LORDS	Terence Taplin, John York
SPIRIT	Hugh Keays Byrne

Number in company	14
Press night	15 October 1970

1974

Director	Keith Hack
Designer	Debbie Sharp, Keith Hack
Music	Stephen Oliver
Lighting	John Watts
ALONSO	Dan Meaden
SEBASTIAN	James Aubrey
PROSPERO	Michael Aldridge
ANTONIO	Jonathan Kent
FERDINAND	Michael Pennington
GONZALO	Richard Griffiths
CALIBAN	Jeffrey Kissoon
TRINCULO	Ian McDiarmid
STEPHANO	James Booth
MIRANDA	Debbie Bowen
ARIEL	Robert Lloyd
Number in company	11
Press night	22 October 1974
Stratford venue	The Other Place

1978

Director	Clifford Williams
Designer	Ralph Koltai
Music	Guy Woolfenden
Lighting	Leo Leibovici

ALONSO	Dennis Edwards
SEBASTIAN	Donald Douglas
PROSPERO	Michael Hordern
ANTONIO	Paul Brooke
FERDINAND	Alan Rickman
GONZALO	Raymond Westwell
ADRIAN	James Griffin
FRANCISCO	Paul Webster
CALIBAN	David Suchet
TRINCULO	Richard Griffiths
STEPHANO	Paul Moriarty
MASTER OF A SHIP	Conrad Asquith
BOATSWAIN	George Raistrick
MIRANDA	Sheridan Fitzgerald
ARIEL	Ian Charleson
IRIS	Catherine Riding (replaced very early by Susanna Bishop)
CERES	Carmen DuSautoy
JUNO	Darlene Johnson

SPIRITS:

Alan Barker, Susanna Bishop (replaced by Juliet Stevenson), Bill Buffery, Avril Carson, Ian Reddington, Ruby Wax

Number in company	24
Press night	2 May 1978

1982

Director	Ron Daniels
Designer	Maria Bjornson
Music	Stephen Oliver
Lighting	Richard Riddell
Choreography	David Toguri

ALONSO	Paul Webster
SEBASTIAN	Jeffery Dench
PROSPERO	Derek Jacobi
ANTONIO	Robert O'Mahoney
FERDINAND	Michael Maloney
GONZALO	Edward Jewesbury
ADRIAN	William Haden
FRANCISCO	Raymond Llewellyn
CALIBAN	Bob Peck
TRINCULO	Alun Armstrong
STEPHANO	Christopher Benjamin
MASTER OF A SHIP	Raymond Llewellyn
BOATSWAIN	Niall Padden
MIRANDA	Alice Krige
ARIEL	Mark Rylance
IRIS	Angela Kazimierczuk
CERES	Christine Botes
JUNO	Theresa Lister

MARINERS, SPIRITS:
Robert Clare, Cathy Finlay, James Gaddas, Tom Mannion, Lesley Sharp, Josette Simon

Number in company	23
Press night	12 August 1982
Transfer	Newcastle, Theatre Royal, 1 March 1983
	London, Barbican Theatre, 13 September 1983
Video recording	22 January 1983 (evening)

1988

Director	Nicholas Hytner
Designer	David Fielding
Music	Jeremy Sams
Lighting	Mark Henderson
Staging of masques	Martin Duncan

ALONSO	Nicholas Selby
SEBASTIAN	Colin McCormack
PROSPERO	John Wood
ANTONIO	Richard Haddon Haines
FERDINAND	James Purefoy
GONZALO	Alfred Burke
ADRIAN	Stephen Jacobs
FRANCISCO	Patrick Miller
CALIBAN	John Kane
TRINCULO	Desmond Barrit
STEPHANO	Campbell Morrison
MASTER OF A SHIP	Peter Lennon
BOATSWAIN	Ken Shorter
MIRANDA	Melanie Thaw
ARIEL	Duncan Bell
IRIS	Vivienne Rochester
CERES	Cate Hamer
JUNO	Julia Lintott

MARINERS/SPIRITS:
Stephen Gordon, Paul Hargreaves, Stephen Jacobs, Peter Lennon,
Patrick Miller, Heather Osborne, Joanna Roth, Ken Shorter

SPIRITS:
Sharon Buchanan, Stephanie Hallworth, Sarah Hamilton, Jemma
Hicks, Hannah Langley, Sian Lewis

Number in company	28
Press night	27 July 1988
Transfers	Newcastle, Theatre Royal, 14 March 1989
	London, Barbican Theatre, 25 May 1989
Video recording	1 January 1989

1993

Director	Sam Mendes
Designer	Anthony Ward
Music	Shaun Davey
Lighting	Paul Pyant
Movement	Terry John Bates
Illusions	Paul Kieve
ALONSO	Paul Greenwood
SEBASTIAN	Christopher Hunter
PROSPERO	Alec McCowen
ANTONIO	James Hayes
FERDINAND	Mark Lewis Jones
GONZALO	Clifford Rose
ADRIAN	David Birrell
FRANCISCO	Richard Clothier
CALIBAN	David Troughton
TRINCULO	David Bradley
STEPHANO	Mark Lockyer
MASTER OF A SHIP	Christopher Robbie
BOATSWAIN	Mike Burnside
MIRANDA	Sarah Woodward
ARIEL	Simon Russell Beale
IRIS	Sian Radinger
CERES	Johanna Benyon
JUNO	Virginia Grainger
SPIRITS	Peter Grimes, Sean Hannaway, Robin Pratt, Sarah Weymouth
Number in company	22
Press night	12 August 1993
Transfers	Newcastle, Theatre Royal, 1 March 1994
	London, Barbican Theatre, 13 July 1994
Video recording	1 January 1994

1995

Director	David Thacker
Designer	Shelagh Keegan
Music	Adrian Johnston
Lighting	Alan Burrett
Movement	Lesley Hutchison

ALONSO	David Weston
SEBASTIAN	Stephen Hattersley
PROSPERO	Paul Jesson
ANTONIO	Daniel Flynn
FERDINAND	David Fahm
GONZALO	Ken Farrington
ADRIANA	Romy Baskerville
CALIBAN	Dominic Letts
TRINCULO	Jeremy Brook
STEPHANO	Ian Driver
BOATSWAIN	Sekai Matimba
MIRANDA	Sarah-Jane Holm
ARIEL	Bonnie Engstrom
MARINERS	Sarah Ball, Helen Blatch, Jeremy Brook, Ian Driver
SPIRITS	Sarah Ball, Helen Blatch, Sekai Matimba

Number in company	15
London venue	The Young Vic
Press night	29 June 1995
Transfer	Stratford, Swan Theatre, 25 July 1995
Tour	National, September 1995–February 1996
Video recording	18 August 1995

1998

Director	Adrian Noble
Designer	Anthony Ward
Music	Stephen Warbeck
Lighting	Howard Harrison
Movement	Ian Spink

ALONSO	Colin George
SEBASTIAN	John Straiton
PROSPERO	David Calder
ANTONIO	David Henry
FERDINAND	Evroy Deer
GONZALO	Alfred Burke
ADRIAN	Rowan McCallum
FRANCISCO	Simon Scardifield
CALIBAN	Robert Glenister
TRINCULO	Adrian Schiller
STEPHANO	Barry Stanton
MASTER OF A SHIP	Jason Baughan
BOATSWAIN	Malcolm Scates
MIRANDA	Penny Layden
ARIEL	Scott Handy
IRIS	Simon Scardifield
JUNO	Lisa Reeves

SPIRITS:
Paul Popplewell, Lisa Reeves, Darren Strange, Alexandra Sumner, Andrew Ufondu

Number in company	20
Press night	25 February 1998
Transfer	Newcastle, Theatre Royal, 6 October 1998
	London, Barbican Theatre, 5 January 1999
Video recording	25 June 1998

2000

Director	James MacDonald
Designer/Video	Jeremy Herbert
Projections	
Costume Designer	Kandis Cook
Music	Orlando Gough
Lighting	Nigel Edwards
Choreography	Peter Darling
ALONSO	Paul McCleary
SEBASTIAN	Antony Byrne
PROSPERO	Philip Voss
ANTONIO	Nicholas Day
FERDINAND	Oliver Dimsdale
GONZALO	Robert Langdon Lloyd
ADRIAN	Ben Casey
CALIBAN	Zubin Varla
TRINCULO	Julian Kerridge
STEPHANO	James Saxon
MASTER OF A SHIP	Thomas Aaron
BOATSWAIN	Michael O'Connor
MIRANDA	Nikki Amuka-Bird
ARIEL	Gilz Terera
IRIS	Hazel Holder
CERES	Gilz Terera
JUNO	Sarah Quist

SPIRITS/MUSICIANS:
Thomas Aaron, Matthew Bailey, Barbara Gellhorn, Hazel Holder,
Michael O'Connor, Sarah Quist

Number in company	18
London venue	Barbican (The Pit), 1 November 2000
Press night	19 January 2001 (Leisure Centre, Macclesfield)
Transfer	Stratford, The Other Place, 30 November 2000
Tour	National and International, November 2000– June 2001
Video recording	13 January 2000

2002

Director	Michael Boyd
Designer	Tom Piper
Music	Craig Armstrong, John Woolf
Lighting	Tina MacHugh
Movement	Liz Ranken
Aerial Choreography	Gavin Marshall
Fights	Terry King
ALONSO	Keith Bartlett
SEBASTIAN	Tom Beard
PROSPERO	Malcolm Storry
ANTONIO	Brian Protheroe
FERDINAND	Alan Turkington
GONZALO	Jerome Willis
ADRIAN	Dylan Charles
FRANCISCO	James Garnon
CALIBAN	Geff Francis
TRINCULO	Simon Gregor
STEPHANO	Roger Frost
MASTER OF A SHIP	James Staddon
BOATSWAIN	James Telfer
MIRANDA	Sirine Saba
ARIEL	Kananu Kirimi
IRIS	Kananu Kirimi
CERES	James Telfer
JUNO	James Staddon

MARINERS AND SPIRITS:
Dan Crute, Gracy G. Goldman, James Hyland, Fiona Lait,
Jami Quarrell

Number in company	20
London venue	The Roundhouse
Press night	7 May 2002
Stratford venue	RST, 12 September 2002

REVIEWS CITED

1946

Birmingham Mail, 22 April 1946, S.
Birmingham Post, 22 April 1946, T.C. Kemp
Birmingham Sunday Mercury, 21 April 1946, W.H. Bush
Daily Herald, 22 April 1947, P.L. Mannock
Daily Telegraph, 22 April 1947, W.A. Darlington
Manchester Guardian, 22 April 1946, G.P.
News of the World, 21 April 1946
Observer, 21 April 1946
Times, 22 April 1946

1947

Birmingham Mail, 10 May 1947, O.L.W.
Shakespeare Survey, 1 (1948), 109, H.S. Bennett and George Rylands
Stage, 15 May 1947
Wolverhampton Express and Star, 10 May 1947, C.J.

1951

Birmingham Post, 27 June 1951, T.C. Kemp
Daily Telegraph, 27 June 1951, Reginald P.M. Gibbs
Daily Worker, 29 June 1951
Leamington Spa Courier, 29 June 1951
Manchester Guardian, 27 June 1951, G.P.
New Statesman, 7 July 1951, T.C. Worsley
Scotsman, 28 June 1951
Shakespeare Quarterly, 2 (1951), 335–6, Alice Venezky
Spectator, 29 June 1951, Peter Fleming
Stage, 29 June 1951

Stratford-upon-Avon Herald, 29 June 1951, Ruth Ellis
Theatre, 1 July 1951, Harold Hobson
Times, 27 June 1951

1952

Daily Telegraph, 26 March 1952, W.A. Darlington
Daily Worker, 29 March 1952, Hugh Philips
Evening Standard, 26 March 1952, Harold Conway
Manchester Guardian, 26 March 1952, Philip Hope-Wallace
News Chronicle, 26 March 1952, Alan Dent
Observer, 30 March 1952, Ivor Brown
Sketch, 29 April 1952, J.C. Trewin
Spectator, 28 March 1952, Peter Fleming
Stage, 26 March 1952, J.C. Trewin
Time and Tide, 5 April 1952, Philip Hope-Wallace
Times, 26 March 1952

1957

Birmingham Evening Despatch, 14 August 1957, Neville Gaffin
Birmingham Mail, 14 August 1957, W.H.W.
Birmingham Post, 21 August 1957, J.C. Trewin
Bolton Evening News, 17 August 1957, John Wardle
Daily Express, 14 August 1957, John Barber (interview with Brook and review)
Daily Mail, 14 August 1957, C.W.
Daily Telegraph, 14 August 1957, W.A. Darlington
Evening News, 14 August 1957, Felix Barker
Evening Standard, 14 August 1957, Milton Shulman
Financial Times, 6 December 1957, Derek Granger (London transfer)
Leamington Spa Courier, 16 August 1957, N.T.
Liverpool Daily Post, 14 August 1957, S.J.
Manchester Guardian, 15 August 1957, Philip Hope-Wallace
Morning Advertiser, 24 August 1957, Geoffrey Tarran
New Statesman, 24 August 1957, T.C. Worsley
Nottingham Guardian, 14 August 1957, W.T.
Observer, 18 August 1957, K[enneth] T[ynan]
Oxford Mail, 14 August 1957, A.O.

Oxford Times, 16 August 1957, F.W. D[arlington]
Punch, 21 August 1957
Shakespeare Quarterly, 8 (1957), 488–92, Muriel St Clare Byrne
Shakespeare Survey, 11 (1958), 134–5, Roy Walker
Stage, 15 August 1957, R.B.M.
Star, 14 August 1957, Robert Wainwright
Sunday Times, 18 August 1957, Harold Hobson
Times, 14 August 1957
Yorkshire Post, 14 August 1957, Desmond Pratt

1963

Birmingham Post, 3 April 1963, J.C. Trewin
Daily Mail, 3 April 1963, Bernard Levin
Daily Sketch, 3 April 1963, Denis Blewett
Daily Worker, 4 April 1963, M.A.
Evening News, 3 April 1963, Colin Frame
Evening Standard, 3 April 1963, J.W.M. Thompson
Financial Times, 3 April 1963, John Higgins
Manchester Guardian, 3 April 1963, Philip Hope-Wallace
News Daily, 7 April 1963, John Percival
Oxford Mail, 3 April 1963, Don Chapman
Scotsman, 4 April 1963, Conrad Wilson
Shakespeare Quarterly, 14 (1963), 423–5, Robert Speaight
Stratford-upon-Avon Herald, 5 April 1963, Edmund Gardner
Sunday Telegraph, 7 April 1963, Alan Brien
Sunday Times, 7 April 1963, J.W. Lambert

1970

Birmingham Evening Mail, 16 October 1970, W.H.W.
Birmingham Post, 16 October 1970, J.C. Trewin
Daily Telegraph, 16 October 1970, John Barber
Guardian, 16 October 1970, Philip Hope-Wallace
Listener, 22 October 1970, D.A.N. Jones
New Statesman, 23 October 1970, Benedict Nightingale
Observer, 18 October 1970, Ronald Bryden
Times, 17 October 1970, John Higgins

1974

Coventry Evening Telegraph, 23 October 1974, N.K.W.
Daily Telegraph, 23 October 1974, Eric Shorter
Evesham Journal, 31 October 1974, V.J.D.
Oxford Mail, 23 October 1974, Don Chapman
Stratford-upon-Avon Herald, 25 October 1974, Sheila Bannock
Times, 24 October 1974, Charles Lewson

1978

Cahiers Elisabéthains, 13 (1978), 104–6, John W. Velz
Daily Telegraph, 3 May 1978, John Barber
Evening News, 3 May 1978, Caren Meyer
Financial Times, 3 May 1978, B.A. Young
Glasgow Herald, 5 May 1978, Anne Donaldson
Guardian, 15 May 1978, Michael Billington
Morning Star, 5 May 1978, Gordon Parsons
New Statesman, 5 May 1978
Observer, 7 May 1978, Robert Cushman
Oxford Mail, 3 May 1978, Don Chapman
Shakespeare Survey, 32 (1979), 202–4, Roger Warren
Spectator, 20 May 1970, Germaine Greer
Stratford-upon-Avon Herald, 5 May 1978, Gareth Lloyd Evans
Sunday Times, 7 May 1978, Bernard Levin
Times, 3 May 1978, Irving Wardle
Yorkshire Post, 4 May 1978, Desmond Pratt

1982

Cahiers Elisabéthains, 22 (1982), 116–17, J. Fuzier and J.-M. Maguin
Daily Mail, 14 September 1983, Jack Tinker (London transfer)
Financial Times, 13 August 1982, Michael Coveney
Guardian, 12 August 1982, Michael Billington
Guardian, 14 September 1983, Michael Billington (London transfer)
Kidderminster Shuttle, 20 August 1982, P.B.
Leamington Morning News, 13 August 1982, Sue Law
Mail on Sunday, 18 September 1983, Paul Vallely (London transfer)
New Statesman, 20 August 1982, Christopher Edwards

Observer, 15 August 1982, Robert Cushman
Oxford Mail, 12 August 1982, Don Chapman
Scotsman, 14 August 1982, Judith Cook
Shakespeare Quarterly, 34 (1983), 85–7, Roger Warren
Shakespeare Survey, 36 (1983), 154–5, Nicholas Shrimpton
Times, 13 August 1982, Ned Chaillet
Times, 14 September 1983, Irving Wardle (London transfer)
Times Literary Supplement, 3 September 1982, David Nokes
Yorkshire Post, 12 August 1982, Desmond Pratt

1988

Cahiers Elisabéthains, 34 (1988), 103–5, Jean-Marie Maguin
Daily Mail, 26 May 1989, Jack Tinker (London transfer)
Daily Telegraph, 29 July 1988, Eric Shorter
Financial Times, 28 July 1988, Michael Coveney
Financial Times, 27 May 1989, Martin Hoyle (London transfer)
Guardian, 29 July 1988, Michael Billington
Guardian, 29 May 1989, Michael Billington (London transfer)
Independent, 1 August 1988, Alex Renton
International Herald Tribune, 3 August 1988, Benedict Nightingale
Observer, 31 July 1988, Kate Kellaway
Punch, 12 August 1988, Benedict Nightingale
Shakespeare Bulletin, January/February, 1989, 9–10, Michael J. Collins
Shakespeare Bulletin, January/February, 1989, 11,Virginia M. Vaughan
Shakespeare Quarterly, 40 (1989), 85–7, Robert Smallwood
Shakespeare Survey, 42 (1990), 147–8, Stanley Wells
Sunday Express, 28 May 1989 (London transfer)
Sunday Telegraph, 31 July 1988, Francis King
Sunday Times, 31 July 1988, John Peter
Times, 28 July 1988, Jeremy Kingston
Times, 27 May 1989, Irving Wardle (London transfer)
What's On, 31 May 1989, Dominic Gray (London transfer)

1993

Cahiers Elisabéthains, 44 (1993), 95–7, Angela Maguin
Daily Express, 12 August 1993, Maureen Paton
Daily Mail, 13 August 1993

Daily Telegraph, 16 August 1993, Charles Spencer
Financial Times, 15 July 1994, Alistair Macaulay (London transfer)
Guardian, 13 August 1993, Michael Billington
Hampstead and Highgate Express, 8 July 1993
Independent, 13 August 1993, Paul Taylor
Independent on Sunday, 15 August 1993, Irving Wardle
Observer, 15 August 1993, Kate Kellaway
Observer, 17 July 1994, Andrew Billen (London transfer)
Shakespeare Bulletin, Winter 1994, 13, Barbara Stuart Farley
Shakespeare Quarterly, 45 (1994), 343–5, Russell Jackson
Spectator, 23 July 1994, Sheridan Morley (London transfer)
Stage, 26 August 1993, Ann Fitzgerald
Sunday Times, 15 August 1993, John Peter
Times, 13 August 1993, Benedict Nightingale
Times, 15 July 1994, Benedict Nightingale (London transfer)
What's On, 18 August 1993, Carole Woods

1995

Cahiers Elisabéthains, 48 (1995), 102–3, Peter J. Smith
Evesham Journal, 10 August 1995
Guardian, 1 July 1995, Michael Billington
Independent, 3 July 1995, Paul Taylor
Plays International, August 1995, Martin Esslin
Shakespeare Quarterly, 47 (1996), 319–21, Russell Jackson
Stratford-upon-Avon Herald, 3 August 1995, Paul Lapworth
Time Out, 5 July 1995
Times, 1 July 1995, Benedict Nightingale
Times Literary Supplement, 28 July 1995, Emily Wilson

1998

Birmingham Post, 26 February 1998, Terry Grimley
Cahiers Elisabéthains, 54 (1998), 123–5, Peter J. Smith
Daily Telegraph, 2 March 1998, Charles Spencer
Evening Standard, 26 February 1998, Nicholas de Jongh
Financial Times, 28 February 1998, Alistair Macaulay
Guardian, 27 February 1998, Michael Billington
Independent on Sunday, 1 March 1998, Kate Bassett

Shakespeare Quarterly, 50 (1999), 196–9, Russell Jackson
Shakespeare Survey, 53 (1999), 237–40, Robert Smallwood
Sunday Telegraph, 1 March 1998, Peter Fleming
Times, 27 February 1998, Benedict Nightingale

2000

Cahiers Elisabéthains, 59 (2001), 106–8, Peter J. Smith
Daily Express, 26 January 2001, Robert Gore-Langton
Daily Telegraph, 22 January 2001, Charles Spencer
Evening Standard, 2 November 2000, Patrick Marmion
Evening Standard, 24 January 2001, Rachel Halliburton
Financial Times, 23 January 2001, Ian Shuttleworth
Guardian, 20 January 2001, Lynn Gardner
Independent, 23 January 2001, Paul Taylor
Independent on Sunday, 21 January 2001, Kate Bassett
Mail on Sunday, 21 January 2001, Georgina Brown
Observer, 28 January 2001, Susannah Clapp
Shakespeare Quarterly, 52 (2001), 113–14, Russell Jackson
Sunday Times, 28 January 2001, John Peter
Time Out, 8 November 2000, Andrew Aldridge
Times, 20 January 2001, Benedict Nightingale
What's On, 8 November 2000, Roger Foss

2002

(All reviews are of the Roundhouse opening.)

Daily Telegraph, 9 May 2002, Charles Spencer
Evening Standard, 8 May 2002, Nicholas de Jongh
Guardian, 8 May 2002, Michael Billington
Independent, 13 May 2002, Paul Taylor
Time Out, 22 May 2002, Dominic Maxwell
Times, 9 May 2002, Benedict Nightingale

ABBREVIATIONS

Birm. E. Desp.	*Birmingham Evening Despatch*
Birm. E. Mail	*Birmingham Evening Mail*
Birm. E. Mer.	*Birmingham Evening Mercury*
Birm. Mail	*Birmingham Mail*
Birm. Post	*Birmingham Post*
Birm. Sun. Mer.	*Birmingham Sunday Mercury*
Bolton E. News	*Bolton Evening News*
Cahiers Elis.	*Cahiers Elisabéthains*
Coventry E. Tel.	*Coventry Evening Telegraph*
D. Express	*Daily Express*
D. Herald	*Daily Herald*
D. Mail	*Daily Mail*
D. Sketch	*Daily Sketch*
D. Telegraph	*Daily Telegraph*
E. News	*Evening News*
E. Standard	*Evening Standard*
Evesham J.	*Evesham Journal*
FT	*Financial Times*
Glasgow Her.	*Glasgow Herald*
Indep. Sun.	*Independent on Sunday*
Int. Her. Trib.	*International Herald Tribune*
Leam. Spa Cour.	*Leamington Spa Courier*
Liv. D. Post	*Liverpool Daily Post*
Mail Sun.	*Mail on Sunday*
Man. Guardian	*Manchester Guardian*
Morn. Adv.	*Morning Advertiser*
New States.	*New Statesman*
News Chron.	*News Chronicle*
Oxf. Mail	*Oxford Mail*
Oxf. Times	*Oxford Times*

Plays Int.	*Plays International*
S. Telegraph	*Sunday Telegraph*
S. Times	*Sunday Times*
SA Herald	*Stratford-upon-Avon Herald*
SB	*Shakespeare Bulletin*
SQ	*Shakespeare Quarterly*
SS	*Shakespeare Survey*
Time & T.	*Time and Tide*
TLS	*Times Literary Supplement*
Wolverhampton E. & S.	*Wolverhampton Express and Star*
Yorks. Post	*Yorkshire Post*

BIBLIOGRAPHY

This bibliography lists all works cited in the text, others that have specific reference to the performance history of the play, and one or two of the major critical articles on the play. The collections of critical essays edited by Virginia and Alden T. Vaughan and by R.S. White provide a good sense of the character of current *Tempest* criticism.

EDITIONS

Clark, Sandra (ed.), John Dryden and William Davenant, *The Enchanted Island*, in *Shakespeare Made Fit* (London, 1997)

Dymkowski, Christine (ed.), *The Tempest*, Shakespeare in Production (Cambridge, 2000)

Gasper, P.A., *An Acting Edition of Shakespeare's The Tempest* (London, 1939)

Kean, Charles, *Shakespeare's Play of The Tempest Arranged for Representation at The Princess's Theatre* (London, 1857)

Lindley, David (ed.), *The Tempest*, New Cambridge Shakespeare (Cambridge, 2002)

Lindley, David (ed.), *Beerbohm Tree's 1904 Tempest* (http://www.leeds.ac.uk/english/staff/projects/treestempest/)

Orgel, Stephen (ed.), *The Tempest* (Oxford, 1987)

Oxberry, W. (ed.), *The Tempest ... as it is performed at the Theatres Royal* (London, 1823)

Vaughan, Virginia Mason and Alden T. Vaughan (eds), *The Tempest*, The Arden Shakespeare (London, 2000)

BOOKS AND ARTICLES

Addenbrooke, David, *The Royal Shakespeare Company: The Peter Hall Years* (London, 1974)

Barker Francis and Peter Hulme, 'Nymphs and reapers heavily vanish: the discursive contexts of *The Tempest*', in John Drakakis (ed.), *Alternative Shakespeares* (London, 1985)

Bate, Jonathan, 'Caliban and Ariel write back', *Shakespeare Survey*, 48 (1995), 155–62

Bate, Jonathan and Russell Jackson (eds), *The Oxford Illustrated History of Shakespeare on Stage* (Oxford, 1996)

Berry, Ralph, *Shakespeare in Performance* (London, 1993)

Brook, Peter, *There Are No Secrets* (London, 1993)

Broomhead, A, '"A most majestic vision and harmonious charmingly"': *The Tempest* in the Modern Theatre, with Particular Reference to Sam Mendes's 1993 RSC Production', unpublished M.A. dissertation, Shakespeare Institute, 1994

Cholij, Irena, '"A thousand twangling instruments": music and *The Tempest* on the eighteenth-century London stage', *Shakespeare Survey*, 51 (1998), 79–94

Cook, Judith, *Shakespeare's Players* (London, 1983)

Dobson, Michael, '"Remember / First to possess his books": the appropriation of *The Tempest*, 1700–1800', *Shakespeare Survey*, 43 (1991), 99–108

Dobson, Michael, *The Making of the National Poet: Shakespeare, Adaptation, and Authorship, 1660–1769* (Oxford, 1992)

Ferris, Paul, *Richard Burton* (London, 1981)

Findlater, Richard, *Michael Redgrave: Actor* (London, 1956)

Gielgud, John, *An Actor and His Time* (in collaboration with John Miller and John Powell) (London, 1979)

Gielgud, John, with John Miller, *Acting Shakespeare* (London, 1997)

Griffiths, Trevor R., '"This island's mine": Caliban and colonialism', *The Yearbook of English Studies*, 13 (1983), 159–80

Gurr, Andrew, '*The Tempest*'s tempest at Blackfriars', *Shakespeare Survey*, 41 (1989), 91–102

Hamilton, Donna B., *Virgil and The Tempest: The Politics of Imitation* (Columbus, Oh., 1990)

Hawkes, Terence (ed.), *Coleridge on Shakespeare* (Harmondsworth, 1969)

Hayman, Robert, *John Gielgud* (London, 1971)

Hirst, David L., *The Tempest: Text and Performance* (London, 1984)

Holland, Peter, *English Shakespeares* (Cambridge, 1997)

Hordern, Michael, with Patricia England, *A World Elsewhere* (London, 1993)

Hulme, Peter, *Colonial Encounters* (London, 1986)

Jackson, Russell, 'Actor managers and the spectacular', in Jonathan Bate and Russell Jackson (eds), *The Oxford Illustrated History of Shakespeare on Stage* (Oxford, 1996), 112–27

James, Heather, *Shakespeare's Troy: Drama, Politics and the Translation of Empire* (Cambridge, 1997)

Kennedy, Dennis (ed.), *Foreign Shakespeare* (Cambridge, 1993)

Kennedy, Dennis, *Looking at Shakespeare* (Cambridge, 1993)

Lewis, Peter, interview with Alec McCowen, *Sunday Telegraph*, 8 August 1993

Lindley, David, 'Music, masque and meaning in *The Tempest*', in D. Lindley (ed.), *The Court Masque* (Manchester, 1984), 47–59

Lindley, David, 'Tempestuous transformations', in Shirley Chew and Alistair Stead (eds), *Translating Life: Studies in Transpositional Aesthetics* (Liverpool, 1999), 99–121

Mannoni, Octave, *Prospero and Caliban: The Psychology of Colonisation*, trans. Pamela Powesland (Ann Arbor, Mich., 1990)

Maus, Katharine Eisaman, 'Arcadia lost: politics and revision in the Restoration *Tempest*', *Renaissance Drama*, 13 (1982), 189–209

Miller, Jonathan, *Subsequent Performances* (London, 1986)

Miola, Robert S., *Shakespeare and Classical Comedy: The Influence of Plautus and Terence* (Oxford, 1994)

Miola, Robert S., *Shakespeare's Reading* (Oxford, 2000)

Morley, Sheridan, *John G: The Authorised Biography of John Gielgud* (London, 2001)

Mowat, Barbara, 'Prospero, Agrippa, and hocus pocus', *English Literary Renaissance*, 11 (1981), 281–303

Nilan, Mary M., '*The Tempest* at the turn of the century: cross-currents in production', *Shakespeare Survey*, 25 (1972), 113–23

Nilan, Mary M., 'Shakespeare illustrated: Charles Kean's 1857 production of *The Tempest*', *Shakespeare Quarterly*, 26 (1975), 196–204

Nixon, Rob, 'Caribbean and African appropriations of *The Tempest*', *Critical Inquiry*, 13 (1987), 557–78

O'Connor, Marion, *William Poel and the Elizabethan Stage Society* (Cambridge, 1987)

Orgel, Stephen, *The Illusion of Power: Political Theater in the English Renaissance* (Chicago, Il. 1975)

Orgel, Stephen, 'Prospero's wife', in Margaret W. Ferguson, Maureen Quilligan and Nancy J. Vickers (eds), *Rewriting the Renaissance: The Discourses of Sexual Difference in Early Modern Europe* (Chicago, Il. and London, 1986), 50–64

Pearce, Brian, 'Beerbohm Tree's production of *The Tempest*, 1904', *New Theatre Quarterly*, 11 (1995), 299–308

Redgrave, Michael, *The Actor's Ways and Means* (London, 1953)

Sales, Roger (ed.), *Shakespeare in Perspective*, vol. 1 (London, 1982)

Sinden, Donald, *A Touch of the Memoirs* (London, 1982)

Sinden, Donald, *Laughter in the Second Act* (London, 1985)

Skura, Meredith Anne, 'Discourse and the individual: the case of colonialism in *The Tempest*', *Shakespeare Quarterly*, 40 (1989), 42–69

Smallwood, Robert, 'Directors' Shakespeare', in Jonathan Bate and Russell
    Jackson (eds), *The Oxford Illustrated History of Shakespeare on Stage*
    (Oxford, 1996), 176–96

Spevack, Marvin, *A Complete and Systematic Concordance to the Works of
    Shakespeare*, 9 vols (Hildesheim, 1968–90)

Suchet, David, 'Caliban', in Philip Brockbank (ed.), *Players of Shakespeare,*
    1 (Cambridge, 1989), 167–79

Symon, Roz, 'Shakespeare's Love of Ambiguity: Readings of *The Tempest* on
    Page and Stage, 1970–1995', unpublished M.Phil. dissertation,
    University of Birmingham, 1998

Thomson, Leslie, 'The meaning of thunder and lightning: stage directions
    and audience expectations', *Early Theatre*, 2 (1999), 11–24

Trewin, J.C., *Alec Clunes* (London, 1958)

Trewin, J.C., *Peter Brook: A Biography* (London, 1971)

Vaughan, Alden T. and Virginia Mason Vaughan, *Shakespeare's Caliban:
    A Cultural History* (Cambridge, 1991)

Vaughan, Alden T. and Virginia Mason Vaughan (eds), *Critical Essays on
    Shakespeare's The Tempest* (New York and London, 1998)

Voss, Philip, 'Prospero', in Robert Smallwood (ed.), *Players of Shakespeare*,
    5 (forthcoming)

Warner, Marina, '"The foul witch" and her "freckled whelp": Circean
    mutations in the New World', in Peter Hulme and William H. Sherman
    (eds), *'The Tempest' and Its Travels* (London, 2000)

Warren, Roger, *Staging Shakespeare's Late Plays* (Oxford, 1990)

Wax, Ruby, in *For Ian Charleson: A Tribute* (London, 1990), 57–63

White, R.S. (ed.), *The Tempest: William Shakespeare*, New Casebooks
    (Basingstoke, 1999)

INDEX

This index includes actors, directors, critics and other individuals mentioned in the main text who are connected with a production of *The Tempest*. It also includes references to other Shakespeare plays. Individual productions, listed under Shakespeare, are identified by director and year. Page numbers in bold refer to illustrations.